GO TELL EVERYONE

GO TELL EVERYONE
Reflections and Commentaries on the Sunday Readings
Cycles A-B-C

James E. McKarns

ALBA · HOUSE NEW · YORK

SOCIETY OF ST. PAUL, 2187 VICTORY BLVD., STATEN ISLAND, NEW YORK 10314

Library of Congress Cataloging in Publication Data

Rev. James E. McKarns.
  Go Tell Everyone.

  1. Church year meditations.   I. Title.
  BX2170.C55M42   1985   242'.3   85-20036
  ISBN 0-8189-0488-7

Nihil Obstat:
Most Rev. James W. Malone
Bishop of Youngstown

Imprimatur:
Rev. James A. Clarke
Chancellor - Cenror Librorum

Designed, printed and bound in the United States of America by the Fathers and Brothers of the Society of St. Paul, 2187 Victory Boulevard, Staten Island, New York 10314, as part of their communications apostolate.

1 2 3 4 5 6 7 8 9 (Current Printing: first digit)

' *Copyright 1985 by the Society of St. Paul*

This book is dedicated to MARY

> She opens her mouth with wisdom,
> and the teaching of kindness
> is on her tongue.
>
> *Proverbs 31:26*

PREFACE

The biblical movement began as a scholar's movement, and high level scholarship remains an important part of it to this day. But within the past few years it has also become a major popular movement, touching every aspect of life and ministry.

Much of the impetus for the popular movement came from Vatican II, beginning with the Constitution on the Liturgy. It is especially in the liturgy that Catholics and others come in contact with the scriptures.

Greater attention is given to the quality of the readings in the liturgy of the word. Prayer groups and Bible study groups as well as personal reading and meditation often focus on the Sunday readings for their nourishment. There is also great concern for the quality of the homily. These are wonderful developments. Together they contribute to the shaping of a dynamic Church, attentive to the Word and seriously committed to fulfilling its promise. Who could have predicted that we would come so far in such a short time?

The homily is a very important biblical moment in our lives. It is in the homily that someone examines the way we have heard the scriptures. The communication of the Word operates at many levels, some of them unconscious. The homily raises these to conscious awareness. When the scriptures puzzle or confuse us, the homily clarifies the puzzlement and dispels the confusion. When the Word challenges us, the homily helps us to face and accept its challenge.

In other words, the homily is a prophetic moment in the

liturgy, and the homilist like a prophet sees deeply into reality, presents the gospel vision, heals our blindness and calls us to fidelity to our story as a community of Christians. The homily gathers our individual Christian stories into a common story. It joins us in a community of mutual support and commitment and builds up the Church.

To do all this, we need the inspiration and enlightenment which comes from good homilists. In recent years, many have shared their efforts in the form of various types of homiletic helps. These are not intended to provide us with ready-to-serve homilies. The Table of the Word is not a cafeteria or a fast-food restaurant. They provide starters, images, ideas, illustrations and suggestions for homiletic preparation.

Father James McKarns has provided us with just such a book. His work is filled with helpful insights. It is also sensitive to tradition. It bears the imprint of a broad Christian culture as well as warm familiarity with God's word and skill at interpretation in a pastoral setting.

Go Tell Everyone will help those who prepare the Liturgy of the Word with its prayers, readings and homily as well as those who pray with the Lectionary or use it in Bible study. May it help many to find a home in the dwelling of God's Word.

Eugene LaVerdiere, SSS

TABLE OF CONTENTS

Cycle A

First Sunday of Advent 3
Second Sunday of Advent 4
Third Sunday of Advent 5
Fourth Sunday of Advent 6
Christmas (Midnight Mass) 8
Sunday in the Octave of Christmas—Holy Family 9
Octave of Christmas—Solemnity of Mary, Mother of God 11
Second Sunday after Christmas 12
Epiphany 13
Baptism of the Lord 15
First Sunday of Lent 16
Second Sunday of Lent 18
Third Sunday of Lent 19
Fourth Sunday of Lent 20
Fifth Sunday of Lent 22
Palm Sunday 23
Easter Sunday 24
Second Sunday of Easter 26
Third Sunday of Easter 27
Fourth Sunday of Easter 29
Fifth Sunday of Easter 30
Sixth Sunday of Easter 31
The Ascension 33

Seventh Sunday of Easter	34
Pentecost Sunday	36
Trinity Sunday	37
Corpus Christi	39
Feast of Peter and Paul	40
The Assumption of the Blessed Virgin Mary	41
All Saints	43
The Immaculate Conception	45
Second Sunday of the Year	46
Third Sunday of the Year	47
Fourth Sunday of the Year	49
Fifth Sunday of the Year	50
Sixth Sunday of the Year	51
Seventh Sunday of the Year	53
Eighth Sunday of the Year	54
Ninth Sunday of the Year	56
Tenth Sunday of the Year	57
Eleventh Sunday of the Year	59
Twelfth Sunday of the Year	60
Thirteenth Sunday of the Year	62
Fourteenth Sunday of the Year	63
Fifteenth Sunday of the Year	64
Sixteenth Sunday of the Year	66
Seventeenth Sunday of the Year	67
Eighteenth Sunday of the Year	68
Nineteenth Sunday of the Year	70
Twentieth Sunday of the Year	71
Twenty-First Sunday of the Year	73
Twenty-Second Sunday of the Year	74
Twenty-Third Sunday of the Year	76
Twenty-Fourth Sunday of the Year	77
Twenty-Fifth Sunday of the Year	79
Twenty-Sixth Sunday of the Year	80
Twenty-Seventh Sunday of the Year	82

Table of Contents xiii

Twenty-Eighth Sunday of the Year 83
Twenty-Ninth Sunday of the Year 84
Thirtieth Sunday of the Year 86
Thirty-First Sunday of the Year 87
Thirty-Second Sunday of the Year 89
Thirty-Third Sunday of the Year 90
Thirty-Fourth Sunday of the Year
   Solemnity of Christ the King 92

Cycle B

First Sunday of Advent 97
Second Sunday of Advent 98
Third Sunday of Advent 99
Fourth Sunday of Advent 101
Christmas (Midnight Mass) 102
Sunday in the Octave of Christmas—Holy Family 104
Octave of Christmas—Solemnity of Mary, Mother of God ... 105
Second Sunday after Christmas 107
Epiphany 108
Baptism of the Lord 110
First Sunday of Lent 111
Second Sunday of Lent 113
Third Sunday of Lent 114
Fourth Sunday of Lent 116
Fifth Sunday of Lent 117
Palm Sunday 119
Easter Sunday 120
Second Sunday of Easter 121
Third Sunday of Easter 123
Fourth Sunday of Easter 124
Fifth Sunday of Easter 126
Sixth Sunday of Easter 127

The Ascension 129
Seventh Sunday of Easter 130
Pentecost Sunday 132
Trinity Sunday 134
Corpus Christi 135
Feast of Peter and Paul (see p. 40)
The Assumption of the Blessed Virgin Mary 137
All Saints 138
The Immaculate Conception 140
Second Sunday of the Year 142
Third Sunday of the Year 143
Fourth Sunday of the Year 145
Fifth Sunday of the Year 146
Sixth Sunday of the Year 148
Seventh Sunday of the Year 149
Eighth Sunday of the Year 151
Ninth Sunday of the Year 152
Tenth Sunday of the Year 154
Eleventh Sunday of the Year 156
Twelfth Sunday of the Year 157
Thirteenth Sunday of the Year 158
Fourteenth Sunday of the Year 160
Fifteenth Sunday of the Year 161
Sixteenth Sunday of the Year 163
Seventeenth Sunday of the Year 164
Eighteenth Sunday of the Year 166
Nineteenth Sunday of the Year 167
Twentieth Sunday of the Year 168
Twenty-First Sunday of the Year 170
Twenty-Second Sunday of the Year 171
Twenty-Third Sunday of the Year 173
Twenty-Fourth Sunday of the Year 174
Twenty-Fifth Sunday of the Year 176
Twenty-Sixth Sunday of the Year 177

Table of Contents

Twenty-Seventh Sunday of the Year 178
Twenty-Eighth Sunday of the Year 179
Twenty-Ninth Sunday of the Year 181
Thirtieth Sunday of the Year 182
Thirty-First Sunday of the Year 183
Thirty-Second Sunday of the Year 185
Thirty-Third Sunday of the Year 186
Thirty-Fourth Sunday of the Year
   Solemnity of Christ the King 187

Cycle C

First Sunday of Advent 191
Second Sunday of Advent 192
Third Sunday of Advent 192
Fourth Sunday of Advent 194
Christmas (Midnight Mass) 196
Sunday in the Octave of Christmas—Holy Family 197
Octave of Christmas—Solemnity of Mary, Mother of God ...198
Second Sunday after Christmas 200
Epiphany 202
Baptism of the Lord 203
First Sunday of Lent 204
Second Sunday of Lent 206
Third Sunday of Lent 207
Fourth Sunday of Lent 209
Fifth Sunday of Lent 210
Palm Sunday 211
Easter Sunday 213
Second Sunday of Easter 214
Third Sunday of Easter 216
Fourth Sunday of Easter 217
Fifth Sunday of Easter 218

Sixth Sunday of Easter 220
The Ascension 221
Seventh Sunday of Easter 223
Pentecost Sunday 224
Trinity Sunday 226
Corpus Christi 227
Feast of Peter and Paul (see p. 40)
The Assumption of the Blessed—Virgin Mary 229
All Saints 230
The Immaculate Conception 232
Second Sunday of the Year 233
Third Sunday of the Year 235
Fourth Sunday of the Year 236
Fifth Sunday of the Year 237
Sixth Sunday of the Year 239
Seventh Sunday of the Year 240
Eighth Sunday of the Year 241
Ninth Sunday of the Year 243
Tenth Sunday of the Year 244
Eleventh Sunday of the Year 246
Twelfth Sunday of the Year 247
Thirteenth Sunday of the Year 249
Fourteenth Sunday of the Year 250
Fifteenth Sunday of the Year 252
Sixteenth Sunday of the Year 253
Seventeenth Sunday of the Year .255
Eighteenth Sunday of the Year 256
Nineteenth Sunday of the Year .258
Twentieth Sunday of the Year 259
Twenty-First Sunday of the Year 261
Twenty-Second Sunday of the Year 262
Twenty-Third Sunday of the Year 263
Twenty-Fourth Sunday of the Year 265
Twenty-Fifth Sunday of the Year 266

Table of Contents

Twenty-Sixth Sunday of the Year .... .268
Twenty-Seventh Sunday of the Year .... .269
Twenty-Eighth Sunday of the Year .... .270
Twenty-Ninth Sunday of the Year .... .271
Thirtieth Sunday of the Year .... .273
Thirty-First Sunday of the Year .... .274
Thirty-Second Sunday of the Year .... .275
Thirty-Third Sunday of the Year .... .277
Thirty-Fourth Sunday of the Year
   Solemnity of Christ the King .... .278

ABBREVIATIONS

Old Testament

Genesis	Gn	Nehemiah	Ne	Baruch	Ba
Exodus	Ex	Tobit	Tb	Ezekiel	Ezk
Leviticus	Lv	Judith	Jdt	Daniel	Dn
Numbers	Nb	Esther	Est	Hosea	Ho
Deuteronomy	Dt	1 Maccabees	1 M	Joel	Jl
Joshua	Jos	2 Maccabees	2 M	Amos	Am
Judges	Jg	Job	Jb	Obadiah	Ob
Ruth	Rt	Psalms	Ps	Jonah	Jon
1 Samuel	1 S	Proverbs	Pr	Micah	Mi
2 Samuel	2 S	Ecclesiastes	Ec	Nahum	Na
1 Kings	1 K	Song of Songs	Sg	Habakkuk	Hab
2 Kings	2 K	Wisdom	Ws	Zephaniah	Zp
1 Chronicles	1 Ch	Sirach	Si	Haggai	Hg
2 Chronicles	2 Ch	Isaiah	Is	Malachi	Ml
Ezra	Ezr	Jeremiah	Jr	Zechariah	Zc
		Lamentations	Lm		

New Testament

Matthew	Mt	Ephesians	Ep	Hebrews	Heb
Mark	Mk	Philippians	Ph	James	Jm
Luke	Lk	Colossians	Col	1 Peter	1 P
John	Jn	1 Thessalonians	1 Th	2 Peter	2 P
Acts	Ac	2 Thessalonians	2 Th	1 John	1 Jn
Romans	Rm	1 Timothy	1 Tm	2 John	2 Jn
1 Corinthians	1 Cor	2 Timothy	2 Tm	3 John	3 Jn
2 Corinthians	2 Cor	Titus	Tt	Jude	Jude
Galatians	Gal	Philemon	Phm	Revelation	Rv

Cycle A

FIRST SUNDAY OF ADVENT (A)
Is 2:1-5   Rm 13:11-14   Mt 24:37-44

There's great optimism in today's liturgy, with Isaiah, the Old Testament seer, peering into the future. He sees peaceful times ahead for his people and country. It will happen, he says, because all will hold the Lord in awe and enthusiastically worship Him. People everywhere will walk in His paths, and the sign of peace will be given when they "beat their swords into plowshares and their spears into pruning hooks." There will be no more training for war, for mutual love will have cancelled it out.

Isaiah's visionary proclamation is similar to Martin Luther King's historic "I Have A Dream" speech, delivered in our nation's capital. Both called for and predicted the end of violence and racism. Yet neither dream has been realized.

We wonder if the people of the world can live in peace with each other, lay down their arms and destroy the weapons of war. Is it an impossible dream? Realistically, it's impossible; but the optimism which springs eternal continues to try to make it happen.

The nations of the world have reversed Isaiah's vision. We are beating the plowshares into swords and the pruning hooks into spears. Our contemporary "swords" and "spears," however, have far greater capabilities for destruction and death than ever before.

Aside from military build-ups, people in general are armed with "swords" and "spears" and we use them continually against each other. Even those who do not engage in violence with guns and knives, contribute to the demise of peace by cruel actions and bitter words. We all have our little weapons with which we slash and cut.

The liturgy calls for us to beat our hate-filled hearts into loving hearts. We have four weeks of Advent ahead, before we celebrate the birth of our Savior. This presents us each year with an exciting challenge to realize the vision of Isaiah.

Just imagine the profound contentment all of us would feel if we lived in a world where one nation would not arm itself against another and no one trained for war. Although difficult to envision, this dream should be tried. Nothing needs to be destroyed—only changed. The first and most important change must begin within ourselves.

SECOND SUNDAY OF ADVENT (A)
Is 11:1-10   Rm 15:4-9   Mt 3:1-12

A cartoon in the newspaper showed several lions and lambs living contentedly in the same pen, with the caption: "Peaceful Coexistence." A man was asking the owner how he had achieved this remarkable result. "Oh, quite easily," he replied, "each day I just throw in a few more lambs."

This scene parodies the hopes of Isaiah in today's passage, where he envisions all the creatures of the world dwelling together in a state of delightful harmony. The message of the cartoon, however, is that things are often not what they seem to be. Regardless of appearance, we know that the powerful dominate the weak both among humans and animals. The distressing experiences of history have made one critic quip: "Peaceful coexistence is found only in the cemetery."

The prophet Isaiah provides us with a long-range view of Advent with his visions and prayers of universal peace. Today, however, the Church introduces a second and more immediate voice of the season in the person of John the Baptist. He appears in the role and costume of Elijah, his famous predecessor, and identifies himself as "a herald's voice in the desert." He is a religious reformer, initiating changes which will be carried to completion by the Messiah, who is near at hand.

Although trained in the sacred traditions of the past, John calls his audiences to abandon anything which fosters a sense of false security. He leads them to take the first step into a new faith by being cleansed in the waters of the Jordan. He promises the gifts of fire and the Holy Spirit, but these will come through the hands of the One he is introducing.

We should heed the annual pleas of Isaiah and John at this ADVENTurous time of the year and reexamine our lives to determine if we are honest and sincere. The Pharisees and Sadducees were berated by John and later by Jesus for performing religious actions without the right spirit.

In the penitential season of Lent, we emphasize reform by being more faithful to our sacred beliefs and practices. Advent calls us to assess the beliefs and practices themselves. Do we place too much faith in the wrong things? Do we say a certain prayer to a particular saint each day and skip Sunday Mass? Or feel assured of salvation if we read the Bible ten minutes a day? Before we can do anything Christian, we must first have a deep and abiding faith in the person of Jesus Christ.

This is the time of year when we can pause to think thoughts of peace, to review our depth of faith in Jesus and examine how we can come to a better way of thinking and living.

THIRD SUNDAY OF ADVENT (A)
Is 35:1-6, 10   Jm 5:7-10   Mt 11:2-11

One of the most impressive events in the whole history of Israel was the Exodus. It confirmed God's unique love for this one nation and showed His determination to protect them. Whenever they doubted His benevolent friendship, they simply needed to recall the Exodus and their sacred trust was reestablished.

Isaiah, too, was tremendously impressed by the Exodus, but he is even more ecstatic about a future happening—the coming of the Messiah. He foresees this spectacular event as a new and greater

Exodus and the Messiah as a new and greater Moses, who will lead the people out of spiritual slavery. Not only those in the bondage of sin, but even the blind and deaf will be released to enjoy the fullness of life.

John the Baptist and Jesus were both aware of the optimistic prophecies of Isaiah. Thus, when John sought the Lord's identification, Jesus simply told the messengers to report back to John that the predictions of Isaiah were being fulfilled. The dead were raised up, the poor heard the gospel, the blind were released from darkness, the deaf freed from their silence and the crippled were given their mobility. In short, the long-expected Messiah had finally arrived and the new Exodus was now in progress.

Neither Isaiah nor John realized how completely the "New Moses" would supersede the old. Who could have known that Jesus would personally offer His life for His people?

If we, therefore, begin to doubt His unique love for us, we need only recall the blood-stained cross at Calvary and the empty tomb. Then our trust in His friendship is reestablished. The redemptive acts of Jesus were so profound and earth-shattering that they continue to vibrate through the world. Each day we can hear and feel them, ever inviting us out of bondage and darkness into a new found freedom.

The Advent liturgy is just another reminder of how important was the coming of the Lord. John was, as Jesus said, one of the greatest men before Him. But any of us can be "greater than he," for we are the recipients of a more excellent gift.

Yes, John, He is the One appointed to come. We need not look for another. After 20 centuries we still avidly hear His words, are thrilled by His miracles and gratefully accept His healing touch.

FOURTH SUNDAY OF ADVENT (A)
Is 7:10-14   Rm 1:1-7   Mt 1:18-24

Advent is something like a four-act play. It began in 700 B.C.

with Isaiah announcing the coming of the Messiah; then followed the prophecies through the intervening centuries; then the birth of the Baptist. Now today we meet Mary and Joseph, and learn that the Child has been conceived.

Here we are presented with the reluctance of Joseph to accept Mary as his wife. He is not only hesitant but seemingly fearful. Why? Various reasons are given. Some think that he questioned her virtue and wondered if the Child truly was conceived by the Holy Spirit, as she said, or by some other man. Another opinion is that Joseph did not doubt her, but was simply confused. A third view is that he accepted her honesty and believed that the Child was conceived by the Holy Spirit—but, being a humble and unassuming man, wanted to disassociate himself from her out of deep awe and reverence. Whatever the situation, the angel's message in the dream confirmed Mary's story and persuaded Joseph to take her as his wife.

Thus the scene was set for the birth of the Messiah, and Jesus was provided with two sensitive and holy people to raise Him to manhood.

Advent is the Church's way to help us prepare for the celebration of the birth of Jesus. Although Christ came long ago, we can always deepen our appreciation of His impressive entry into our history. When we envision the world without His teachings, we can be thankful for our Christian heritage.

With our many customs for this pre-Christmas season, we should be careful not to overlook the essential elements. We can have Christmas without the snow, presents, a festival meal or midnight Mass; but there would be no real Christmas without genuine love in our lives and the sharing of it with others.

The fourth candle now burns on the Advent wreath, our churches and homes are decorated, the presents for our loved ones are being wrapped and the children whisper their requests in Santa's ear.

We all would do well to whisper a prayer to the Savior for His eternal friendship and the precious gift of salvation which He has freely given and continues to give each day.

CHRISTMAS MIDNIGHT MASS (A)
Is 9:1-6   Tt 1:11-14   Lk 2:1-14

There resides within the human heart an untiring curiosity to probe beneath the surface, to analyze the hidden and explore the mysterious. We want to understand ourselves, other people, the world and beyond. Christmas is a time when we can all be starry-eyed and lost in wonderment—but unfortunately, so many stop at the surface level with songs, lights, presents and of course the Christ Child. This event should grab our minds and imaginations to carry us off in flights of joy and glory.

We often hear the slogan, "Keep Christ in Christmas"—which is good advice, for many lesser things can crowd Him out. An example is the radio announcer who said, "Christmas is pine cones and mistletoe." In reality, it is the birthday celebration of the world's most important Person. In that sense, we need to keep Christ in Christmas—but in another sense we need to get Him out of Christmas.

Too many of us keep Him there so that we know exactly where to find Him next year at the same time. These are the Christmas-Christians. For them Jesus is always the cute Baby, quietly sleeping in His little crib. They fail to see beyond the manger or hear His voice echoing through the ages. If we can keep Christ in His crib, He won't threaten our life style and it will be easy to be a good Christian.

Imagine how absurd it would be if the parents of a teenage boy would invite his friends each year for his birthday celebration and always display his baby pictures, little rattle, first booties and teddy bear. Although they would want him to remain their little child forever, he no doubt would shout, perhaps angrily, "Hey, I've grown up."

The same is true of Jesus. It is in the mature Christ that we find the answers to the tough questions in our lives—not in the Infant. The Jesus of Christmas cannot give an appropriate response to the family just split by divorce; the young woman dying of cancer; to crime in the streets and hatred among nations. Here we must turn to the Christ of Good Friday and Easter.

Christmas is a birth, a beginning, a first step—but the road leads from an empty crib. We can stop and pause there, but are not meant to stay. That road winds its way through valleys and mountains, across rivers, lakes and wind-blown deserts, in success and failure, in tears and prayer. The road winds on from an empty cross and on again from an empty tomb.

We are invited to pursue those divine footprints and echoes, on into the mysterious future. And so it is that we can find Christ in Christmas but we cannot keep Him there. It's only the beginning—the easy part of life. The heroic challenge is to follow Him.

SUNDAY IN THE OCTAVE OF CHRISTMAS
HOLY FAMILY (A)
Si 3:2-6, 12-14   Col 3:12-21   Mt 2:13-15, 19-23

A three-hour TV special was presented by NBC several years ago entitled "The American Family: An Endangered Species?" Prior to the showing, *TV Guide* commented: "Only one family in four makes up the traditional family, with a working father, a homemaking mother and one or more dependent children. Nearly 4 in 10 marriages end in divorce which is a 700% increase since 1900. There are 6 million working mothers and 6 million single parents." Against this modern background of a radically changing family life style, the Church presents today the traditional religious celebration of the Holy Family.

There is obviously a world of difference between a single mother on ADC and food stamps, trying to raise four hungry children and the Holy Family in the temple, hearing saintly people speaking about Jesus under the inspiration of the Holy Spirit. If true to her mission, the Church cannot ignore the former case. Since we need ideals to live by, we can extol the virtues of the Holy Family at Nazareth—but we can't expect families to minutely imitate them.

On Holy Family Sunday perhaps the Church's best objective is to announce to all people that the old values are still praiseworthy and should be pursued to the best of our ability. The Church understands that many marriages were not "made in heaven" and that divorce or separation is often the only alternative. It would also be fine if mothers of young children did not have to work outside the home, but millions must for a variety of reasons. The Church also recognizes that certain tax laws make living together for some people more advantageous than getting married. This is not condoned but understood to be the case. We likewise are well aware of homosexual and lesbian "marriages" and believe that the mission to minister must include rather than exclude them.

It would be beautiful if all parents were like Mary and Joseph and every child was a little Jesus, but that family was one of a kind. Our families must be encouraged to find holiness in their own circumstances.

Whatever our particular relationship to our family is, we should give a little thought and prayer this day on how to improve those natural ties of togetherness. If your family is close, loving and happy, should you not offer a prayer of thanksgiving?

We all need some kind of family or trusting community where personal weaknesses are forgiven and small victories are applauded. Our families are so precious that we must hold them together to the very best of our ability and make them holy.

OCTAVE OF CHRISTMAS
SOLEMNITY OF MARY, MOTHER OF GOD (A)
Nb 6:22-27   Gal 4:4-7   Lk 2:16-21

Now that a week has passed since our celebration of the birthday of the Savior, our liturgy invites us to sit beside Mary and review the mysterious events of Christmas one more time. We remember the long journey south; the closed doors of the inn and Christ's birth in Bethlehem's stable. There, the angel tells the shepherds the "good news of great joy"; then a choir of angels sings "The Gloria"—our Lord's personal delegation from His world to welcome Him to ours. These and other events happened so rapidly that Mary didn't have time to analyze them; so today she sits and ponders their profound meaning.

We can also pause to consider the impact of Jesus' birth on our lives. There are different approaches. 1) Some simply memorize the stories and recite them to others—often complete chapters and verses. It may make one appear intelligent, but there is probably little understanding present. This was not Mary's approach. 2) Others continue to marvel at the good news, by getting excited and jumping about with ecstatic joy. This wasn't Mary's way, either. 3) Her response to the birth of Jesus is told by Luke in today's Gospel. "Mary treasured all these things and reflected on them in her heart." I think "reflected" is the key word. It includes hearing and marvelling but goes beyond them. It seems like something that Mary would naturally do—just quietly think and pray, basking in God's gentle love. 4) The final step is living one's reflections, which she also did.

Although history has delicately placed her beside Jesus, she can easily stand alone, for her value and virtue do not depend upon her being the mother of Jesus. This obviously enhanced her quality, but did not establish it. Her famous Son, Himself, attested to that when, during His public life, a person in the crowd shouted, "Blessed is the womb that bore you and the breasts that nursed you" (Lk 11:27). Jesus replied, "Rather blessed are they that hear the word of God and keep it." She was called "blessed" not for being His mother but for hearing God's word and living it.

Mary offers much encouragement to us all. She, like the rest of us, had to pray and reflect at each step along the way. God didn't make it easy for her to discover the meaning of His life or hers.

Our reflections on this glorious season should usher us confidently into the new year, for "A Savior has been born, who is Christ the Lord." His mother is from our human family, which makes us related to God. That's a beautiful mystery, which we certainly would want to treasure and reflect on in our hearts.

SECOND SUNDAY AFTER CHRISTMAS (A)
Si 24:1-4, 8-12   Ep 1:3-6, 15-18   Jn 1:1-18

Many books and speakers today are promoting leadership values and inspiring people to lead successful lives. I heard one speaker stress that a wise person will sometimes openly say this four word sentence: "I made a mistake." If we have the responsibility of making many decisions, we will sometimes make a wrong judgment—but the mistake can be gracefully, even willingly, admitted. We can be actually proud of our mistakes because they mean that we have been accepting our duties and making decisions.

If we continually try to avoid all mistakes, then we will be neglecting decisions—and many times the failure to make a decision is in itself the wrong decision.

Today's liturgy stresses wisdom, especially in the first reading from Sirach. Wisdom is attractive and to be sought as a guide for daily living. It's encouraging to realize that there's wisdom even in our failures, which can give us added glory by displaying our honesty.

Our spiritual wrong decisions—sins—also need to be admitted in order to grow in God's love, for unless we acknowledge our sins how can we be forgiven or make any future improvement?

The sacred wisdom referred to in Sirach is said to come from the "mouth of the Most High." It came to earth to dwell in the midst of His people and to be a real part of our lives. To live in wisdom is to live in God. This is why others are attracted to wise people and seek their counsel.

Foolishness like sin may appear attractive but is ultimately repelling, especially when foolish people will not admit their ignorance and weaknesses.

One popular speaker constantly encouraging others to develop themselves and increase in their inner wisdom is Charles T. Jones. He says that we will be the same in five years as we are now except for two things: "the people we meet and the books we read."

To be wisdom-filled Christians we read Sacred Scripture and reflect on the elevating thoughts recorded in those inspired pages. The readings can also bring us into contact with many saintly people who long ago lived by divine guidance and in turn can become role models for us.

Do others think of you as a wise person? Do you think of yourself as a wise person? The more wisdom we possess the more like God we are and the better we can work His will in the world, with calm confidence in His trusting guidance.

Wisdom lives among the people, as the reading says, and it's meant to be found in us, whoever we are. By it we are inwardly directed along our path through this world and become an unfading light for others.

EPIPHANY (A)
Is 60:1-6   Ep 3:2-3, 5-6   Mt 2:1-12

One of the liturgical topics suggested by today's Epiphany celebration is: Our Search For God. Since He is both our origin and destiny, we seek Him to better understand ourselves and find future security. In the Sermon on the Mount, Jesus said, "Seek and you shall find . . ." (Mt 7:7), but the Magi had already fulfilled those words before they were spoken.

We might think that since we have known God from our youth, we don't need to seek Him—but we are continually challenged to deepen our appreciation. St. Teresa speaks of God often concealing Himself from us, as a parent playfully hides from a toddler, to encourage the child to walk.

Most of us can easily see God in our successes and good fortunes, but we feel deserted by Him in our sicknesses, failures and rejections. Yet faith counsels us that it is His presence there that makes these sad conditions tolerable.

Epiphany might reawaken within us a certain "homing instinct," like that found in many other forms of life on this planet. Many are the stories of dogs and cats which have traveled hundred of miles to return home. The same homeward pull is present in the salmon and the carrier pigeon. Whether they walk, swim or fly, these creatures possess a mysterious tug to the familiar. Our souls, like doves, are set free from the fingers of God, but always retain an innate desire to someday return to His outstretched hand, to be securely at home, forever.

We are the modern day Magi, walking by faith, inspiration, reason and intuition, on our long and mysterious journey to the Kingdom. We are the 20th century spiritual stargazers, in search of the one Super Star.

We carry our gifts of virtue and goodness, like nuggets of gold fit for a King. They will be presented when we arrive. Also, we bring our pains—the myrrh. We offer, too, the mystic frankincense—our prayers, which drift skyward through the days and nights of life.

We celebrate today the Light of the World, Who has made the night a little brighter by His wondrous presence. John speaks of Jesus as "the true light." What light do we follow through life?

Those who pursue the light of faith, good reason and clear conscience, regardless of hardships or distances involved, will find their God and King. We don't need to travel far to find God, for He is not far from any of us.
May we all discover the guiding Star which will lead us home.

BAPTISM OF THE LORD (A)
Is 42:1-4, 6-7   Ac 10:34-38   Mt 3:13-17

Jesus was baptized as a 30 year-old adult. Later He would call His followers to be baptized as a commitment to Him. In the very early Church, baptism was for adults only. Before they received it there was an extended period of prayer, instruction and personal decision. It was both a time for sadness and gladness, for although the person was beginning a demanding way of life, at the same time they were receiving a pledge of sustaining grace and future reward.

When the candidates would first present themselves to the baptized community of believers, they would speak of their personal lives, their views of God, church, prayer, etc. Then the church members would relate to the candidates their beliefs and teachings on these and similar subjects. Following this mutual discussion and prayer, the church membership would decide which aspirants should be accepted for instructions and which should be rejected or postponed. Those accepted would then begin their entrance programs which culminated with their reception into the Church on the vigil of Easter. That evening still remains the most opportune time to receive adult converts into full communion.

The baptism of children did not become commonplace until about the 5th century. In each case the parents were to speak in behalf of their children, and had to promise to raise their youngsters in the faith, before they could be baptized. This also is still the practice today, and the modern Church is reemphasizing its importance.

The deep significance of baptism is that it is the entrance into a new life of faith, intended to grow and blossom into eternity. As a ceremonial pouring of water, baptism is received only once. But it is also a day by day consignment of one's life to the risen Lord. The funeral liturgy is a solemn reminder of our baptismal dignity. When the white pall shrouds the casket, it is a symbolic reminder of the small white robe that veiled this person as a baby many years before. "On the day of his (her) baptism," the priest prays, "he (she) put on Christ; in the day of Christ's coming may he (she) be clothed with glory."

The baptism of Jesus, like our own, is viewed as a public pledge to do more than the minimum and to accept the responsibility to be our brother's keeper. A baptized person becomes a contradiction if he or she grows selfish with possessions and narrow-minded in outlook. When we see the many social sins around us, we should feel some responsibility to make improvements—and in some cases a sense of guilt for having contributed to them.

At our baptisms we don't see any doves or openings in the sky, but we do believe that the sacrament makes us a better person and that God's favor rests upon us.

FIRST SUNDAY OF LENT (A)
Gn 2:7-9, 3:1-7   Rm 5:12-19   Mt 4:1-11

Some common-sense explanations need to be applied to this Sunday Gospel. It pictures salvation's two archrivals—Jesus and the devil—having an animated conversation with each other on a mountain and at the pinnacle of the Temple. The best interpretation seems to be that this did not literally happen. The temptations were presented to the mind of Jesus. He had to subdue His inward temptations, urging Him to use His power and glory for His own good as the devil had done. The temptations were in the areas of bread, glory and possessions.

1. BREAD: This is the lure of catering to bodily comforts, giving free rein to all our appetites for food, drink, sex, leisure, etc.—the easy life. It's only natural to want the best if we can get it, and forget about self-denial and discipline. Jesus knew, however, that this was not the way to prepare for the cross, where He would be thirsty, naked and tortured. So He resisted the temptation.

2. GLORY: Here He was tempted to show off and be spectacular. He could, if he had wanted, put on a dazzling display and the people would have jumped with excitement and applause. He could even convince Himself that it would be good for His cause, for it would have attracted an enthusiastic following.

How often we love to be the center of attention and be popular in the eyes of others. Sometimes this clouds our minds, causing us to say and do foolish things. Jesus had to be in control, for later He would be challenged to come down from the cross and save His life. He wouldn't do that, either. In resisting this temptation, He manifested the divine strength which destroyed our sins.

3. POSSESSIONS: Just imagine all the things that people do for the sake of money. They kill for pay; endure cold, darkness and fear to obtain gold and riches. Some sacrifice every decent principle to obtain an exalted position. The devil doesn't truly own the world and couldn't give it to Jesus. But he could remind Him of His freedom to forsake His Father's will and take possession of the world. Abandoning the Father was tantamount to worshipping the devil and the tough Redeemer told His adversary to get lost. "The devil made me do it," has no application here.

This passage causes us to ask: Can Jesus really be tempted? Some would say "no," for He is divine. Others respond "yes," for He's human.

One thing is sure. We can be tempted, but when the mind is

resolute, evil will flee. Then peace, like a ministering angel, will gently settle within our souls.

SECOND SUNDAY OF LENT (A)
Gn 12:1-4   2 Tm 1:8-10   Mt 17:1-9

A common expression used to refer to one's religious life is, "My Spiritual Journey." From the French, *jour* (day), it describes one's daily progress in walking with the Lord and each other. The word "journal," also from the same root, means a daily record of events. Each person's journey is unique and must always be treated as such. We have different times of beginning and ending, and a lifetime of varieties in between. The important similarity of all journeys is that we move through life according to the same measured pace of time. We know that change is inevitable and that we are subject to it, willingly or otherwise.

We can appreciate the unwavering faith of Abraham in the first reading, as he obeys the call of his God to leave behind his father's house and native land, to journey into the uncharted future, into a totally new type of life. We increase our admiration when we realize that he was 75 years old at the time.

Abraham is for us an inspiring model of faith, who was willing to trust God completely by letting go of earthly securities, as he ventured out of what is currently Iraq to Palestine. There, he was given a new name and became the father of a new nation and a new religion. Because of Abraham, we should never say or even think that we are too old to make a change for the better.

Another type of spiritual journey occurs in today's Gospel, in the lives of three chosen apostles. They climb steep Mount Tabor with the Master and, once on top, soar into ecstasy as they behold the transfigured Savior conversing with Moses and Elijah. Their doubts are for the time being removed, for they have seen the glory of the Lord. It was a mystical journey into the brilliance of paradise.

God promises this same reward to any of us willing to abandon the safe places and familiar faces for a faith-filled journey into the night of the unknown. An act of simple trust is the first step that will bring us face to face with the transfigured Jesus.

The season of Lent is a constant reminder of our invitation from the Master to always seek the better life. We hear the Church reassuring all pilgrim people that their efforts are far outweighed by the divine glory to be gained. The stories presented in today's liturgy are not meant to glorify Abraham or the Apostles, but to make us believe that these grace-filled adventures can also be ours. Our journeys can all have happy endings, provided we are willing to venture forth each day with trusting faith.

THIRD SUNDAY OF LENT (A)
Ex 17:3-7   Rm 5:1-2, 5-8   Jn 4:5-42

In Wyoming, there is an inspiring natural phenomenon—a tree growing out of a solid rock. A plaque explains its history. "The original line of the Union Pacific Railroad passed within a few feet of this point, and supposedly was deflected slightly to avoid destruction of this tree. The fireman of each passing train never failed to drench the tree with a bucket of water."

How many people are there who, like that struggling tree, would have withered and died if it had not been for the care that others have freely bestowed upon them?

The popular caption, "Bloom where you are planted," is not as easy as it sounds. Our roots are very different and some environments encourage the fullness of life, while others stifle it. Those who live in blindness, in abject poverty, in wheelchairs, in sickness and in a thousand other harsh and hostile situations, cannot bloom or even survive without the generous help of other caring people.

The strong, rich and healthy also often stand in need of assistance and ministry. To some degree, everybody does. Even Jesus, the most self-sufficient Person ever to walk this earth, in today's Gospel asks for a bucket of water from an unknown Samaritan woman. Warmed by the noonday sun, both Savior and sinner sit on the edge of Jacob's Well, discussing their past journeys and sharing a brief glance into the future. The God of the Universe is momentarily in the role of recipient. In exchange for the kindness of this woman, He promises her the living waters of eternal life. The modern-day pilgrim to the Holy Land can still visit this sacred well, view its 90 foot depth, sample its soft water and feel spiritually uplifted.

If we consider ourselves too insignificant or unworthy to assist other people, we are totally wrong. Our possibilities for doing good are limitless. If the Samaritan woman—a five-time divorcee—could minister to Jesus, we certainly can minister to each other in His name.

If God can bring water out of a rock, as in today's first reading, He surely can give even better gifts to us, if we only allow Him to do so.

A fitting Lenten project might be to discover someone who is having a hard time in life. In a spirit of genuine love, bring that person a few extra buckets of water.

FOURTH SUNDAY OF LENT (A)
1 S 16:1, 6-7, 10-13   Ep 5:8-14   Jn 9:1-41

There are many blind people in today's Gospel who could have been healed by Jesus, but only one was cured. He was the man who was born blind. The others in the story, by contrast, believe that they are able to see perfectly well. In reality, the blind man had better vision than the others, for his blindness pertained only to his eyes; theirs was much deeper—affecting their very minds and souls.

Concerning this passage, Bible scholar Bruce Vawter comments: "As sheer drama, this trial scene is one of the most brilliant passages in the gospel." We note the variety of pressures at work which distort the views of the various people involved.

The *disciples* show their lack of vision by asking the Lord whose fault it was that the man was blind, instead of asking how they could help him. We share their blindness, if we overlook people in need and only concern ourselves with the abstract question of evil in the world.

The *parents and neighbors* were blinded by fear, and therefore would not stand up for the healed man or support his statement that Jesus had cured him—which they knew very well was true. The parents were afraid of being expelled from the synagogue if they befriended Jesus. Fear makes us close our eyes and turn our backs on many unpleasant situations.

The *Pharisees* could not see through the thick fog of their exaggerated pride. It was their goal to prove that Jesus was an impostor. Thus, they deliberately rejected the truth, to "convince" themselves and others that Jesus could not have worked a miracle.

The cured *blind man* possessed deep insight and was not afraid to declare his belief in Jesus. The Pharisees could not refute his words, so their rage took charge—and rage is blind.

No doubt most of us have never thought of ourselves as blind. But are we? Can we see other people's points of view, even though we don't accept them? Are we blind to our own faults? In order not to face them, do we always blame others? Is our faith too weak to see any good beyond our present sorrow? There are many kinds of blindness which have nothing to do with the quality of our eyes.

During the penitential season of Lent, the Church hopes that this Gospel story will inspire us to look within and pray for light. We must ask Jesus to make us see, and then speak the truth even in the face of opposition.

FIFTH SUNDAY OF LENT (A)
Ezk 37:12-14 Rm 8:8-11 Jn 11:1-45

He was a good man; a personal friend of Jesus. He became very ill, and his two caring sisters immediately thought of asking Jesus for help. They sent this simple message: "Lord, the one you love is sick." Jesus heard their plea and remembered his deep love for them, yet He delayed several days, and did not even reply. In the meantime, the man died. Then, amidst their tears, He came to them and restored life to their brother, extending joy to the family and the entire neighborhood.

Today we can pull this story of Lazarus out of the hills of Bethany and relocate it in our own cities, homes and hearts. This event displays the power of Jesus, foreshadows His own death and resurrection and gives some rare insights into His dealings with people. We can consider three of them.

First: Note that holy people who are close friends of God can get very sick, and suffer great misfortunes, pains and ultimately deaths. None of these misfortunes indicate any lessening of holiness or divine friendship. People who suffer should not be made to feel guilty by being told that a stronger faith in God would solve everything. Jesus loved Lazarus, and yet Lazarus got sick and died. The Lord's earnest love and concern for him, however, remained constant. This scriptural teaching should give us hope, for God knows that we all have plenty of troubles. We don't need to falsely add to our miseries by thinking that God has abandoned or is punishing us.

Secondly: Hear the one-line prayer which these close friends of Jesus offered to Him. "Lord, the one you love is sick." It's short, direct and filled with trust. The Bible shows that it's effective. We might say those very words when praying for those suffering from physical, mental or emotional ills. This prayer could be used for ourselves also—even for such moral sicknesses as anger, pride, lust or greed.

Thirdly: See how Jesus refuses to be either rushed or delayed. The sisters wanted Him to come immediately. The apostles tried to discourage Him from going at all, out of concern for His safety. He must do things His way, even if it seems like He is ignoring our prayers. The Bethany plea is like the Cana request. At first He showed indifference, but in both cases the prayers were answered with spectacular miracles.

We will pray effectively if we clearly state our views and let Him respond His way. The vital thing is to have sincerity, which the Lord cannot ignore. "Lord, the one you love is sick." Come give us life and set us free.

PALM SUNDAY (A)
Mt 21:1-11   Is 50:4-7   Ph 2:6-11   Mt 26:14-27:66

If we were in Jerusalem today, we could participate in a memorable event. As the Patriarch of Jerusalem (or his representative) rides a donkey down a steep mountain road, across a broad valley and up into the city, we would be invited to stand along the way, waving palm branches and singing religious songs, welcoming him to the ancient city. This annual palm procession follows the route which tradition says that Jesus traveled, in His triumphant entry. Each year, thousands of pilgrims come from far-off lands to participate in this time-consecrated ceremony in its original setting. The religious and emotional impact is of lasting memory.

We are transported to the actual scene today through the words of scripture. To help us better envision and appreciate these Holy Week events, we might want to keep in mind a few geographical features of the area.

Jerusalem is built on the crest of a mountain. Thus, travelers from any direction use the phrase, "going up to Jerusalem." Although 2400 feet above sea level, the ancient city must still look up to Mount Olivet—located to the east and towering 300 feet higher. Between Jerusalem and Mount Olivet is the deep and dangerous Kidron Valley. This erratic area of peaks and valleys still stands in silent memory as a symbol of the highs and lows of the salvation drama which happened there.

In our liturgy this day we reenact the sacred palm procession and then move swiftly to the tragic account of the passion.

Reading Matthew's Gospel this year, we devoutly follow Jesus and His disciples from the Last Supper at the Upper Room in Jerusalem, through one of the many gates in the stone wall, across the Kidron Valley, to the top of Mount Olivet. The view of the city would have been spectacular and panoramic from this vantage point. It was here that Jesus had earlier foretold the destruction of Jerusalem and taught the Lord's Prayer. From this same location, six weeks later, He would ascend into Heaven.

At the base of Mount Olivet is located the Garden of Gethsemani with the large surface rock where Luke says that Jesus sweat blood. There He was betrayed by Judas and captured. Today that rock forms a large section of the sanctuary in the Church of All Nations. After a brief skirmish in the garden, Jesus was roughly led across the Kidron Valley, back to the city for His trial and crucifixion.

The events narrated on Passion Sunday are as harsh as Easter is happy. Yet Jesus willingly submitted to the forces of sin in order to conquer them. The passion theme today takes precedence over the palm theme; thus, the traditional name for this Sunday has been restored. It was the most pain-filled week in the life of Jesus. We should always remember that our salvation came at a very high price.

EASTER SUNDAY (A)
Ac 10:34, 37-43   Col 3:1-4   Jn 20:1-9

Let us imagine that we are attending the impressive celebration of Easter in Rome. We find seats in one of the balcony sections overlooking the vast piazza of St. Peter's Basilica, on a warm sunlit morning. From there, we watch nearly a quarter of a million people streaming to the world's largest church to worship with the Holy Father on this liturgical anniversary of the Resurrection of Jesus.

When the solemn Mass is over, the Pope leaves the elevated outside altar near the entrance of the Basilica to assume a higher position on a balcony above the main door. There, looking over the vast international crowd, he wishes his fellow Christians "Happy Easter" in many different languages. When citizens from particular countries hear the greeting in their native tongue, they loudly cheer and applaud. We experience in these joyful sights and sounds both a sense of the diversity of Christian customs and a close sense of unity demonstrated in the way all share at the one altar and are united in the Risen Lord.

Let's also imagine that a week before this Easter morning, we had been on a pilgrimage in the Holy Land, seeing the actual sites of Jesus' death and resurrection. What was happening now in Rome, we realize, is only possible because of what had happened nearly 20 centuries earlier in Palestine. Those events alone give meaning to the Mass in Rome.

Of course, we don't need to be at the center of the Christian world to appreciate the beauty of Easter Day. Wherever and whoever we are, we can chant the Hebrew word "Alleluia" as we cherish the fact that Jesus both showed His victory over death and promised eternal life to His followers.

We encounter many pains and hurdles along our journey in life, but the big barrier—the huge stone—has been rolled from our path by our mighty Savior. Because He laid down His life and took it up again, we can face the barren coldness of the grave with renewed courage. With Him our spirits can wing their way to eternal freedom. "In Him, through Him and with Him," we rise and shine in shared victory. Without Him, we can do nothing. All Christendom knows what Jesus did on Easter morning, and in spite of our many customs, languages and other differences we share today a common unity. Today we skip with joy, sing alleluia and wave the victory pennant, walking with Jesus into the brave new world of tomorrow. How can we not celebrate?

SECOND SUNDAY OF EASTER (A)
Ac 2:42-47   1 P 1:3-9   Jn 20:19-31

The teenaged girl blushed and giggled as the palm-reader spoke slowly while examining her hands; then she excitedly ran back to join her friends. "She says I'm intelligent, will meet a very loving man and have a long life." "All that just from looking at your hands?" asked one of the group. "Sure, you see this mark? That's my long lifeline; this one shows intelligence, and the long curving line indicates my future romance." Another teenager smiled skeptically and patted her friend on the shoulder. "I hope it all comes true for you," she said, as they sauntered down the midway of the amusement park.

The pseudo-science of palmistry obviously cannot predict the future by analyzing our hands. At best, it's just a game of make-believe. Today's Gospel, however, does beckon us to analyze the hands of Jesus to understand his character and to see what the future holds. On our Lord's hands the usual lines are obscured by the nail scars. These scars reveal His true character in clear and certain terms. They tell us that He suffered and died for others, and was treated as a criminal—not because He was so bad, but because He was so good. The scars show that He persevered until His painful task was finished and that He was, is and ever will be true to His word.

If you don't feel as close to God as you used to, you should ask yourself, which one of you moved away. In His hands we read His faithfulness and eternal friendship.

The Lord did not carry a driver's license or social security card, but He had the best identification possible—the indelible marks of the nails. These scars in the glorified body of Jesus are the lifelines for fallen humanity.

Thomas was not satisfied with only seeing the face of our Lord to determine His identity. The face can change its expression and deceive others. The face can smile when sad and cry when happy, but the hands cannot change their expression. Jesus understood what Thomas meant, and He said to him, "Take your finger and examine my hands."

There's a beautiful variety of expression in the many varied hands which are raised to receive the Eucharistic Lord. Some are soft and well-manicured; others are shadow-thin and shaky. There are the strong and calloused hands of laborers and the little fingers of children. All reach out for Jesus. Jesus reaches back with hands which will bleed no more—but the blessed scars remind us of the day they did.

John says that this story of Jesus and Thomas is told "to help you believe that Jesus is the Messiah, the Son of God, so that through this faith you may have life in His name."

THIRD SUNDAY OF EASTER (A)
Ac 2:14, 22-28   1 P 1:17-21   Lk 24:13-35

The Eleven were assembled in their old familiar meeting place in Jerusalem, wondering among themselves: "Where's Jesus?" The women who had gone to the tomb before dawn and failed to find Him, asked in their puzzlement: "Where's Jesus?" The two travelers on the road to the little town of Emmaus were engaged in asking: "Where's Jesus?" When we sincerely pray and the prayer seems to return empty, like a hollow echo; when we hurt and beg for help but are not healed, we cry out: "Where's Jesus?"

Today's Gospel reading asks that same intriguing question and provides an exciting answer. It's a classic story which can be read dozens of times and still provide new insights into the age-old search for Jesus.

The Lord walks with us seven days a week, as surely as He walked the seven miles to Emmaus, with Cleopas and his unnamed companion. Even though we don't invite Jesus to walk with us, He still runs to our side and joins us for the journey—whether for seven miles, seven days or seventy years. He walks with us and talks with us and tells us of His love. If only we could recognize Him!

We can't find Jesus by returning to the places where He used to be, as the apostles went to the meeting room and the women went to the grave site. The tomb is empty and the Lord is on the road again, right where we are. He predicted that where two or more are gathered in His name, we should expect His presence. For that reason, we dare not ignore the stranger in our midst.

When we have traveled with Him a mile a day, at the end of the seventh day we invite Him to eucharistically stay with us, for evening is at hand and we want His security and light to dispel the darkness

There is so very much we don't know about the Lord; but as we gather around His table at the end of seven miles, we can watch Him take, bless, break and give Himself to us. He is our spiritual strength for the next mile and for every step of the journey ahead. It's His unique way of staying and sharing our company even though we might think He is far away. Each time we receive His glorified body in Holy Communion, our minds are opened to more deeply appreciate His marvelous revelations. Repeatedly He vanishes into the Bread and the Bread vanishes into our lives to make us like Him.

We, in turn, can become the mysterious Stranger, giving

courage to the doubtful, that their hearts will burn with love and that, rising up, they will walk through the night and find their way back home.

So where can we find Jesus? On the road, in deeds of kindness, in believing hearts, in the words of Scripture and in the breaking of the Bread.

FOURTH SUNDAY OF EASTER (A)
Ac 2:14, 36-41   1 P 2:20-25   Jn 10:1-10

In the catacombs of St. Priscilla, in the northern section of Rome, you can clearly see the artistic illustrations of the faith-filled Christians of the second century. Colorful frescoes are still etched on the walls of what was originally an underground cemetery, meeting area and place of worship. One particular painting is that of the "Good Shepherd."

The colors of red, brown and green which highlight the Shepherd are amazingly vivid after nearly 1900 years. Jesus, the Good Shepherd, is wearing a rugged loose-fitting garment above the knees which extends over His left shoulder, leaving the right side of His upper body uncovered. He carries a sheep on His shoulders and is flanked by trees, birds and other sheep. His right hand is openly extended, inviting all to Him. This calm pastoral scene is bordered by a nearly perfect red circle with the Shepherd in the center.

It is inspiring to realize that the Shepherd theme which was so prevalent in the early Church is still an integral part of our religion. In fact, it is the subject of today's liturgy.

One of the best known references to God as Shepherd in the Old Testament, Psalm 23, is read at this mass as the responsorial. We can be sure that Jesus knew and prayed this psalm. Most likely, He used it as a basis for His own teachings of the Shepherd and sheep.

We should note that the Latin word for "shepherd" is "pastor"—which designates the leader of the community of believers, the Church. The duties of the pastor are those of the shepherd: to provide food (Eucharist), lead to fresh water (Baptism), give shelter (a place to worship) and protect against enemies (prayer and education). The shepherd of each church is called to model his or her role on that of the Good Shepherd.

Jesus ultimately is the Shepherd of all of us, who lavishes affection on each. He Himself said that the true test for the genuine pastor is to lay down his life for those in his care. This Jesus personally did for us. He took up His life again as He had promised, and now leads us on toward a better and eternal pasture.

In our journey through the valley of darkness, we can all individually pray with the psalmist: "The Lord is my shepherd... He guides me in right paths... I fear no evil... There is nothing I shall want." Regardless of our various roles and titles in the Church, we are all members of the one flock and have but one Shepherd. He alone is in center place, surrounded by His redeemed creation, as pictured in the catacombs. The Lord is my Pastor.

FIFTH SUNDAY OF EASTER (A)
Ac 6:1-7 1 P 2:4-9 Jn 14:1-12

Between the turn of the century and the First World War, countless families immigrated from Europe to the United States. In many cases the father would come first, leaving his family in the old country. He would find a job and prepare a place for his wife and children. Then he would return for them or, in most cases, send money for their voyage. He was their ticket to a new life in a new world.

A similar arrangement exists between Jesus and his family of faith. When He spoke to His disciples about the way which leads to the eternal Kingdom, Thomas retorted: "We don't know where you are going. How can we know the way?" Jesus replied with ten words which have inspired generations of Christian believers: "I am the way, and the truth and the life."

Through His redemptive death, the Lord has booked passage for us to a better life in a better land. He has assured us that there is room for all who wish to dwell in His Father's House. For the present, we stay busy in the old world. But when Jesus sends for us, we will be ready to leave—confident that our new home will be waiting.

Although we have many concerns about our everyday world (and rightly so), Jesus challenges us to keep in mind our ever-better future in the new world, even though it is hidden in profound mystery. Trust in Jesus is our ticket, for He said: "Do not let your hearts be troubled. Have faith in me." Someone humorously said that living a decent life on earth is difficult, but "the retirement is out of this world."

The first book of the Bible tells how Adam sinned in his attempt to be like God. He reaped only death. Jesus, the fullness of life, willingly accepted death and thereby achieved eternal life for all.

Some people avoid using the word "dying" to describe one's departure from this world. In its place, they say "passing." I used to think that this was a refusal to face reality. Now I believe that the term "passing" is an excellent choice. "Dying" implies a stopping, a negation; but "passing" indicates a journey into a new life.

With this in mind, let us look in faith to the time when Jesus sends for us with the message, "Your home is ready."

SIXTH SUNDAY OF EASTER (A)
Ac 8:5-8, 14-17   1 P 3:15-18   Jn 14:15-21

We are members of the Catholic Church because of certain beliefs, practices and values which we have that identify us as such.

We profess the existence of God; the Holy Trinity; that Jesus is Lord and Savior; the reality of the future life. We interpret the teachings of the Bible as our directives for daily living—our code of morality. We acknowledge the central importance of the sacraments in our spiritual lives. The particular ways we view, value and adhere to these and other basic truths, makes us unique—it makes us Catholic. Yet how many of us are truly informed about our religion?

If a non-Catholic asked us about the meaning of the Mass or the presence of Jesus in the Eucharist or the reason why we confess our sins to a priest, would we have intelligent answers? Could we explain in a meaningful and convincing way our enduring hope in eternal life?

Today we read part of a letter from the first Pope to his fledgling flock, encouraging them to have answers about their faith, both for themselves and others. He insists that they be informed members of the Church—in fact, they are the Church. The early Christians were to teach Christ to the world. It was not their mission to tell the inquirers to "see a priest." They had to provide the information on the spot for those who were seeking it.

St. Peter's words are just as vital for 20th century Catholics as for those of the first century. The need for quality adult education grows ever greater in the Church. But the sad truth is that many adults stopped learning about their religion when they graduated from their Catholic school or C.C.D. program. They are living their adult Christian lives with their childhood religious guidelines.

We might also become too preoccupied with the "how's" of our religion and not pay enough attention to the "why's." How to receive Holy Communion—on the tongue or in the hand—is not important compared to why we receive Communion. The reality of sin in our lives is essential to understand. The question of how to confess—face to face, or behind a screen—is relatively unimportant.

Our deep personal beliefs are to help us in our daily struggles and to enable us to assist others in theirs. St. Peter reminds us to present our views "with gentleness and humility," lest we appear to be arrogant.

The call goes forth for us to be informed Catholics by reading quality books and articles; attending theological lectures; listening to tapes and watching informative TV programs. Also helpful are Bible reading, personal meditation and prayer. We must do whatever we can to know our religion, for we may be the only gospel our neighbor will ever read.

THE ASCENSION (A)
Ac 1:1-11   Ep 1:17-23   Mt 28:16-20

The major events in the life of Jesus have all been artistically and liturgically expressed in many ways through the centuries. We note a few examples in connection with the celebration of His ascension into heaven. The 19th century poet, Matt Bridges wrote:

> Rise glorious conqueror, rise
> Into thy native skies
> Assume thy right.
> And where in many a fold
> The clouds are backward rolled
> Pass through those gates of gold
> And reign in light.

The painter, De Cramer has pictured the ascension with the apostles on the Mount of Olives looking upward and viewing two scarred feet disappearing into the sky. Below are His footprints left on the surface of the earth.

The ascension of Jesus to His native home has been celebrated in church music, in the second glorious mystery of the rosary and in various other ways and places. One of the best expressions is found in the Gospel of St. Luke.

The liturgical celebration of the feast always comes 40 days after Easter and 10 days before the observance of Pentecost. In the early Church this was a time for enthusiastic rejoicing; during this period there was to be no fasting. Prayers were generally said in a standing position to express the joyful spirit of the season—that of arising. The vestments worn for Mass were to be white.

In conformity with the life of Jesus and the history of our religion, on this Ascension Thursday we lift up our minds and hearts. Although He has ascended, He still remains with us. In the profession of faith we say "He rose from the dead and ascended into heaven," yet before He did, He said that He would be with us always. There are a variety of opinions as to what or where this heaven is to which Jesus ascended. The point is, however, that while He bodily disappeared and is with the Father, at the same time through the Spirit Jesus remains here living in each one of us.

One of His last requests was to tell His disciples to make other disciples of all nations. "I go," He said, "to prepare a place for you," signifying that we don't have a permanent place here. Whether heaven is up there or out there or whatever the direction, the point is that our future is not earthbound.

If we are the ascension people, then we are not to live like we'll stay here forever. In thought and prayer today we try to ascend into heaven with Jesus, for the Church tells us that we are to expect and prepare for our own ascension day.

SEVENTH SUNDAY OF EASTER (A)
Ac 1:12-14   1 P 4:13-16   Jn 17:1-11

Last Thursday, we celebrated the Ascension of Jesus into Heaven. Next week, we will commemorate the coming of the Holy Spirit. This intervening Sunday serves as a bridge between these two outstanding liturgical events.

The first reading, from the Acts of the Apostles, captures the spirit of the early Church. This vivid account shows the apostles (in fact, the entire Church) gathered in the Upper Room for a combination business meeting and spiritual retreat. The pressing business at hand was to select someone to replace Judas. There was an urgency about this, since the Church membership numbered 120 (Ac 1:15). This was the minimum number necessary, in Jewish law, for an official Sanhedrin—a people's court. The Jewish law also stated that the officers of the organization should be one tenth of the membership. A replacement for Judas therefore was necessary to make 12 leaders—the one tenth requirement.

This passage also mentions that Mary, Mother of Jesus, was present at this gathering. It's the last mention of her in Sacred Scripture. She too had been the bridge between the old and the new. Her first scriptural appearance is found in the first chapter of Luke's gospel, where she is asked to be the mother of Jesus. Her final appearance is in the first chapter of Acts, Luke's second book. Here she is the mother of the newborn Church which is struggling to grow. Before she leaves the salvation scene, her work completed, Mary will assist the infant Church to stand and walk on its own, as she had done for the child Jesus.

The "Upper Room" is also an intriguing part of this story. It's the original central office of Christianity, although as yet the members were not known as Christians but simply as "the Brethren." They would be called Christians only later, at Antioch.

Missing the physical presence of Jesus and anxiously awaiting the Holy Spirit, the Brethren find strength in nine days of prayer in their favorite meeting place. Here they participate in the first novena with the intention of opening their lives to the influence of the Holy Spirit and conditioning themselves to be at His service.

The Church today, now grown to millions of parishioners and encircling the entire world, still calls us to imitate the "Brethren" in a pre-Pentecost novena. As we gather together in the Upper Room—our own parish churches—we can reflect on the long road of the past and our pressing needs for today. Here we can pray that the Spirit will move and direct us—the Christian brothers and sisters of the 20th century.

PENTECOST SUNDAY (A)
Ac 2:1-11   1 Cor 12:3-7, 12-13   Jn 20:19-23

Dale Carnegie, the author of *How To Win Friends and Influence People*, once remarked that he had heard the "confessions" of thousands of men and women. These people timidly confided that they were "scared to death" to stand in front of an audience to give a speech. Many of these crowd-frightened individuals were otherwise fearless in their beliefs and highly successful in their careers.

Those "confessions" led Carnegie to write another book: *On Public Speaking*, and moved him to establish courses to help people speak in public without suffering from paralyzing fears. These classes have helped many people and are still very popular today.

The Bible tells us that the apostles suffered a similar fear of facing the public after Jesus had ascended to His Father. For a brief time they floundered in their helplessness to preach to the world, until divine assistance was sent to them.

Pentecost is the day we celebrate the anniversary of the gift of this power from on high, which converted fearful fishermen into courageous preachers and launched them on their world-wide mission.

The liturgical observance of this Spirit-filled day can also be the occasion for renewed encouragement to those of us who are too timid to take a stand for the things we know we should. We are all in need of this divine strength from above, to speak out and live out our convictions.

We don't want to imitate the shiftless hobo, who was seen wandering aimlessly about town. When asked about his destination, he replied, "No place in particular." "Well, how do you decide which direction to go at the beginning of the day?" He replied: "I always travel with the wind at my back."

Many ill winds blow through our world to carry us in their directions, but Pentecost is the wind and fire from Heaven that pushes us toward the Kingdom.

The sacrament of Confirmation is our personal Pentecost, where we open our lives to divine guidance, lest we become spiritual drifters.

Without the strength of the Spirit, the apostles would have been assigned to a mission impossible. Having received the Spirit, they were now able to accept the victor's crown of martyrdom and the ultimate affirmation from their Master.

The first step to fulfill our missions in this world is to believe that we can, because the power of the Spirit takes away our fears and energizes our lives. Once freed from our crippling anxieties we can, like the apostles, walk bravely and talk confidently on our journey to the Kingdom.

TRINITY SUNDAY (A)
Ex 34:4-6, 8-9   2 Cor 13:11-13   Jn 3:16-18

We begin our private prayers and church services in the name of the Father, Son and Holy Spirit, because we belong to a trinitarian religion. This means that we profess God to be three distinct Persons, who share one common nature. Jesus is God. In the Bible, He speaks of His divinity and does astonishing deeds that are proper only to God. He prays to God, His Father, and expresses His unity with Him. Jesus also sends His equal, the Holy Spirit, into the world to continue the process of salvation. Therefore, belief in the Trinity is the central and basic truth of our faith. Because God's nature is so far beyond our comprehension, we constantly preface the word "mystery" to the Holy Trinity. Had Jesus not revealed this profound secret to us, we would never have known God's true, intimate nature.

It is challenging to accept even the simplest concept of God, for His reality is difficult to grasp and consequently many deny His existence. To envision three Persons with one nature staggers the imagination and defies the most brilliant intellect.

God's intimate nature will ever be beyond us. There are no adequate analogies for comparison. This, like countless other religious mysteries, will never be solved. They are not meant to be. They must be accepted on faith rather than reason. Those who say that the Second Vatican Council has taken away much of the mystery from our religion, by its changes, are thinking and speaking foolishly.

The Church's teaching on the Trinity has been consistent from the beginning. St. Peter begins his first letter by referring to the "sanctification of the Spirit . . . the foreknowledge of God the Father and obedience of Jesus Christ . . ." (1 P 1:2). The various ecumenical councils through the centuries have continued to teach and clarify this sacred and central conviction of God's inner nature. Jesus' own unity with the Father and the Holy Spirit inspired Him to call for community among His followers. This is repeated by Paul in today's second reading: "Live in harmony and peace and the God of love and peace will be with you."

Trinity Sunday has been celebrated since the time of Pope John XXII in the early 14th century. It always follows Pentecost and officially closes the Easter season.

"We believe in one God, the Father, the Almighty . . . We believe in one Lord, Jesus Christ, the only Son of God . . . We believe in the Holy Spirit . . ." We believe that God is pure existence, everlasting perfection and an inexhaustible source of wonderment.

CORPUS CHRISTI (A)
Dt 8:2-3, 14-16;   1 Cor 10:16-17;   Jn 6:51-58

One of the most pleasant and natural reasons for families and friends to gather together is to share a meal. This has been a universal custom since the beginning of history.

The ancient Hebrews, with their profound familial and religious practices, found many occasions to assemble around their sacred banquet tables. A very significant meal was the one to celebrate the Passover, which commemorated their deliverance from slavery.

Jesus and His apostles, faithful to their Jewish heritage, also observed the Passover each year. It was in conjunction with the Passover festival that Jesus initiated another sacred meal, the Last Supper. "Do this in memory of me" are solemn words which Christians have always observed, honoring and fulfilling the command of the Savior, given the night before He died. When we assemble at Mass, we celebrate and perpetuate this directive of Jesus, spoken at the original Holy Thursday meal.

The feast of Corpus Christi, observed today, calls our attention to the dignity of the Last Supper and the precious heritage of the Lord's presence in our midst when we gather in faith around His table. It is the body of the risen Lord which we receive, and we are humbly reminded of His eternal love for each of us. His power, wisdom and friendship come to us in the reception of the Bread of Life.

An Italian lady once told me how her father used to serve his homemade wine at their annual family celebrations for many years. The members around the table would sip the wine and compliment him on its good quality. He would smile with inward satisfaction, happy that his family appreciated both him and his labors. He died, leaving many of his untapped bottles in his wine cellar. "Now," she said, "when the family gathers for anniversaries and holidays, we continue to share a bottle of dad's wine." Brushing aside a tear, she said that it helps them to remember the good times of the past. In the wine they sense his presence as still being with them.

The Holy Eucharist is something like that, but is much more. It is the real presence of the Risen Lord abiding with His people in His glorified body. It's His unique way to be with us always.

Corpus Christi evokes memories from the Upper Room, the multiplication of the loaves, the manna in the desert and more. It's a memorial of the past.

Corpus Christi speaks to the present. Jesus said, "*I am* the living bread." That is, right now, today. Through my reception of the Living Bread, I am being strengthened this very moment.

Corpus Christi carries a future promise, an everlasting pledge: "Anyone who eats this bread will live forever."

FEAST OF PETER AND PAUL (A)
Ac 12:1-11   2 Tm 4:6-8, 17-18   Mt 16:13-19

Peter and Paul are two of the biggest names in the history of Christianity; contemporaries of the Lord Himself, chosen by Him to lead and guide the early Church. Although they are linked inseparably in this annual liturgical celebration, in the names of churches and institutions and in the minds of believers, they at times openly opposed each other.

Peter was recruited from the fishing boat, was one of the famous Twelve and soon became their spokesman. Paul was raised and schooled in the circles of legalistic Pharisaism, and opposed and persecuted the early Christians. Although not one of the original Twelve, he was an Apostle and considered himself their equal.

Peter was the first Pope of the infant Church and Paul its greatest missionary. These two religious giants had radically different temperaments, cultural backgrounds and opinions. Paul at times openly opposed Peter and "withstood him to his face" (Gal

2:11). They pushed against each other like the weighty buttresses on either side of a magnificent cathedral. Their differing opinions and influences were vital, for they held the center intact and kept the structure growing tall and strong. Had both been on the same side of every question, the cathedral might have toppled.

One carries the sword, the other the keys. Both wear the martyr's crown and stand linked in this one feast day. Although both these religious superstars seemed undaunted in their post-pentecostal lives, they showed a deep reverential fear of the Lord Jesus. "Depart from me Lord, for I am a sinful man" was said by Peter. The ever-courageous Paul admitted to the Corinthians that he severely disciplined himself "lest after having preached to others he himself would be lost."

Through the centuries, Popes and missionaries have continued the work of their founding fathers. The average reign of the Popes has been 7½ years, and over 26 of them began and ended their office within the same year. In contrast, there is the 32 year reign of Pius IX; but no Pope has surpassed the 33 years of St. Peter. It was the demented Roman Emperor Nero who cut short the careers of both Peter and Paul. Their fate has been shared by many other Popes and missionaries, to the present day.

Today we offer heartfelt prayers for all who serve in the various levels of church leadership and for the self-sacrificing men and women in the missions, facing hardships to bring to others the message of Jesus.

We remember that every Christian is expected to be a leader and a missionary. We are all called to inspire others with divine wisdom and to unify and sanctify the world for Jesus.

THE ASSUMPTION OF THE BLESSED VIRGIN MARY (A)
Rv 11:19; 12:1-6, 10   1 Cor 15:20-26   Lk 1:39-56

A person who has been given rare gifts and honors is called a privileged character. Mary must be regarded as such, considering the many glorious favors handed her which other people have never received. There's the exclusive gift of the Immaculate Conception which protected her from original sin. The unparalleled dignity of being Mother of Jesus places her in intimate association with the divine. Her deep and docile faith at the conception of her Son and her quiet resignation at His death, are models ever to be admired by the rest of humankind.

Mary indeed stands in a class of her own, with qualities and dignities far superior to ours. Yet there is one privileged blessing which she received that we can not only hope for but actually obtain—the one celebrated in today's liturgy. She was taken into heaven at the end of her life on earth, and we hope for the same happy ending when our existence here is finished. We too are privileged characters.

Our Gospel reading contains Mary's perfected formula for successful living, based on her life style of profound faith in her Maker and tender love for all creation. The luminous views of the Magnificat are a striking summary of her convictions about faith and good works. Mary shows that her lofty thoughts did not center on self-love but that she identified with the lesser people of earth. She sees the proud "deposed" and the mighty "dethroned" but the lowly (like her) are lifted up to inherit "every good thing." The Magnificat, more than any other scripture passage, gives precious glimpses into the hallowed soul of the Virgin Mary. It's her jubilant theme song.

We remember Jesus' glorious baptism, when the clouds of heaven opened for the descent of the Holy Spirit and the Father's voice was heard: "This is my beloved Son." The clouds opened another time (although this occasion is not recorded in the Bible) when the mother of Jesus was taken home. We can imagine the eternal welcome which awaited her on the other side, and the celestial voice of the Father: "This is my beloved daughter."

It's exciting to know that God can love a human being so deeply. With this in mind, we should never doubt our own self-worth even though we are lowly and hungry. In those situations we are not being abandoned but are in a position to be lifted up in glory. If our spirits (like Mary's) can find joy in our God and if we can proclaim His greatness in words and deeds, then we are living the Magnificat. We too have a kingdom promised to us and we have many reasons to joyfully sing that the Almighty has done great things for us.

ALL SAINTS (A)
Rv 7:2-4, 9-14   1 Jn 3:1-3   Mt 5:1-12

The opinionated world to which Jesus hurled out His challenging invitation to perfection was dominated by three major power groups. Each was consolidated in its own custom-laden traditions.

1. There were the Greeks, well known for their famous philosophers with a wide reputation for wisdom and scholarly pursuits. They believed that knowledge alone could make them completely fulfilled, and they strived for it beyond all else. Their "patron saints" were Socrates, Plato and Aristotle.

2. The Romans made everyone intensely aware of their military presence. They professed complete faith in their mighty army, believing that it could conquer any rival. Power was the god they worshiped, guided by the moral dictum that might is right. Their leaders thrived on conquered riches, luxurious comforts, delicate food, lavish entertainment and plush villas. Where the Greeks worshiped the wise, the Romans deified the strong.

3. The Jews were the third class to whom Jesus extended His proposal for a new kind of integrity. They were steeped in hundreds of ritualistic laws and traditions, faithfully handed down from their ancestors. For the most part they lived by the minute letter of their legal codes, believing that they contained the ex-

pressed will of God. To be just in the eyes of God, they had to know and observe the law exactly. The religious lawyers therefore attracted the veneration of the people.

In today's Gospel reading Jesus stands on the mount, like Moses on Mt. Sinai 1300 years earlier, speaking a strange doctrine—His new commandments for holiness. What would the Greeks' reaction be to the teaching that love was superior to knowledge and how would a loyal Roman accept the suggestion that a peacemaker is better than a conqueror? The Jew would object that the new commandments were not superior to the old law.

We might deepen our appreciation for those adventurous men and women who accepted the beatitudes of Jesus and began to live according to His standards. It is easy to see why so many first generation Christians died martyrs' deaths.

The word "saint" comes from the Latin *sanctus*, meaning "holy," which in turn means "whole" or "well." Thus a saint is one of proven strength and virtue. The saints are not odd or eccentric individuals but honest and straightforward people. They are neither two-faced nor half-hearted. They are our heroes and heroines.

Although technically a saint is one in heaven, we don't start becoming saints the day we die but the day we are born. It's a lifelong objective and heaven is the fulfillment. No one is enshrined in the hall of fame unless he or she has been severely tested and proven on the field of competition and conquest.

Today we honor all those strong, innocent and reformed people who lived for and loved their God and now share His Kingdom. We pray for renewed strength and grace to continually accept the paradoxical wisdom of Jesus in such a way that He will find us worthy to enter the Kingdom.

THE IMMACULATE CONCEPTION (A)
Gn 3:9-15, 20   Ep 1:3-6, 11-12   Lk 1:26-38

In the Mass there are several times when we observe silence. These are for reflection in order to develop our appreciation of the liturgy. There is the moment of quietness at the beginning of Mass to thankfully remember God's mercy. Silence after the readings enables us to savor their message. This is true as well in the silence following the homily and again after the reception of communion.

Moments of peaceful silence become even more meaningful when we celebrate the various feasts in honor of the Blessed Virgin Mary, for her entire life was one of quietness. She is not remembered for any stirring public speeches, although she would have been well qualified to deliver them. She must have believed that wisdom is conveyed as much by the things we don't say as those we do. It has been observed that important people are recognized by the things they don't say. Jesus was often completely silent, especially in trying times—a quality no doubt learned from His mother.

Mary listened to God and responded quietly as an obedient servant girl. Yet her dignity was absolutely staggering for she was a woman without sin, mother of Jesus and future queen of heaven. Nonetheless we never hear her boasting of any exalted position. She does acknowledge that she is blessed—not to call attention to herself but to offer a prayer to the One who made her blessed.

Today, when people seek to acquire important-sounding titles, the lowly label of servant does little for our image. But it was that title which Mary used to describe herself, and she gloried in its meaning. "Behold the handmaid of the Lord." Who of us could have moved in the circles of divine royalty and been privileged to share in the intimate life of God Himself and still have been silent in conversation and totally humble in mind?

Success, honor and praise can easily change a person for the worst. They can make them the very opposite from what he or she was originally. Mary is the model of continuing success as she calmly demonstrates how to handle dignity with grace and class. She passed that same humble dignity to her Son, who in later years would say, "I am humble of heart."

A study and imitation of her life can help us avoid pitfalls and give timely directions for peaceful living. Mary is an excellent role model for both men and women on how to love and minister with grace and how to be blessed forever.

Immaculate Mary, servant of God, pray for us.

SECOND SUNDAY OF THE YEAR (A)
Is 49:3, 5-6   1 Cor 1:1-3   Jn 1:29-34

The Lamb. That's what Jesus is called in today's Gospel. This gentle symbol would never be considered as a fitting logo for the mighty people of today. Imagine a football team being called "The Lambs." The hard-hitting players and avid fans prefer names like Lions, Tigers, Panthers, Bulls, etc. Isn't it strange that the Almighty would choose to be known as The Lamb? Does it not clarify for us the Lord's understanding of real strength, and give us the deeper spiritual meaning of true power?

The Lamb symbol has a rich history and is intimately associated with some tremendous salvific events. The lamb was ceremonially eaten in Egypt on the eve of the Exodus. The lamb again was present on the Last Supper table, the night before Jesus died. It has often been shown in Church art as wounded yet triumphantly holding aloft a pennant-shaped victory flag. The Lamb has won the pennant. The animal that sacrifices its flesh, wool and skin is God's victory sign.

Its symbolism is not confined to the Jewish and Christian religions. The courageous Hindu, Mahatma Gandhi found the lamb image deeply significant of his concept of pacifism, which he preached as the only way to ultimate triumph.

Our religion overflows with paradoxes. So many of its teachings are exactly the opposite from what we would expect. Thus, we preach that the lamb is stronger than the lion. At each Mass we cry out the triumphant chant, not once but three times: "Lamb of God, who takes away the sins of the world." By this we profess that humanity's most admirable Servant walked through this world, showing us that gentleness is toughness.

We are invited to follow that same paradoxical tradition and find glory in our weaknesses. St. Paul said it well: "I am content with weakness . . for when I am powerless it is then that I am strong" (2 Cor 12:10).

Whenever we try to act as a dominating master instead of a humble servant, we are ignoring the "lamb theology." Jesus told us that church and civil authority are radically different. In the state, the leaders "lord it over" their subjects. But to His disciples, Jesus says, "It cannot be like that with you. Anyone among you who aspires to greatness must serve the rest" (Mt 20:25).

So it was that He lived and preached, and although He was led to the slaughter and was as mute as a lamb before the shearer, He won a greater victory than anyone has ever done.

THIRD SUNDAY OF THE YEAR (A)
Is 8:23-9:3   1 Cor 1:10-13, 17   Mt 4:12-23

St. Paul did not hesitate to admonish the infant Christian community of Corinth for its lack of unity. Naturally he realized that there would be divisions, but he expected a deeper unanimity than was present. In our reading today, he paternally reprimands his recent converts, crying out: "Let there be no factions; rather be united in mind and judgment."

His words have a timely meaning for the many and varied Christian Churches today. We still have our factions and contradict one another, while each of us claims to understand and possess Jesus in His fullness.

Each year at this time, in the cold deadness of winter, we celebrate Church Unity Week. It is a time we try to heal past divisions with those of other churches. This Unity Week is not just another change flowing out of the Second Vatican Council. Although the Council did augment its thrust, Unity Week has been observed in the U.S.A. since 1906.

Our efforts toward Christian unity fall under the category of ecumenism. This is an attempt to foster understanding and mutual respect between separated Christians. Our past divisions are the fault of both Catholics and Protestants, and these generations of hostility are not easily forgotten. It is therefore understandable why many find it hard to abandon their ghettoes of isolation to engage in friendly dialogue.

For your thought and discussion, I have listed some ecumenical guidelines, suggested by the noted scholar, Fr. Avery Dulles, S.J.

1) The church of Christ, as it should be, is not found in any Church today; we are still moving toward that objective.
2) The Christian Churches have more that unites them than divides them, and this should be expressed in common worship.
3) All religions have something good to offer.
4) Ecumenism calls people to be strong in their own religions, but understanding of others.
5) We cannot be good Catholics without some sense of ecumenism, for Jesus and His disciples prayed and worked for it.
6) Unity is a gift of God which will come only through prayer and change of heart.
7) We need to have a kindly attitude toward those who work for unity and not view them as half-hearted. They are zealous members, trying to accomplish the very thing for which Jesus died.

Although our oneness with each other helps us to more

completely be one with God, we are never to be pressured into the sacred bond of religious agreement. We must always be invited.

FOURTH SUNDAY OF THE YEAR (A)
Zp 2:3; 3:12-13 1 Cor 1:26-31 Mt 5:1-12

Long ago, Moses received the Ten Commandments from God and taught them to his people. The Commandments are a mere fraction of the total number of Jewish laws; the Old Testament contains whole books of laws, such as Leviticus and Deuteronomy. Yet the Ten Commandments were afforded an unrivaled dignity because they are so basic to daily life. Even to this day, they hold an exalted position in both the Jewish and Christian religions.

These Ten Commandments support the Jewish belief of the goodness of life on this earth. The fourth commandment, "Honor your father and mother," for example, has a promise attached: "that you may have a long life" in this world (Ex 20:12). If these ten holy rules were faithfully observed, this would indeed be a wonderful world, but not necessarily a Christian one, for Jesus demanded more. He added a further moral dimension to the Commandments—the Beatitudes, which we read in today's Gospel.

Christians view the future life as being more important than this one. The Beatitudes are future oriented.

A present misfortune, for the ancient Hebrews was viewed as a sign of the loss of the good graces of God. The Christian should see it as a hidden blessing, which will produce a greater future good. Jesus said, "Blest are the sorrowing; they *shall* be consoled. Blest are the lowly; they *shall* inherit the land." We therefore do not view the poor as cursed nor the rich as necessarily blessed. If we really believed in the Beatitudes we would not complain about sorrows, poverty and hunger, for they would be recognized as signs of future blessings. This does not mean that we should passively accept such conditions. Jesus' ministry was one of healing the sick, the blind and the lame. We are called to do all we can to relieve the sufferings of others.

Can we personally accept discouragements, reversals, and even tragedies, by seeing them as blessings? Do we believe that these bitter hurts are a sign of a rich future glory?

Moses climbed his mountain to receive the Commandments. Jesus likewise climbed His mountain and gave the Beatitudes—the new Commandments, which enrich the old.

After the Lord taught the world how suffering leads to glory, He gave an unforgettable example. He was agonizingly killed on Friday afternoon but rose gloriously on Sunday morning. His life, death and resurrection are the best commentary on the Beatitudes that we have.

FIFTH SUNDAY OF THE YEAR (A)
Is 58:7-10   1 Cor 2:1-5   Mt 5:13-16

Drummond Erskine tells a story of a mother and her small child as they drove past the restored home of Abraham Lincoln in Springfield, Ill. It was night, and the national shrine was brightly lit. "Look, mama," the child said excitedly, "Mr. Lincoln left his lights on." The mother smiled. "Yes," she replied, "he left them on for the whole world to see."

Although Lincoln has been dead since 1865, he is still a tremendous inspiration to all people. There is general agreement that he is the most popular of all the presidents, and the World Book Encyclopedia calls him "one of the truly great men of all time."

As a young man we know he read every book he could find, including the Bible. He must have read and perhaps meditated on today's passage from Matthew: "You are the salt of the earth . . .

you are the light of the world." Salt both gives flavor and acts as a preservative. Light gives direction and encouragement.

Lincoln proved to be a guiding light especially when he signed the Emancipation Proclamation, which was the beginning of the end of slavery. He was also a preserver—of the Union during the Civil War.

In our reading today from the Sermon on the Mount, Jesus tells his disciples that they are the light of the world and the salt of the earth. He doesn't say that we are to *become* that, but that we *are* that already. As dedicated Christians, we follow our Leader—Christ, who according to our creed is "God from God, Light from Light . . ." No world leader has been more effective or left a more lasting impact than Jesus Christ. He is the shining beacon for all people, of all times. He calls us to let our lights shine to encourage those in darkness. Jesus openly defended the truths he professed. No one had to guess where He stood.

Good people often encourage crime by failing to condemn it. When too many lamps are hidden under tables, the night becomes darker and crime and sin increase and thrive.

The prophet Isaiah gives us the same message today. He encourages us to good works, promising a brighter world and the healing of old wounds. God has selected each of us for our own particular time in history, to be a part of the light of the world.

How can I dispel darkness, heal wounds and preserve peace? Certainly not by crawling under the kitchen table to hide in fear. We are to consider it our religious duty to do good works with the light and salt that is within us.

SIXTH SUNDAY OF THE YEAR (A)
Si 15:15-20   1 Cor 2:6-10   Mt 5:17-37

The Sermon on the Mount has been called our Lord's Inaugural Address, since it was delivered early in His public career and contains a clear summary of His teachings. This is the third Sunday in a series of six that we read from this famous mountain discourse, found in chapters 5, 6 and 7 of Matthew's Gospel. Today's passage from chapter 5 highlights our internal thoughts and desires, and stresses their moral consequences for good or evil.

Jesus clearly teaches that sins are committed in the human mind if one has the definite intention of doing wrong, even if the decision is not acted on. If we hate someone so bitterly that we want to kill them, Jesus says that we are guilty of murder. Of course, the consequences would be much worse if we actually murdered someone, but from God's point of view we have already committed murder.

To escape "murder by intention," Jesus counsels us to avoid thoughts of anger. They can twist our minds and lead us to violent and vicious deeds.

The same advice is offered in the case of adultery. One may say that he has never been unfaithful to his wife. If accused of adultery, he would deny it. Yet the Lord says that if you lust for another in your heart, you are guilty of committing the sin and the Lord sees it as such. This refers to deliberate intentions which for one reason or another are not acted on, and not to passing thoughts. These are indeed very high codes of conduct and they go contrary to many of our present day standards.

We have a grave personal responsibility to monitor all the stormy debates which rage within us and not allow ourselves to act from hatred, passion or ignorance. It is vitally important that we have a correct conscience to direct our choices in daily living. "Conscience" literally means "with knowledge." It must be our true guide for action.

We must not imitate our first parents, who chose to believe the serpent (the deceiver) rather than consult with God as He "walked in the garden in the cool of the evening." The more we keep in touch with the Source of truth, the less we will be dominated by thoughts filled with unworthy motives and suspicions. Since our deeds follow our ideas, honorable thinking is a great blessing.

This Christian teaching echoes an old Buddhist saying, from about 300 B.C.: "All that is, is the result of what we have thought."

SEVENTH SUNDAY OF THE YEAR (A)
Lv 19:1-2, 17-18   1 Cor 3:16-23   Mt 5:38-48

We might consider the ancient law of revenge— "an eye for an eye and a tooth for a tooth"—to be cruel and barbaric, but actually it was a law of mercy. It limited the retaliation to no more than the original injury. For example, if a person in anger knocked out one of your teeth, you could retaliate by knocking out one of his—but that was it. If someone struck you in the eye, you could return the "favor" but no more.

Jesus dissented from this old principle and in today's Gospel He presents a real challenge: "love your enemies, pray for your persecutors." Loving friends and praying for benefactors is fine, but enemies and persecutors? The Lord says that even the pagans love their friends, and there's nothing exceptional about that. Christians are expected to do more. In fact, we are asked to forego self-defense in the face of physical violence.

The noted scripture scholar John L. McKenzie, S.J. calls this rejection of self-defense one of the Lord's "most paradoxical sayings." It would be difficult to envision a group of people who absolutely refused to fight to preserve their property or lives. McKenzie further comments, "the Christian world has never been able to live according to this ethic." If we did, we would all be avowed pacifists.

However, there is another point of view in the interpretation of this difficult passage. Perhaps Jesus did not mean it to be taken 100% literally. He may have intended it as a deliberate overstatement, to impress on His hearers the necessity of being at peace with others. We may criticize our government for not acting in line with this teaching, but none of us are living the spirit of complete peacefulness, even in our private lives. How many grudges do you carry about, simmering within you? Are the slights and putdowns you received years ago, still waiting for the right moment to strike back? Forgiveness is one message we can put into effect immediately and unilaterally. Why don't we? We might consider the length of our enemy list and see whose name is on the top. It's also interesting to speculate on who would write our names on their enemy list, and if they are justified in doing so.

In an effort to be loving and forgiving people, we extend the hand of friendship at Mass. It means that we are on good terms with everyone, for the few we greet are symbolic of it.

If your worst enemy was right behind you in church today, would you be willing to turn and sincerely offer a peaceful greeting? The revengeful would not turn. The Christian would.

EIGHTH SUNDAY OF THE YEAR (A)
Is 49:14-15   1 Cor 4:1-5   Mt 6:24-34

There is an old Latin saying: "Age quod agis." It means literally, "Do what you do." A few examples will show how it should be applied.

When we come to church, for instance, we should come intending to pray to God and deepen our faith. It's a time to sing the hymns, hear the readings, apply the homily, offer a peaceful hand and receive Holy Communion. It's a time to really do what we're there to do. The same applies to our jobs. We should give a full day's work for a full day's pay. When the day's work is finished, we ought to engage ourselves completely in other activities.

If we go to a movie, we should involve ourselves in the plot, discern what the producer is trying to do, and see how well the stars are performing. One lady says that whenever she attends the theater with her husband, he gripes through the first half: "You mean we paid $8.50 to see this?"—and then he always wants to leave early to beat the traffic out of the parking lot. It's the classic case of not doing what you're doing.

Prayer, work and recreation have long been recognized as the three essential ingredients for the rhythm of life. These were clearly preached by St. Benedict in the 6th century and incorporated into his Rule. We're expected to neither overdo nor underdo any of the three—but whichever we are doing at the time, it should have our full attention.

Isn't it encouraging to realize that it was Jesus who said we should live for today and "stop worrying about tomorrow"? In short, He was saying "Age quod agis."

The Lord explains in today's Gospel that the birds in the sky show more common sense than some people. They put in a good day's work, refurbish their nests, feed their young, chase away predators and peacefully go to sleep. He says that the birds don't worry, and advises us to follow their example.

The wild flowers also really enjoy life, brightening the valleys and hillsides and never fretting over which is the prettiest. Shouldn't we free our minds from the constant competition of making money, climbing socially, etc. to simply enjoy the world of beauty about us? We need to take time to watch the birds and smell the flowers to both stay in touch with reality and remain in harmony with God and each other. Don't think that only the poets, artists and inventors need leisure time—we all do.

You might want to circle Matthew 6:24-34 in your Bibles and read the passage often. It is the most beautiful section of the Sermon on the Mount, and one of the outstanding passages of the entire Bible. It flows with a free and open style, telling us to relax, stop worrying and be at peace. It was the way, long ago, that Jesus told us to "have a good day."

NINTH SUNDAY OF THE YEAR (A)
Dt 11:18, 26-28   Rm 3:21-25, 28   Mt 7:21-27

Anthony was an outstanding miler during his senior high school year. He was successful because he knew how to motivate himself. Several days before each race he would decide how fast he should run, then write the challenging time on a small piece of cardboard and carry it in his pocket.

Sometimes before big meets, he would ink the desired time on the back of his hand or tape it to his bedroom door. Through these constant reminders he mentally "ran and won" dozens of times before the starting gun sounded. When he finally lined up for the actual race, he was mentally and emotionally ready. Anthony impressed others with his tremendous motivation to run fast, endure pain and win—which he nearly always did.

This same style of motivation is presented by Moses in today's reading from the Book of Deuteronomy, where he tells the people to bind the commandments to their wrists and foreheads. In this way, they would be inspired to both learn and observe these sacred laws of God, and adhere to them even when severely tempted.

Just as Moses inspired the Hebrews to internalize God's directives, so did Jesus in the Sermon on the Mount. Those who merely mouth the words without conviction will not enter the Kingdom. The Lord explicitly warns us that we cannot talk our way into Heaven. The person admitted, He says, is not the one shouting, "Lord, Lord," but the one "who does the will of my Father in heaven."

Picture the embarrassment of those who excitedly rushed to Jesus to enter the Kingdom and were told that He didn't know their names. Confused but still optimistic, they reminded Him that they had spoken His name often during their lives; but He gave the same answer as before. The meaning of the passage is that they truly didn't know Him.

We must seriously ask ourselves if we know Jesus. Do we really talk to Him in prayer and do our works for His glory? Do we, too, say "Lord, Lord" thoughtlessly and do our good works for our own glory?

Ash Wednesday invites us to the annual season of penance. We are called to purify our motives and strengthen our bond of love for the Master, for His friendship must be daily developed and never presumed.

When the lifeless ashes are placed on our foreheads, it should remind us that what we build on the sands of pride will be reduced to ruins, but that a life constructed on the rock of Christ will not collapse.

TENTH SUNDAY OF THE YEAR (A)
Ho 6:3-6   Rm 4:18-25   Mt 9:9-13

A good teacher conveys wisdom to students by speaking clearly and also by way of example. The word "teach" is of Anglo-Saxon origin, meaning "to show."

In this passage from Matthew, the enemies of Jesus want to discredit Him as a teacher by saying that by "eating with tax collectors and those who disregard the law," He shows Himself to be a bad example. Like an alert teacher, aware of classroom murmurings and whispers, Jesus "overhears the remark," and responds that they, the hostile and narrow-minded Pharisees, are not His sole concern. His mission as teacher is to the general public and especially to those considered of little worth.

A banquet consisting of tax collectors, prostitutes and other assorted sinners would not be regarded as the social event of the year; yet it would be an outstanding occasion, if Jesus were present. The tax collectors especially were hated, and often rightly so. Fr. John L. McKenzie explains that they were native Israelites who obtained their jobs by competitive bidding and would often cheat and gouge clients. Since they frequently over-charged for personal gain and collected the tax money from their native people for the Romans, they were viewed as traitors.

This reading does not excuse sinners. It simply acknowledges the existence of evil and states that the Lord is willing to forgive—in fact, that's His mission, His reason for being here. He is the Savior, who brings spiritual healing to all people, for all times. Fortunately, that includes all of us.

Since we are recipients of His mercy, we in turn should extend that same compassion to others who stumble and fall. Jesus says that unless there are sick people, there is no real need for the doctor. Sinners, he implies, need his forgiveness even more than the physically sick need the physician, for nobody can say, "I am free from sin." There's a bit of the drunkard, the cheater, the prostitute, the unjust tax collector in each of us which cries out for the merciful Physician.

If we refuse to admit our spiritual sicknesses, we can't see any real need for the saving Jesus. We may consider ourselves healthy and holy—but if we, like the snobbish Pharisees, disdain others, we are sick. If we think ourselves to be above reproach, we're sick. If we talk and act as if we have personally accomplished our own salvation without the suffering Savior, we are really sick. Maybe we endlessly praise ourselves for keeping the civil laws better than some—but what about the law of charity?

This Gospel passage probes into our spiritual health. How many infectious spiritual diseases do we have? How urgently do we need to call upon the healing Lord?

Fortunately, we are welcome at His table—for he "eats with tax collectors and those who disregard the law." Jesus personally invites you to His supper. R.S.V.P.

ELEVENTH SUNDAY OF THE YEAR (A)
Ex 19:2-6   Rm 5:6-11   Mt 9:36-10:8

A little boy had a four-year-old sister with a rare disease, who was in dire need of a blood transfusion. The blood would have to come from a relative with the same blood type, and the boy was suggested as the logical donor.

"Son," the doctor asked him, "would you be willing to give your blood so your sister can live?" A shocked expression came over his face. Finally he bravely replied: "Sure, I'll do it."

The necessary blood had been taken and he was still lying on his cot when the physician walked by. "Doctor," he asked, "when do I die?" Only then did the doctor realize the little boy had misunderstood—he thought he had to give ALL his blood for his baby sister. The doctor quickly reassured him that they had taken only a small amount of his blood and that he would not die.

Jesus gave ALL His blood for His sisters and brothers. "By His blood we are saved." The Savior is forever our best model of self-sacrifice, One who both lived and died a life which was a total gift to others. As a baby He had "no crib for a bed," and as an adult there was "nowhere to lay His head." He remarked that the birds and foxes had nests and dens but as He journeyed through life, there was no place for Him to call home.

Paul marvels in today's second reading that Jesus walked the road to execution and willingly accepted death, as a type of hostage in our behalf. The ironic part of it was that Jesus gave His blood not for family nor friends but for billions of people who neither knew Him nor loved Him.

Matthew recounts in today's Gospel reading how Jesus was moved with pity for the crowd. He saw them as helpless, dejected sheep and thus He selected the first twelve shepherds to lead, feed and heal them. We cannot accuse Jesus of deceptively luring the disciples with promises of earthly securities and comforts. Ministry is a gift, and it's to be given as a gift.

Those who shepherd in the field of religion must find their security in Jesus, now and in the future. Life insurance policies, pension plans, retirement funds, etc. are all good and necessary, but we must remember that "we have not here a lasting kingdom."

Can we see our lives and blood as gifts from God and give them in behalf of others? Can we look beyond death and see life on the other side of the grave?

The readings for today are very challenging. They invite us to give of our precious selves. The Lord gave His blood and the apostles gave likewise. We at least can give our attention to the closing words of the Gospel reading: "The gift you have received, give as a gift." What does that mean for us on our pilgrim way through this world to the Kingdom?

TWELFTH SUNDAY OF THE YEAR (A)
Jr 20:10-13   Rm 5:12-15   Mt 10:26-33

Jeremiah was a very unhappy and persecuted man, as the book of Scripture which bears his name tells us. Although he desperately tried to do what was right—and precisely because he did—he was denounced, gossiped about and tormented. His condemners constantly tried to maneuver him into a trap.

Many people today suffer the same fate as Jeremiah, especially those with public responsibilities. They are often the objects of vicious attacks and merciless gossiping. These are the odious tactics of small, vicious people too stupid and cowardly to face their supposed opponents and voice their objections in person.

If a person is continually subjected to harassments it can cause them to become bitter and filled with hate. When we meet a disgusted person with a negative attitude about most things, very likely they have been fashioned by someone's viciousness.

Contrast the reading from Jeremiah with that from the

Gospel of Matthew. Here we encounter a bright and cheerful mood, with optimistic thoughts and feelings. Jesus says: "Do not let men intimidate you." The Lord promoted long ago the type of positive thinking which is so common in our time. We have numerous books, tapes and lectures available today, presented by dynamic achievers who want to convey to others their secrets of success. They say that attitude is the most important factor in determining our degree of happiness and success.

If we have a poor and negative attitude toward our jobs, other people and life in general, then we are prone to failure. On the other hand, if we exhibit a positive, strong and aggressive attitude toward our tasks, then we will succeed.

The Lord's insistence that others not intimidate us is so very current and correct. Why should others be permitted to put us down and make us feel inferior? No one is sin-proof and no one lives a life without making poor judgments and other mistakes. Remembering that we are as good as the next person (and especially that God has told us that we are personally worth more than a flock of sparrows) should help us to raise our self-esteem if it has fallen.

Someone has said that it is our attitude rather than our aptitude which will determine our altitude. Jesus counsels us to be strong-willed, prudent, persevering and filled with faith. If God loves His created birds so much that not one will fall without his consent, then we should rejoice that He loves us "more than a whole flock of sparrows." Paul, like Jeremiah, was a very persecuted person—but this never dimmed his dynamic enthusiasm, for he found strength to conquer every difficulty and discouragement with the courage Jesus gave to him.

When we have to contend with the whisperings and gossip which surely will come our way, we need not be defeated, for the Lord commands us to be unintimidated. Regardless of the evil forces which pull us down, His graces are far stronger to lift us up.

THIRTEENTH SUNDAY OF THE YEAR (A)
2 K 4:8-11, 14-16   Rm 6:3-4, 8-11   Mt 10:37-42

"It's time for you to go to bed, honey," a father told his five-year-old girl. She didn't want to and when her father insisted in a louder tone, her pleading eyes filled with tears. She saw his frown and asked: "Daddy, do you love me?" He immediately replied: "Why yes, darling, I love you." "How much do you love me, daddy?" He extended his long arms as far open as possible and replied, "That much." He then asked his daughter if she loved him. In imitation, she extended her little arms as open as possible. They smiled and hugged each other. The father explained that his love for her made him insist on doing what was best for her; if she truly loved him, she would now be obedient and run along to bed.

In today's Gospel reading the Lord gives some clear guidelines about the quality of love which He asks us to give to Him. The norm, He says, must be greater than the love we have for parents and children—that is, two of the most intimate and tender types of love. So we view the highest and best we humanly have to offer others, and know that our love of God must be more, although we can't see Him face to face or throw our arms around Him. It is a demanding love indeed; one intimately bound up with a deep and lively faith. We know that He opened His arms on the cross as far as possible to show for all time His tremendous love for us.

A bit further in this Gospel, the Lord says that we are worthy of Him only if we take up our crosses and follow Him. A cross normally reminds us of pain and death, but the messages of love and life are even more deeply imbedded in the cross of Christ.

We do not truly love one another if we only consider our own selfish interests. The kind of sacred caring of which Jesus speaks is very costly. Kindness, patience and trust do not come easily for most people. Real love does not stop at words but hands a cup of cold water to another in need.

Unless we carry a cross and follow the Lord, we are not

worthy of Him. Since we want to be worthy of His love and trust, we should clarify what it means "to carry a cross."

When we welcome an insignificant person and treat them with honor and respect, we are carrying a cross. That's not too difficult. When we do our work well and uncomplainingly even though we don't feel like it, that's carrying a cross. When we suffer a terrible tragedy and still believe in God's eternal goodness, we are carrying a cross.

Jesus left heavenly Father and earthly mother for us, and we were His cross. Our crosses are to carry whatever life hands us and to walk through this world back to Him. The cross is basic to Christianity. It signifies the present cost of living, of loving and of following the Lord.

FOURTEENTH SUNDAY OF THE YEAR (A)
Zc 9:9-10   Rm 8:9, 11-13   Mt 11:25-30

On the pedestal of the Statue of Liberty is a poem entitled "The New Colossus," written by Emma Lazarus. It contains over one hundred words, but many people remember only one sentence. "Give me your tired, your poor, your huddled masses yearning to breathe free . . ." Holding her torch 305 feet above the base of the pedestal, the copper-garmented lady speaks to the people of the world about our philosophy and values.

Today's Gospel passage is about as long as "The New Colossus," and contains a similar line from the lips of Jesus. "Come to me, all you who are weary and find life burdensome, and I will refresh you." He extends a gentle invitation to all people of all times to come to Him for rest and peace. Since everyone at times feels weary and burdened, it certainly is encouraging to know where to turn for relief. The Lord, like the Statue of Liberty, points out a harbor of safety and opportunity for those seeking a better life.

Although there are many things wrong in our country, we are still very fortunate. The world should be thankful for the existence of the U.S.A., for no nation has ever extended itself more to assist the tired and poor. This generosity has benefited both those who have come to our shores and those who have not. Food, medicine, money, and foreign and domestic aid of all kinds have been freely given by our country. The Statue of Liberty does speak the truth.

Yet the best of earthly blessings cannot satisfy all the longings of the human heart. We possess deeper needs, and only the Lord can speak to them.

The poor and weary are those who feel an inner emptiness, and it is to them that the Lord promises His refreshments. We might think that material blessings would be better than spiritual ones, but actually they are the lesser gifts. Wealth can easily bring more pain than joy. A peaceful mind and a calm sense of security is by far a greater possession. Temporary benefits have a built-in sadness by the very fact that they are temporary. The quality of a gift is ultimately determined by its capacity to endure.

The Lord of all nations invites the tired, the poor, the huddled masses, to triumph over their weariness and burdens of life by discovering the spiritual strength of His gentle and humble heart. His promised refreshments do not disappear with time. They are faith, trust, courage and genuine love, which lift us up and make us live forever.

FIFTEENTH SUNDAY OF THE YEAR (A)
Is 55:10-11   Rm 8:18-23   Mt 13:1-23

A young man who joined a fundamentalist church once told me that the intellect can be very dangerous and can get in the way of the Holy Spirit working in our lives and teaching us the scriptures. I objected to his statement, but could not persuade him to reevaluate the need for scholarship. He simply said that the Holy Spirit "inspired the writing of the Bible and inspires each person with the correct interpretation, and there is no need for study."

Common sense tells us that the intellect is our best ally. The more we develop it, the better for ourselves and others. It seeks the truth, and God knows we need to know and live the truth. When the scripture scholar, Bruce Vawter was asked about this anti-intellectual approach to the Bible, he replied, "Fundamentalism is not a biblical religion; it is a travesty and a parody of biblical religion."

In today's Gospel we have the parable of the Sower and the Seed, presented and interpreted by Jesus. As He explains the parable to His apostles, notice how He stresses that faith does not take root in the "footpath" people because they lack *understanding*. The seed (message) is sown in the *mind* but stolen from it. It cannot penetrate the minds of those who are hardened in their narrow views and who refuse to even consider anything new or different.

The Bible is not one continuous flow of literal historical fact. It is a collection of literature of many kinds in need of various interpretations. Parables, for example, are fictitious stories told for the purpose of making one or sometimes several general points. The parable of the Sower and the Seed teaches us to have open minds to accept God's word and reproduce it in our own lives.

This parable also refutes the idea that true faith will deliver one from all disappointments and pains. Jesus says that setbacks and persecutions will come; when they occur, it does not mean that our faith is weak. Some of the world's holiest people have suffered the most. Christ Himself is the greatest example of that.

The Lord commands His loyal followers not to be sidetracked by foolishness but to be single-minded in the pursuit of wisdom and truth.

O God of all wisdom, we pray that You sharpen our minds to pursue the truth, which You have promised will set us free.

SIXTEENTH SUNDAY OF THE YEAR (A)
Ws 12:13, 16-19   Rm 8:26-27   Mt 13:24-43

In a fifth-grade class there were two boys by the name of Fred. One Fred, the smaller one, bothered the teacher with his undisciplined antics and his refusal to study. Because of him, she frequently questioned the wisdom of becoming a teacher.

At the first P.T.A. meeting a polite lady entered her classroom and introduced herself as Fred's mother. Assuming that she was the mother of the other Fred, who was one of her favorite students, the teacher lavishly praised him and said that he was a fine boy and a real joy to have in class.

The following morning, little Fred came dashing into the classroom before the other students and threw his arms around his teacher. "Thank you," he half sobbed, "for telling my mother I was one of your favorite students and a joy to have in class." Shocked by his words but remaining prudently silent, the teacher realized the mistaken identity. "I haven't been good—but I will be." She softly patted his down-cast head and turned away in tears. She never revealed that she had thought the nice lady was the mother of the other Fred. Little Fred was changed from that moment. He did become one of her favorite students and was a joy to have in class.

The story of the two Freds in a way illustrates the parable of the Weeds and the Wheat in today's Gospel. In real life, weeds don't become wheat but ugliness can be changed into beauty. We are naturally proud of the "wheat" people and often irritated with the "weed" people. Like the servants in the story, we might want to pull up the weeds and throw them out. We forget that it is too soon to tell how they will turn out. Many good citizens might have grown up to become criminals, had not someone convinced them that they could do better and had encouraged them to try.

Not only children but all people need the affirmation and encouragement of others. The good and the bad are never isolated but live side by side through the years. No one becomes a saint or sinner in an instant. The seed grows slowly, but God is patient.

Every small deed of kindness is like the mustard seed in the Gospel which can lead to great and glorious results, multiplying itself thousands of times. Many giant organizations are the lengthened results of one little idea. Many lifelong friendships have started with one tiny smile. On the other hand, bitter fights and even wars have begun from small misunderstandings the size of a mustard seed.

If we could eliminate the tiny hurts, the giant troubles would not have to be solved. They would not exist. Little seeds of kindness and love, carefully planted by each of us, can make this world a paradise where we could peacefully live and grow together.

SEVENTEENTH SUNDAY OF THE YEAR (A)
1 K 3:5, 7-12   Rm 8:28-30   Mt 13:44-52

The prolific 20th century writer, W. Somerset Maugham once said: "It wasn't until late in life that I discovered how easy it is to say, I don't know." He had an in-depth knowledge of medicine, government and life in general (as shown in his plays, short stories and novels), yet he could calmly admit his lack of understanding.

We are very foolish to think that we must have an answer to every question, in order to keep our credibility with others. The day we realize and openly admit how pitifully little we really know, is the day we become truly wise.

In today's liturgy we heard the thoughtful conversation between God and the young Solomon, who has just been chosen as King of Israel. In his dream, he is invited to make a wish and is promised it will come true. Solomon's prayerful wish is for wisdom, that he may know what is right and wrong and may judge people fairly.

In his position as king, Solomon needed to possess deep

understanding to fulfill his office—but don't we all? Regardless of our particular job or vocation, we are constantly in need of wisdom—both for our personal lives and especially for dealing with others. No matter how intelligent we are, our knowledge has not yet exceeded the limit and there's plenty of room to grow.

Do we ever think of praying for wisdom, like the young king did? Solomon already showed his intelligence simply by knowing that he should pray for more. If we don't know that we should pray for wisdom, that shows how much we need it.

God was very pleased with Solomon's request for most young men, given the opportunity to have anything they wanted, would have asked for a long life, great riches or revenge against their enemies.

When asking for something in prayers of petition, we should say to ourselves, "if it's God's will." It is His will for us to possess wisdom, for the more we acquire the more we become like Him. True wisdom can only benefit us; it is an ideal request. Perhaps we will receive not only our request but also the things we didn't ask for, as happened with Solomon. After much prayer and study, we still should not be ashamed to admit that we don't have all the answers. To know that we don't know is a sign of intelligence. "I don't know" doesn't mean that we didn't try to know.

So what shall we pray for today? A long life, good health, money, power, revenge? Why not go for the valuable gift of wisdom? Then we can better understand our God, ourselves and others. Then, when judgments are necessary we can be fair and honest.

EIGHTEENTH SUNDAY OF THE YEAR (A)
Is 55:1-3   Rm 8:35, 37-39   Mt 14:13-21

A few years before his death, Bishop Sheen underwent open-heart surgery. There was great concern about his ability to endure the operation because of his advanced age. After his recovery, a reporter asked him if he had been afraid of dying. The Bishop replied that he had not been worried. "If I should leave this world," he said, "I will be in heaven with Christ and if I remain, Christ will be here with me." He had faith that there was no way he would be separated from his Lord.

St. Paul states in today's second reading that there is nothing which will separate him from Christ; not persecution, hunger, danger or even death. He feels very secure about the eternal stability of this divine relationship.

How confident are we of our lasting love and union with the Lord? Aren't there many temptations which can lure us away from our baptismal promises to be friends of Jesus forever? Why is our love so shaky and uncertain, while many others are so confident?

Bishop Sheen's unwavering trust flowed to a great extent from his daily holy hour which he observed for many years, using the time for deep personal prayer with God. He always spent his sacred hour in a church, wherever he happened to be, and he constantly and enthusiastically recommended the practice to others.

Paul had a mystical experience of the risen Jesus and heard His admonishing voice. He then continually talked to the Lord in prayer, especially thanking Him for past blessings. Thus he developed a deep trust in Jesus.

With sincere, daily prayer, our confidence in the Lord can increase greatly. Without it, we will flounder in fear.

Scripture often compares the Christian's relationship to the Lord with that of a husband and wife, yet we know how easily and quickly marriages can be dissolved.

A civil judge once explained to a group of clergy the reasons why so many marriages end in divorce. He listed parents' inability to handle children, unemployment, cruelty, infidelity and alcohol. "But the major cause of divorce," he said, "is the lack of communication." He explained that the average "common time" for many working couples amounts to 27 minutes a day.

Our lack of meaningful communication with Christ can also lead to a break-up with Him. Both human and divine love are mysterious and delicate. Neither dies suddenly. They bleed to death slowly—one drop at a time.

As we admire Paul's confidence that nothing will ever separate him from Jesus, we can joyfully renew our own love affair with our God. Each day we write another page of our lives with Jesus, and someday we hope to pen the last sentence: "And they lived happily ever after."

NINETEENTH SUNDAY OF THE YEAR (A)
1 K 19:9, 11-13   Rm 9:1-5   Mt 14:22-33

No one is exempt from feelings of depression—even to the point of having thoughts of suicide. We meet a man in today's first reading who is terribly dejected and wants to die. It is Elijah the prophet. In his zeal to promote true worship he has incurred the wrath of the wicked queen Jezebel, who has vowed to kill him. Alone and afraid, Elijah has retreated to the mountains in search of strength for his hurting soul. There in the calm, fresh mountain air he discovers his comforting God. This sacred experience repels the thoughts of death, lightens his heavy spirit and enables him to return to his noble work, a renewed and confident man.

Since we are affected by similar pains and trials, we need to have a "mountain retreat" where we can regroup our wearied energies before we return to the mainstream of daily life. Contemplation and solitude are necessary today, for we live in the fast lane with its loud noises and constant pressures.

The great spiritual teachers of the past recognized the vital need to set aside time to regroup one's strength and establish an abiding relationship with God. It was the pattern of Benedict and Francis and today we can still visit their mountain retreats at Subiaco and Assisi, where they found quiet guidance from above.

In our Gospel we see Jesus calmly walking to His disciples, in the midst of violent winds and a raging sea. He moves lightly across the troubled waters which are unable to engulf Him. He is in the midst of turmoil but is unaffected by it, for He has just returned from His spiritual retreat in the mountains where He has communicated with His heavenly Father.

This walk upon the water inspired Peter to imitate the Lord but he failed, for his mind had not been calmed by a mountain meditation. He was too immersed in the sea level fears around him to move above them. They pulled him in, but the outstretched hand of Jesus saved him.

Jesus lifts us up also, lest we be engulfed and drowned in the raging sea. Both the example of Elijah and the Savior Himself show us the need for frequent contemplation.

The Lord said, "Don't let your hearts be troubled. Have faith in me." Notice that He did not promise freedom from all troubles, for such is life. Instead, He promised us untroubled hearts, meaning that we will not be shaken or exhausted to the very core of our being. Faith in Jesus will enable us to keep that vital inner strength so that we can calmly walk with Him through turmoil and confusion and not be swallowed up by it.

May we, like Elijah, find our gentle God in the soft breezes of life and recognize Him as He passes by.

TWENTIETH SUNDAY OF THE YEAR (A)
Is 56:1, 6-7   Rm 11:13-15, 29-32   Mt 15:21-28

Perseverance is an intriguing word. It originates from two Latin words meaning "to severe through"—like running an obstacle course. If there are formidable barriers between the contender and the final goal, the objective will not be achieved without consistent determination.

The Gospel today tells the story of a woman who possessed

great perseverance. She had her goal firmly fixed in mind, which was to obtain a miracle from Jesus for her daughter, who was possessed by an evil spirit. There was nothing which would derail her cause. She sought and fought for it as though it were her only reason for living.

Her cause did not look like it would succeed. She was a foreigner in the eyes of these men from Israel, and her timing for her request was completely wrong—for it appears that Jesus and the Twelve were on vacation. They most likely had come to her country of Phoenicia, north of Israel, to escape for a little while the very kind of thing she was requesting. The encounter took place not far from the present-day city of Beirut. No doubt they were looking forward to some rest in the warm Mediterranean breezes in a setting where they could be anonymous. This miracle-begging woman irritated them when she recognized the famous group and loudly clamored for a cure. The apostles bluntly told Jesus, "Get rid of her!"

To encourage her to leave them alone, they gave her the silent treatment, which would have discouraged most people. Next came a blunt rejection, which she weathered equally well. Finally she passed the third and harshest test of being insulted. This not only failed to deter her but provoked a malice-free retort which must have made Jesus smile.

If we isolate her words, we can easily see the intensity of her appeal: "Have pity on me . . . Help me, Lord." How could Jesus ignore anyone who spoke so sincerely? He couldn't. He praised her and performed the miracle that she had so earnestly requested.

Here is a woman who refused to believe that her pleas were going to the dogs. She deeply believed in the Lord, but it was only through her perseverance that she obtained her request.

Such determination may or may not get us the things we work and pray for. But if we do come up on the short end, we are at least better people for having made the effort. "Thy will be done," is also a God-inspired prayer of persevering trust in Him. The Lord is compassionate even when it seems that He is not. We must be able to endure being ignored, rejected and hurt, for these are the real tests of perseverance.

The poet Longfellow wrote of this in his *Psalm of Life*:

> "Let us then be up a doing,
> With a heart for any fate,
> Still achieving, still pursuing,
> Learn to labor and to wait."

TWENTY-FIRST SUNDAY OF THE YEAR (A)
Is 22:15, 19-23   Rm 11:33-36   Mt 16:13-20

A Methodist minister once came to speak to a youth group and began his talk by asking the name of the first Pope. "St. Peter," they all shouted. "No," he replied, "that's wrong." He then "interpreted" today's Gospel passage by saying that Jesus referred to the first Pope as "Simon, son of John"—i.e., "Johnson"—and then called him "Rock." "So you see," he concluded with a wink, "the name of the first Pope was Rocky Johnson."

This well-known scriptural passage has indeed been subjected to great scrutiny, for it is the basis and key text for the whole governmental system of the Catholic Church. It is our clear and traditional teaching that the words of Jesus about building the Church on the foundation of rock, refers directly to the person of St. Peter. The promised "Keys to the kingdom of Heaven" are bestowed upon him as a sign of authority along with the power of binding and loosing on earth and in heaven. These words are packed with incredible power and responsibility.

Protestant theologians take a different view of the passage saying that all of this refers not to one person but to the Church in general. Therefore, the human governing authority in the Protestant Churches resides in the people and their representatives.

The Orthodox Christians claim that these powers were given to the bishops as a group, and that at most the Pope is first among equals. In general there is close agreement between Catholics and Orthodox on most religious questions, with the exception of papal authority.

Catholic teaching traditionally views the Church as a type of pyramid with the Vicar of Christ at the pinnacle, directing the people through the cardinals, bishops and priests. Another, more modern concept of the Church is to see it as a concentric circle with all members on the same level and the Pope in the center, offering unity and cohesiveness to the entire world community.

The title "Pontifex Maximus" is often applied to the Pope. This term literally means "greatest bridge builder." It signifies that he is to help people bridge their hates and misunderstandings and also to bridge the distance between this world and the next.

Popes in recent times are much more visible to the world than their predecessors because of television and jet planes. John Paul II is the most traveled Pope in history.

Even though St. Peter was given a very noble position, he still had to work out his own salvation amidst personal problems as well as those of the universal Church. The members of the early Church fervently prayed for him, especially during difficult times (Ac 12:5).

Today's Gospel is presented to help us appreciate the structures of our Church and to solicit our prayers for those who serve as our religious leaders. May they bring the glad tidings of Jesus to many and proclaim His holy name throughout the world.

TWENTY-SECOND SUNDAY OF THE YEAR (A)
Jr 20:7-9   Rm 12:1-2   Mt 16:21-27

In his book *Mr. Citizen* (1960), Harry Truman speaks of the necessity of making irrevocable decisions. "Some men," he says, "can make decisions and some cannot. Some men fret and delay under criticism. I used to have a saying that applies here, and I note that some people have picked it up." We've all heard this famous saying: "If you can't stand the heat, get out of the kitchen."

Jesus never told us just how He arrived at His decision to die on the cross to redeem fallen humanity. We do know that He fully intended to die as a victim for us and that He knew that this would happen in Jerusalem. With Him it was never a question of changing His mind. His resolution was firm and it was simply a matter of time before He could carry it out. It was what He called His "Father's will," and it was a part of everything He thought and did.

When Peter therefore tried to convince Him to take another route than that of suffering and death, Jesus became infuriated with His fickle apostle and future Pope. Peter was acting more like an enemy—like the devil, when he tried to dissuade Jesus from His goal in the temptations in the desert. Jesus therefore ordered Peter to get in line, for he was giving bad advice.

Sometimes our friends—even those who may be future saints—can be as much a hindrance to us as our avowed enemies. They don't intend to impede or sidetrack us, but they can easily do it if we follow every bit of "advice" they offer. Had Jesus been persuaded by Peter, humanity would have been unredeemed and the Lord would have failed to fulfill His mission. There are simply some things we have to do our own way, regardless of what others think or say.

The Church has always taught that the ultimate factor in every decision is our own conscience. We recognize that advice is vital, but we must also remember that it can be harmful to follow it against our better judgment.

We can follow wrong advice from our friends by giving up on a marriage; by disregarding vows made in religious commitments; by negating promises and legal contracts. We thank God that Jesus had a stronger will and a deeper commitment.

The Lord in this Gospel reading does not call us to carry our crosses simply for the sake of pain—but in order to fulfill our objectives, which often can be achieved only if we are willing to suffer them through. The easy way out is often the wrong choice.

May we be faithful to our personal convictions and honest to God, that our lives will be fulfilled in lasting peace.

TWENTY-THIRD SUNDAY OF THE YEAR (A)
Ezk 33:7-9   Rm 13:8-10   Mt 18:15-20

Some people are too submissive. They continually back off and are afraid to voice an objection, and this gives them a sense of diminished self-worth. Others are too aggressive. They push people about in an arrogant and dominating manner. These are the people with an exaggerated view of self-importance. Abraham Lincoln spoke to this issue when he said: "As I would not be a slave, so I would not be a master."

Between these two extremes is found the ideal quality for good human relationships—assertiveness. Assertive people neither cower from fear nor threaten with force. They frankly express their feelings and hopes to the person or people with whom they are having difficulties. Assertive people are strong, open and peace-loving.

Hurts and wrongs often go undiscussed and unattended because it is hard for us to talk about them. Although we avoid direct confrontations, we often resort to making complaints behind the scene.

"When your brother offends you," says Jesus in today's Gospel, "go to him and discuss the matter between the two of you." This is simply a call to be assertive. Such an action can save untold hardships and enable us to quickly solve many problems which otherwise could linger on for years or even a lifetime.

If your neighbor plays the TV or stereo so loudly that you are continually disturbed, go and talk to him about it. You may be surprised how quickly and peacefully it can be settled. If your husband makes an offensive remark about you at a party, face him openly on the way home. Perhaps the matter will be solved by the time you pull into the driveway. Otherwise these hurts will simmer for days before exploding.

If we cannot solve our difficulties with others, Jesus recommends that we seek the help of a third person—not to provide an answer but to be an arbiter so that the disputants can better arrive at a mutual solution.

If the conflict still continues, it should be submitted to the Church for a group decision or the assistance of one who is skilled in that area. This biblical approach to conflict management seeks to achieve peace between people and to avoid lawsuits. It especially seeks to avoid the use of violence to solve problems.

We are expected to love one another in an atmosphere of unity and openness, without playing the role of either slave or master.

The virtue of assertiveness does not diminish the other person. Through openness, it speaks and listens and achieves a peaceful understanding.

TWENTY-FOURTH SUNDAY OF THE YEAR (A)
Si 27:30-28:7   Rm 14:7-9   Mt 18:21-35

In his poem "To Know All is to Forgive All," Nixon Waterman writes:

> "If I knew you and you knew me—
> If both of us could clearly see,
> And with an inner sight divine
> The meaning of your heart and mine—
> I'm sure that we would differ less
> And clasp our hands in friendliness;
> Our thoughts would pleasantly agree
> If I knew you and you knew me."

The less we know of other people, the easier it is to be suspicious of their motives and unforgiving for their hurtful actions. If we would honestly communicate with people who confuse us, we could find some agreement and offer forgiveness, were it called for. Forgiving simply means that we cease to feel resentment against another. Forgiveness is more than words—it involves a change of feelings.

Today's liturgy takes a strong stand in favor of forgiveness—from the reading from Sirach, through Psalm 103, to the parable of Jesus. In spite of all this, we still might ask, "Why should I forgive others?"

Sirach presents several reasons for extending a private amnesty to others. The main reason is that it is of the nature of God to forgive and we should be like Him in all ways possible. Imagine begging God's forgiveness for some sin and hearing Him reply, "No, I will never forgive you." How despairing a situation that would be. Yet that is what we do by our refusals.

In the opening sentence, Sirach says: "Wrath and anger are hateful things, yet the sinner hugs them tight." We tightly grasp our selfishness like a small child clinging to a doll.

In Jesus' parable, God is the king and we are the officials. We beg for some limited mercy and He gives a total pardon. He is the great forgiver. Have we grown accustomed to His mercy, whenever we ask, although we still continue to betray Him?

We can be very demanding with others, like the ungrateful official. We forget the many kindnesses which have been extended to us by the Lord and by our fellow men and women.

The Lord's advice to forgive 70 times 7 is more than a mere figure of speech. When we live in close contact with others—whether in marriage, work, or as neighbors—we must literally give pardon at least 490 times in order to keep peace and remain on good terms. Forgiveness, like love, has no restrictions placed upon it.

Since we don't keep count of the times we tell others we love them, so we shouldn't begrudgingly count the times we give pardon. Whoever says that three times is the limit of their forgiveness is not reflecting Christian standards.

TWENTY-FIFTH SUNDAY OF THE YEAR (A)
Is 55:6-9   Ph 1:20-24, 27   Mt 20:1-16

As citizens of a highly industrialized country, we are well acquainted with the many and varied disputes between management and labor. We know that feelings can often be bitter. Sometimes violence irrupts, resulting in personal injuries and property destruction.

There is a small labor dispute in today's Gospel and Jesus himself is the judge. If we review the case and analyze the logic presented by Jesus, we can discover some clear Christian guidelines to be used in our own lives. So we have the case of The Wage Discrimination, as presented in Matthew 20:1-16.

The Grievance: A group of employable men was hired by a vineyard owner to work from 9 to 5 for the flat rate of $10.00 a day. The beginning and quitting times and wages were clearly understood and freely agreed to by both sides. The employer felt an urgency to have the grapes harvested as soon as possible, and he periodically through the day requested the assistance of other men, who happily complied. These later groups did not negotiate with the owner but simply agreed to work and receive whatever he would see fit to give them.

At 5 P.M. everyone who had labored in the vineyard that day received $10.00, even those who had worked only from 4 P.M. The first group therefore filed a grievance claiming discrimination and requesting more money for the day's labor.

The Judgment: Jesus rendered the decision: no injustice had been done by management, and labor in this case had no legitimate complaint. He reasoned that those who had contracted for $10.00 a day got exactly what they had agreed to. The others, who had not contracted for certain hours or definite pay, were simply given a generous reward which was purely at the proprietor's discretion. Therefore, the grievance was rejected.

The Summation: People can be happy with their jobs until they discover that some others are getting a better deal. Then comes the temptation to feel cheated and to complain. Why can't people rejoice in the good fortunes of others instead of becoming intensely jealous?

We can live our entire lives feeling sorry for ourselves, since we can always find many who earn and possess much more money than we do. We can also feel richly blessed with our priceless possessions—life itself, freedom, love, good health, etc.—and realize that these are worth much more than a few extra dollars. We can be as miserable or contented as we want to be.

TWENTY-SIXTH SUNDAY OF THE YEAR (A)
Ezk 18:25-28   Ph 2:1-11   Mt 21:28-32

The singing of religious hymns is central to our worship. These sacred compositions can inspire, unite and instruct us in the truths of our faith. An ancient Christian teacher once remarked that it didn't matter who wrote theology for the people. Just let him write the songs, and he would have a greater influence on their thinking.

There is a long and glorious history of singing as an ideal way of offering praise and thanksgiving to God. In the Old Testament, Miriam led the Israelite women in songs of thanksgiving after their safe passage through the Red Sea (Ex 15:20). There's the Song of Deborah (Jg Ch. 5), proclaiming Israel's great victory on the battlefield. The best known of all biblical songs are the Psalms, which were the 150 top hymns of the day. They express a variety of feelings from praise to thanks, from sorrow to joy. They were used extensively in Jewish worship services and continue to be vital in our Christian liturgies.

In his letter to the Philippians, read today, Paul quotes what scholars say are the lyrics of a very ancient song (composed soon after the resurrection of Jesus. It would be worthwhile to meditatively read that hymn and consider the rich and penetrating truths it contains. We might even sing or chant it according to our own melodies, to appreciate it more.

These verses—the second half of the reading—contain an apt summary of the eventful journey of Jesus from His exalted throne in heaven to earth, where He "took the form of a slave" and died for humanity. It concludes on the glorious note of His triumph over death with "every tongue proclaiming" that "Jesus Christ is Lord." This venerable old hymn consisting of five stanzas is one of the most inspirational passages of the Bible. Besides its use on this Sunday, it is read every year on Passion Sunday to introduce the mighty deeds of Holy Week.

Through the centuries sensitive men and women have continued to put to music the sacred deeds of Jesus, to help us "lift up our hearts to the Lord."

If you feel reluctant to sing in church (as many do) remember that singing is simply praying and that no one, especially the Lord, expects you to be flawless. If the birds in the trees would not sing until each was artistically perfect, the forest would be silent.

Our efforts to fully participate in the liturgy will lead us to concentrate on the scripture readings, the homily and the songs. There's a message for us in every hymn which we are invited to search out, sing out and live out in our daily journey toward the Kingdom.

TWENTY-SEVENTH SUNDAY OF THE YEAR (A)
Is 5:1-7   Ph 4:6-9   Mt 21:33-43

Are you discontented, searching for happiness? Then give your attention to today's reading from St. Paul, especially to the opening sentence. If you can do what he says, you will find a deep and lasting peace. DISMISS ALL ANXIETY FROM YOUR MINDS. Paul then explains how to do it and confidently predicts the results.

Webster defines anxiety as "a painful uneasiness of mind over some anticipated ill." It is not the same as fear; fear is a reality, but anxiety is only imaginary. For example: if you *see* a robber with a gun entering your home, you've got a real fear to deal with. If, on the other hand, you hear a noise and you *imagine* it's a robber breaking into your home, you have an anxiety. Most anxieties never materialize into real fears, but they can drive us crazy with worry. Paul says to dismiss them, send them away, and don't let them clutter up your mind. Recall that Jesus told Martha that she was "anxious about many things," especially about serving food, cleaning the house and trying to make Him feel welcome. He told her to sit down and relax, as Mary had done.

A major step toward dismissing anxieties is to tell our needs and troubled feelings to God in prayer, and to place renewed confidence in Him as a loving Father. We have two strong knees which can lessen the strain of an anxious heart. Tensions and worries can cause heart attacks, but we've never heard of anyone dying from a knee attack. So calm your anxieties, and quiet your heart and let your knees do the talking.

There obviously are many situations which we can't control. But we can learn to accept and defuse our anxieties by realizing God's constant love for us. We must confidently trust that all will work for the best.

One day, a lady sitting in a hospital waiting room noticed a man staring at her. She became upset and angrily glared back at him, but he didn't turn away. Finally, she walked up to him and said, "I don't appreciate you staring at me." He replied, "I wasn't staring at you. I'm blind." How often we become our own worst tormentors.

At each Mass we pray that worries be driven out so that we can experience peace of mind. It is said following the Our Father and just before the sign of peace. Perhaps today we can pray it with renewed trust and hope.

"Deliver us, Lord, from every evil, and grant us peace in our day. In your mercy keep us free from sin and protect us from all anxiety. . . ."

TWENTY-EIGHTH SUNDAY OF THE YEAR (A)
Is 25:6-10   Ph 4:12-14, 19-20   Mt 22:1-14

For several Sundays we have been reading Paul's letter to the Philippians. It is warm in tone, deep in thought and practical for daily living. Paul had nurtured a close and enduring friendship with the people of Philippi and freely shared many of his deep feelings. It was at Philippi that Paul had first proclaimed the Good News in Europe. Of all the churches he founded, this was the only one which had contributed material aid to him. There was mutual admiration and a lasting bond of friendship between the mission church of Philippi and the missionary, St. Paul.

He tells his friends in today's reading that he has experienced life's highs and lows, its good times and bad. We all know what he means, since we have the same variety in our lives. Paul also reveals his secret for successful living. It is his ability *to cope*.

There are thousands of areas where we come face to face with harsh realities. Some can handle them and some cannot. How have we or would we cope with illness, unemployment, divorce, inflation, personal losses, tensions, etc.? Like Paul, we must learn to adjust. We can bend a bit like the hickory branch, or else stand rigid and crack like a pretzel under pressure. Not many people could say with Paul that we are happy whether rich or poor, well fed or hungry.

An elderly preacher once explained that when he was a young man in ministry, he tried to solve every problem which came his way. Now, he said, being older and wiser, he didn't try to solve problems but just cope with them. Perhaps this minister had taken to heart the advice in the fourth chapter of Philippians.

Most of us respond to circumstances somewhere between the heights of toughness and the depths of despair. We may react with peaceful acceptance and tolerance, or with negative indifference and bitterness. Paul had the uncanny ability to peacefully accept whatever happened to him, for he knew that nothing could throw him off center. He viewed events as God's will. If they were hard to accept, he willingly suffered in union with Christ.

We can understand why the liturgy tells us about Paul's internal convictions, for in him we have a strong role model for endurance. When we have some tough problems to face, we might read the fourth chapter of Philippians and find the strength to cope with whatever lies ahead.

Paul's courage can be ours. It flowed from Christ and we all have access to the same divine source. Whether we are starved or well fed, rich or poor—if we want to, we can truthfully say: "I have strength for everything."

TWENTY-NINTH SUNDAY OF THE YEAR (A)
Is 45:1, 4-6   1 Th 1:1-5   Mt 22:15-21

There's a splendid sermon in your pocket—the sermon that Jesus delivered the day He silenced His critics by asking them to explain the image and inscription on a Roman coin comparable to our penny.

Money can "talk" in various ways, and even the insignificant penny can utter profound wisdom and demonstrate a worth far beyond its monetary value. This one cent coin can contribute its proverbial "two cents" to help us appreciate the delicate relationship between church and state.

At the invitation of Jesus in today's Gospel, we take the penny in hand and examine the image and inscription on the face of this small copper coin.

We recognize the familiar strong profile of our country's 16th and most popular president, Abraham Lincoln. His name is often prefaced by the adjective "honest," and his silent face reflects a basic and immortal goodness. No one ever served that office at a more critical time than Abraham Lincoln, and no one ever served it more nobly. His name and face will ever be a shining light and the image of what civil leaders should strive to be.

Haloing the pensive head of Lincoln are those famous words which have been gracing coins since 1864—"In God we trust." The image and inscription blend naturally, challenging us to think of cooperation between religion and government rather than of hostility. The penny proclaims an ideal and a dream worth pursuing.

Both church and state can boldly subscribe to the motto "e pluribus unum"—one from many—which the penny carries on its back. The people of our country are fused into one nation from many around the world. Similarly, the Church unifies people from every state of life in the saving grace of Jesus.

Unfortunately, the image and inscription are not often lived out. We ignore unity and honesty in favor of personal gain and fame. Although our coins loudly proclaim our trust in God, we don't put that fearless faith into effect. Perhaps it would be more honest to write on the coins, "In Power we trust" or "In Wealth we trust."

This little copper coated coin stands in contrast to all the other silvery ones. In a way, it is symbolic of the Blacks and Indians whose rights have so often been violated. We continue to ignore the message of the penny when we discriminate civilly and divide religiously.

So take a coin; examine the image and inscription, and ask what they mean to you. Try to imagine ways in which you might be a better citizen and a more loving Christian.

THIRTIETH SUNDAY OF THE YEAR (A)
Ex 22:20-26   1 Th 1:5-10   Mt 22:34-40

Diet books are always popular with the general public. An author named Emmet Fox proposes an unusual type of diet—a 30 day diet for the mind.

Picture the mind as an eater. The foods it consumes are the images and ideas we give to it. These are digested and become a part of us. Mr. Fox suggests that we do not feed the mind any negative thoughts, on any subjects, for 30 days. He claims that this "selective mental consumption of ideas" is beneficial in improving one's outlook and attitude.

Of course, a Christian can only apply this up to a point. We cannot, even for a limited time, pretend that the ills of this world are not there. Paul and Jesus would have condemned this at once as self-deception. But we can try not to dwell on old hurts and to concentrate on positive emotions. We should do this at all times, but as a tool to help us attain this, a 30 day "diet" might be useful.

A variety of mental and spiritual foods are available to us each day, just like those on a restaurant menu. We alone decide which we want to partake of. We may choose what is good and wholesome, or what is harmful both for body and mind. Many thoughts, which our minds grab and devour so readily, can cause us mental indigestion. Eventually, they begin to eat *us*. When we're moody or impatient, someone may ask, "What's eating you?" It's probably something negative which we swallowed that is now causing a mental or emotional reaction.

The 30 day mental diet can help us to fulfill the divine command spoken by Jesus in today's Gospel: "Love your neighbor as yourself." The person who does not care for and respect him or herself cannot respect others.

Genuine neighborly love cannot exist in a person whose mind is gorged full of suspicions, half-truths and gossip. There will always be plenty of people anxious to feed us their gossipy morsels seasoned with choice words, appropriate gestures and mimic tones. We can say, "No thanks, I don't care for any," or we can eat the whole thing and end up hating our neighbor.

Just imagine what a steady diet of prayer, forgiveness and patient understanding could do for our spiritual health. We would feel better and be able to view the world with a more loving spirit. What we think shapes us into what we are.

Why not put a bit of discipline into your life through good positive thoughts, which are essential for health and happiness. Give the 30 day diet a try and discover the improvement. You will increase your love and appreciation of the people around you, and others will genuinely appreciate your improved attitude.

THIRTY-FIRST SUNDAY OF THE YEAR (A)
Ml 1:14-2:2, 8-10   1 Th 2:7-9, 13   Mt 23:1-12

In today's Gospel Jesus makes a startling remark about His traditional rivals, the Pharisees. Although He did not approve of their actions—seeking honors and important titles and imposing heavy burdens on others—He still told His disciples to follow their teachings because they were legitimate successors of Moses. The Lord respected their status as religious teachers and supports their right to preach and be obeyed, even though they did not practice what they preached.

We might not approve of the personal conduct of some people in authority, but if they hold legitimate offices we have an obligation to respect their positions. Who can be perfectly consistent in word and action every moment of life? If Jesus could show such merciful tolerance to the irritating Pharisees who rarely matched words and deeds, can't we afford some understanding for the inconsistencies of others? Even St. Paul said that he knew what he should do but often did the opposite because he was weak—yet he continually invited others to that perfection which he personally could not attain.

Parents, for example, may restrict their children from smoking and drinking, yet they themselves both smoke and drink to excess. Does that mean that the children have no obligation to obey their parents? They should both respect and obey them. Jesus would advise adherence to what the parents say, but not to what they do. The parents, like the Pharisees, are not following their own advice—but it doesn't mean that their advice is bad.

A person running for a pubic office may be an atheist, and on that fact alone we reject them. In doing so, we may deprive the country of an excellent leader. Again, simply because a person is not all that we expect him or her to be, it doesn't mean that they have nothing good to offer.

Before we begin condemning the "Scribes and Pharisees" of our neighborhood, we might look within ourselves and see that we are pretty much like them. Jesus alone had that heroic consistency between what He said and did, but the rest of us often fall short of the ideal. This example of the Lord's broad-mindedness to the Pharisees is reassuring, for then we can expect His tolerance as well.

There are, of course, many different ways to imitate Jesus. But trying to imitate His benign mercy to others should be at the top of our list. In our efforts to be totally committed Christians, we cannot make the mistake of expecting perfection in others. We cannot forget the divine virtue of tolerance, which must often be applied—even to our own contradictions.

Although continually condemned for their weaknesses and

inconsistencies, the Pharisees still had something beneficial for others. Jesus saw it and affirmed it, and so should we.

THIRTY-SECOND SUNDAY OF THE YEAR (A)
Ws 6:12-16   1 Th 4:13-17   Mt 25:1-13

The calm voice of inner wisdom resounds in today's liturgy, from the Wisdom of Solomon to the Gospel of Matthew. Human wisdom is defined as the ability to judge soundly and deal with facts as they relate to life and conduct. It is similar to knowledge but superior to it, for knowledge can produce vile results as well as honorable ones. A genius could, for example, turn his "talent" to the stealing of cars and the forging of checks. Wisdom, however, will never lead us into evil. We can never possess too much of it, for the more we have the better for us.

Scripture calls us to develop and clarify our personal wisdom—our philosophy of life. It is extremely valuable for us and others if we have intelligent views on major questions and can explain and define them. Regardless of our jobs, abilities or states of life we need to understand the truth, for "the truth will make us free."

A successful dairy farmer in California categorized his thoughts of practical wisdom and printed them for distribution on his business cards. Here are some of them:

> The greatest sin is fear.
> The greatest mistake is giving up.
> The most satisfying experience is doing your duty.
> The best action you can do is to keep your mind clear and your judgment good.
> The biggest fool is the person who lies to self.
> The most certain thing in life is change.

The greatest joy is that of being needed.
The most clever person is the one who does what he or she thinks is right.
The greatest opportunity is the next one.
The most majestic thought is God.
The greatest triumph is the victory over self.

It is the duty of a caring religion to make us think for ourselves, rather than simply issuing "answers." The Church therefore calls us today to consider our philosophy of life and determine what it is and where it comes from. We should ask ourselves: do we have solid views and convictions, or do we live by the cheap maxims promoted on TV?

Many young people, in their efforts to reject cheapness and gain wisdom, become entangled in the clutches of a modern cult. There they are more deeply enslaved under the guise of wisdom and freedom.

In the parable narrated at this Mass, Jesus talks about ten people, of whom five are wise and five foolish. Would that same ratio still hold true today? Are only about half the people really wise?

Scripture reminds us that "the fear of the Lord is the beginning of wisdom." This doesn't mean that we cower and tremble in His presence, but that we genuinely respect God and understand His dignity and ours. We try to see the whole of creation and the meaning of life from His viewpoint—and that's wisdom.

THIRTY-THIRD SUNDAY OF THE YEAR (A)
Pr 31:10-13, 19-20, 30-31   1 Th 5:1-6   Mt 25:14-30

Today's parable told by Jesus is quite lengthy, running at least 400 words—but we could summarize it in five words: USE IT OR

LOSE IT. It's the Lord's call for action to His people to accomplish worthwhile deeds.

We all have so many fine qualities of mind, soul and body which have been freely given to us, like the silver pieces handed by the master to his servants before he left on his trip. What do we do with these valued treasures? Experts say that the average person uses only 10% of the mind. Imagine what would be possible if we used 50% or even 100%. We would never tolerate our car operating at only 10% of its capacity. Similarly, our Maker expects a higher percentage of performance from us. Talents are to be used, not hidden or left idle.

If we would pour out all the love of which we are capable, there would be enough to radically change the whole face of the earth. To fulfill our lives, we don't need more of anything except the motivation to use what we already have. Notice how God, in the person of the master, is terribly upset with the man who was not productive. "You worthless, lazy lout," he says, go out "into the darkness." The other two, who both had 100% increases, were privileged to hear the words, "Well done, you are industrious and reliable servants, come share your master's joy."

Perhaps the use of our abilities depends on our philosophy of life and why we think we're in this world. Some would say that we're here simply to save our own personal souls. Isn't that a rather narrow view? Personal salvation is not the whole story. We are here to live productive lives, just like Jesus did during the time He spent on earth, for He was continually on the move doing good deeds for others.

The money in the parable is used as an image for the human soul. The third individual, who was punished for his non-use of the talents, could have argued: "Look, I didn't lose your money. I saved it." The master replied that the servant was expected not to save it but to use it—or, perhaps more correctly, to multiply it.

This famous Gospel passage supports the need to do good works in order to be fully Christian. It tempers the teaching, often presented, that salvation comes from faith alone. Although faith is basic to religion, it is expected to blossom forth into good works—both to promote God's glory and to assist our fellow men and women. True faith in God and genuine love of neighbor will naturally lead us to service and ministry. In the helping of another we will also be saving our own soul.

THIRTY-FOURTH SUNDAY OF THE YEAR (A)
SOLEMNITY OF CHRIST THE KING
Ezk 34:11-12, 15-17   1 Cor 15:20-26, 28   Mt 25:31-46

The liturgical year comes to a close with this annual celebration of the Feast of Christ The King. The 52 Sundays of the year, like a full deck of playing cards, have been shuffled and dealt out—each with its own particular message. Today we hold the last of the 52—the King of Hearts—as the Gospel tells of His coming in glory at the end of time. The Lord will be escorted by His angels to bless those who have ministered to the hurting people of the world, for by doing so they have served their King.

Jesus is not the king of clubs, ruling with ruthless force and power. The club is the extension of the fist rather than the heart. He is not the king of spades, for the Lord throws no dirt on others nor does He need to cover His actions or bury His past. His reign is open for all to see and imitate. Unlike some earthly rulers, the Savior is not the king of diamonds, desirous of wealth, glory and glitter. His glory comes from another world. "I am a king," He said, "but my kingdom is not of this world." As the four suits, like the four seasons, reflect the cycle of the year, it's encouraging to know that Jesus has chosen to be "The King of Hearts."

Jesus is as central to our lives as the heart is to the body. "Learn of me," the King said, "for I am meek and humble of heart." If our hearts have been broken for whatever reason, know that His was broken for us. He is the wounded healer. Jesus is the Shepherd of lost sheep, Savior of sinners, Teacher, Lover and King of the world.

Our association with Christ The King has brought us both duties and dignities, of which one basic obligation is to observe His golden rule. If we could do unto others as we would have them do unto us, the world would know a new reign of peace. To the King we also owe allegiance and recognition that He holds first place. The dignities He confers upon us are greater than the duties, for it is a privilege to be His servant. We know that we will not be pushed beyond our strength, and that we are invited to be permanent residents of His eternal Kingdom.

Today's Gospel passage from Matthew is regarded by some scripture scholars as the "Ten Commandments of the New Testament." It spells out the do's and don'ts of Christian life and explains how our entire salvation hinges on the manner in which we care for the less fortunate. It is another clear teaching of the necessity of good works.

"Come, you have My Father's blessing. Inherit the Kingdom . . . for I was hungry and you gave Me to eat. . . ." This is His simplified way of living. It is possible for all to imitate and it carries an everlasting promise. We have it on the word of the King Himself.

Cycle B

FIRST SUNDAY OF ADVENT (B)
Is 63:16-17, 19; 64:27   1 Cor 1:3-9   Mk 13:33-37

"Be constantly on the watch!" is the Gospel advice for the first Sunday of Advent. Watch for opportunities to let God into our lives. Watch and prepare for that day when He will invite us to share his eternal Kingdom. This is the countdown time for the annual celebration of the rebirth of Jesus. The Advent wreath is a weekly reminder of the days remaining. In addition to the beautiful liturgical and devotional ceremonies, there are other "liturgies" outside the church which can be spiritualized and centered on Christ.

1. *Christmas Shopping* — This ritual highlights the individuality of people. Parents, siblings, relatives and dear friends all have their particular preferences and we must choose the gift with these in mind. We are unique persons, different from each other. This fact must be appreciated. The Messiah was born for all, regardless of race or human condition.

2. *Sending Christmas Cards* — A message of love is so fitting at this joyful season. Religious cards with their nativity scenes and scripture verses speak directly of Christ's birth. But other cards with inspiring scenes of nature can reflect the glory of creation and give insights into the mind of the Creator. Even a Santa Claus card tells the traditional message of joy, and of caring love from the hand of the sender.

3. *Decorating for Christmas* — The colors and lights which we display so freely speak a language of warmth and show a spirit of kindness. These, mingled with nature's new-fallen snow which softly shrouds the earth, make the world a pretty place. We do not decorate our homes and lawns for our own enjoyment only, but also for those who will stop to visit or just pass by on the road. Is it not a work of love and an attempt to give happiness to others? The more beauty we can bring into others' lives the better we fulfill the nature of Advent. Jesus will be present in the person of those who visit, for

He lives within people. Thus, we are also decorating for Him.

4. *Preparing the Christmas Meal* — During this season we prepare for one of the lavish meals of the year. We all have fond memories of years past when the family gathered, with some coming from a long distance. We didn't understand as children but now realize that those who sat around the table were much more important than what was on the table, for now they sit with us only in memory. The current work of Advent is to unite the separated and those not speaking to each other, so that all can share a joyful feast and break the bread of lasting friendship.

There are many ways to be "Advent people," with a variety of "liturgies" for this season. We surely can find one meaningful to us and by our efforts of four weeks, bring to birth a bright image of the long-awaited Lord.

SECOND SUNDAY OF ADVENT (B)
Is 40:1-5, 9-11   2 P 3:8-14   Mk 1:1-8

It was a religious practice in the ancient world for a person to be anointed with oil. After this ceremony the recipient was then considered to be sacred. Many kings were anointed by either a priest or a prophet, and sometimes one prophet was anointed by another. Because the reception of this ceremony produced "holiness," it was simply taken for granted that the long-awaited Savior would be anointed. That is the reason why He was called "Messiah," for it's a Hebrew word which means "The Anointed One." The Greeks too viewed the Savior as sacred and gave Him the name "Christ" — a Greek word which also means "The Anointed One."

Our present-day Advent liturgy continues to proclaim the coming of the Anointed One as we read the prophecies of Isaiah, saying that the Messiah will change the face of the earth. We believe that the Lord has come, but He has not leveled the mountains or filled the valleys in a literal sense. If we expected that to have been done in an external manner, we would conclude that the Messiah has not yet arrived. The prophet is speaking in a figurative or poetic sense. This passage, like many others in scripture, applies only to the healing of the internal life of the people.

The Messiah is sent from heaven to the inner person with a mission to speak to the human mind. He has leveled for us the mountains of fear, filled the valleys of despair and calmed those divided within and caught in an internal civil war. God's sacred Anointed One counsels us with these encouraging words: "Don't let your hearts be troubled."

Although the Messiah has come to the world in general, He may not yet have been invited to your own little world. If such is the case, note well what John the Baptizer preaches today. The Savior will "baptize you in the Holy Spirit." This is a call to personal holiness. This is an ideal time to invite Jesus into our lives, whether for the first time or as a renewal of many previous invitations. He is the essence of holiness — the Anointed One. His mission is to help us make sense out of life.

Each of us can ask a timely Advent-question: Have I received my Messiah, or am I still looking for another? The Advent liturgy is not just an empty remembering of the ancient past. It is a timely invitation to accept His presence, to be anointed with the oil of gladness and become sacred. Even though at present we are living the Christian life, we can be Advent-minded people — for it is the nature of the Messiah to continue to reveal Himself to us and through us.

THIRD SUNDAY OF ADVENT (B)
Is 61:1-2, 10-11   1 Th 5:16-24   Jn 1:6-8, 19-28

One of the most perplexing problems in our modern economy is what the experts call "run-away inflation." It imposes enormous hardships on many people, especially the poor, by depriving them of adequate purchasing power.

There's another serious inflationary problem with a long history which thrives today — psychological inflation. That is, an exaggerated idea of one's own self-importance. Everyone has an intrinsic priceless value, yet it's so easy to overlook the worth of others and imagine that we are so much more important than they. If some people wish to be known as the big name celebrities of the world that is OK, but it doesn't mean that they're any better than the ordinary people.

In the Gospel John the Baptizer, who is a divinely made celebrity, wants to play down his personal importance and simply identify with the common people. The crowd stands in awe of him, suggesting that he's the Messiah, or the reincarnation of Elijah or one of the famous prophets of old. John categorically denies all their inflated views, although later on Jesus himself said that "history has not known a man born of woman greater than John the Baptizer." (Mt 11:11) John, however, saw himself as a solitary voice in the wind — a dim light in the darkness, announcing the arrival of the Messiah but unworthy to touch even His sandal strap. Humble people like John need very little space in this world, and they're sensitive to the most gentle nudges of the Master.

This Gospel reading invites us to reflect on the questions: "Who are you?" and "What do you have to say for yourself?" The honesty of our spiritual lives hinges to a great extent on how we relate to psychological inflation. Do we mentally stand and applaud ourselves? Do we feel puffed up because we've met or associated with some celebrities? When others say we're the greatest, do we believe it? When we hear it said of someone else do we think it's said only to be polite but not really meant, as in our case?

John the Baptizer can help us glory in being part of the common people without trying to be some kind of a heavenly-sent dignitary. As we joyfully await the birthday celebration of Jesus we bask in the golden glory He has shared with us, and acclaim Him as the one true Celebrity whom we adore. Happy to have the dignity of being His servants, we testify to the Light but realize that we ourselves are not the Light.

FOURTH SUNDAY OF ADVENT (B)
2 S 7:1-5, 8-11, 16   Rm 16:25-27   Lk 1:26-38

The scholarly religion book by Father John Hardon, S.J., entitled *A Catholic Catechism*, is a fine modern treatment of our faith. In the opening sentence of the section pertaining to the Blessed Virgin Mary, he says, "Catholic Christology is unintelligible without knowing the role of Christ's mother."

Christology and Mariology gracefully blend into the time-honored story of salvation. The life and teachings of Jesus are not complete unless we likewise appreciate the vital place which Mary has in His life and ours.

Some religious educators, in their praiseworthy zeal not to detract from the glory of Jesus, fear that Catholics give too much honor to Mary. A common reply to this concern is that God Himself bestowed a sublime dignity on Mary by choosing her as His mother. That distinguished honor far exceeds any human praise which we might offer. Listen to what the angel Gabriel says to her and about her in today's Gospel reading.

"You have found favor with God. The Holy Spirit will come over you. Your child will be Son of God. Blessed are you among women." Since all these praises and privileges were freely conferred upon one woman by the Creator Himself, then that woman must surely deserve our admiration.

Mary is vital to our faith today for another reason. We need to see her practicality in dealing with even the most sacred things. On the question of bearing a child, she could have simply smiled and been silent, trusting that God would expertly handle all the delicate details. After all, she was His favorite. She was deeply holy but sensibly practical. "How can this be?" she immediately asked, since she was not married. We see a beautiful tinge of toughness in this woman who trusted yet questioned and gave her consent on the condition that the information was correct — "Let it be done to me as you say."

Mary was a woman who knew her own mind and what she was about, for she calmly brushed aside the angelic accolades as one might shoo a fly and simply stated "I am the maidservant of the Lord." She, like John the Baptizer (as we noted last week), was not overly impressed with herself, although she had even more reason to be. What an impressive lesson for all of us lesser people to learn!

Who, better than Mary, can help us prepare for the birth of the Christ Child? Our imitation of her virtues can also make Christ present within us, and through us His light can illumine the world. Even if you feel rejected and sinful, you're still invited to the Lord's birthday party. Come rejoice, pray and sing. Let Mary introduce you to Jesus and you will be healed, for she tells us what the angel told her: "nothing is impossible with God."

CHRISTMAS MIDNIGHT MASS (B)
Is 9:1-6   Tt 2:11-14   Lk 2:1-14

Carols, cards, trees and gifts are only a few of the many traditions which annually come alive with the celebration of Christmas. They are all tied together with various meanings and memories from as long ago as our childhood days. These customs, beautiful as they are, do not touch the very heart of Christmas, but are only extensions of its central meaning.

If we are looking for the real message of this day, we should not search for it on the department store shelves or in Bob Hope's TV Christmas Special. We turn to the Church to hear why this day has such deep significance, although we have heard the story a thousand times before.

The most meaningful Christmas sermon ever heard was not preached by Bishop Sheen, Norman Vincent Peale nor Billy Graham, nor by any pope or saint. It was not spoken by any human but delivered in song by an anonymous choir of celebrating angels. We find their melodious words in the second chapter of Luke's Gospel: "GLORY TO GOD . . . PEACE ON EARTH . . ."

That message from heaven, delivered on the night of the Savior's birth, holds the everlasting key to the attitude we should have toward Jesus, His earthly birth and the objective of His mission.

"Glory to God" is a brief but powerful prayer of adoration acknowledging His unexcelled dignity. It tells of His infinite power and our weakness in comparison; His wisdom in the face of our foolishness. Glory to God! How can we ever understand the depths of His love for His wayward people? We realize the insignificance of our thanks for His blessings freely given, and we can only gratefully repeat: "Glory to God."

"Peace on Earth" is the Lord's mission statement set to music. We still pray and work for it, for our distraught world is filled with violence, hatred and mutual mistrust. The Lord Jesus has been born, but His golden objectives are still awaiting birth on our tiny island in space. We have not taken seriously the message of the Peacemaker.

You give glory to God when you extend yourself to another and thereby create a small atmosphere of peace on earth. Your kind words naturally invite other kind words from your neighbor, and that could start a pleasant chain reaction to produce peace on earth. Selfishness breeds contempt, and hatred turns to war — but love, like a seed, germinates and grows into everlasting goodness.

In this Christmas Mass, as well as in our other liturgies throughout the year, we happily join our prayers with those of the angels. We re-echo once again the meaning of the day, the message of the Church, the mission of Jesus and the song of the angels, "GLORY TO GOD ... PEACE ON EARTH ..."

SUNDAY IN THE OCTAVE OF CHRISTMAS
HOLY FAMILY (B)
Si 3:2-6, 12-14   Col 3:12-21   Lk 2:22-40

Jesus, Mary and Joseph — the sacred trio of Nazareth — are normally portrayed as the ideal family. We picture them living in perfect harmony and mutual trust, all wearing shining haloes. The only hint of any family rift is when Jesus gets lost in the temple.

Lest we think they are too ideal for us to relate to, we should remember that they were in many ways very common people. They were poor economically, struggling with the ordinary hardships of making a living. Even their privileged status with the Almighty did not free them from the common lot of trying to decipher His will. The family was holy and successful, and it enabled the child Jesus to develop in three major areas: wisdom, age and grace. Those same threefold guidelines could serve as a measuring stick of success for our own families.

1. WISDOM — The school does not have the sole nor even the primary responsibility for a child's advancement in learning and wisdom. The school is dedicated to the promotion of learning among the young but its efforts are weakened without the constant support of the family at home. Parents should ask themselves if they reflect the proper attitude toward their children's learning, and if they encourage them. Do you as parents take time to look over their textbooks, help them with their homework, attend school functions and have conferences with their teachers? Learning, to children is often important only to the degree that their parents promote it in the home. It's part of being a holy family.

2. AGE — Some parents can't discuss the "facts of life"

because they themselves cannot accept the reality that their children are growing older and need to know. Sexual and emotional developments are therefore often left undiscussed. As the young gradually move toward adulthood they need to listen to their parents, who in turn need to "listen" to their children. It's also good to remember that the commandment, "Honor thy father and mother," is always binding regardless of the ages of children or parents.

3. GRACE — The home is responsible for the children's spiritual development. The church assists the parents but is not solely responsible for the religious formation of the young. In the family setting the children best learn their prayers, the basic commandments and the common Bible stories. Time should be set aside for these religious needs during the long years of growing up.

Are the members of your family at peace with each other? When at home, does your family really feel at home? Or are some tension-filled and restless and feel more "at home" when away from home?

What family do you consider the ideal and why? Do you think anyone considers your family to be an attractive model?

In the beginning of the year when we make those annual promises, we might think of a family resolution. What can we, as a caring group of familiar, close-knit people do, to make our lives and home a better place for all to advance in wisdom, age and grace?

OCTAVE OF CHRISTMAS
SOLEMNITY OF MARY, MOTHER OF GOD (B)
Nb 6:22-27   Gal 4:4-7   Lk 2:16-21

Today we begin a new year amidst the annual celebrations of revelry and noise. December has delayed its departure with a full month of 31 days. Now, like a spent old-timer, it silently leaves the scene, as all eyes focus on the newborn baby of January 1. The past year is history, for better or worse, and we sense a revived hope of exciting opportunities in the future.

Our religion celebrates New Year's Day in a calm fashion by inviting people to church in honor of the mother of Jesus, with the newborn baby still in her arms. The passing of the old and the hope of the new is reflected in her eyes and His. The ancient Simeon, like the old year, has steadied his trembling hands to hold the child, for the Holy Spirit will soon take him from the scene, along with the aged Anna. The elderly pair in the temple wave good-bye to Joseph and Mary with their infant Savior.

The silence of the Lord's mother does not indicate sadness or doubt but a deep and determined sense of purpose. We would do well to see the women of today in that same dignified role and affirm them in their rights, equality and strength. It is often said that Mary did not speak much. But how clearly and loudly this strong woman speaks through her Son! She is the one who gave birth to Him who would in turn give life to the world. All who are born again in the baptism of Jesus, cannot forget that He in turn was born of Mary. From her, He is reborn every year in our liturgical celebrations.

Last year on this day I hung up two calendars, one in my office and the other in the kitchen. The kitchen one wished me "a very happy and prosperous New Year"; it was from the local bank. The other, from the church, announced the octave of Christmas and displayed the picture of Mary. So we celebrate a new beginning with thoughts of the young mother, whose child changed the calendar from B.C. to A.D. We are privileged to live in the love as well as in the year of the Lord.

Time-wise we are living as close to Christ in A.D. as Abraham did in B.C. — about 2000 years either way. We are the new Israel, the family of Abraham. Jesus reaches out His arms to touch and unite us in His one common effort.

Science says that the world has existed for nearly five and one half billion years and will probably continue for a few more billion. Viewing the whole span of time, the actual birth of Jesus is actually a very recent event, and we are much closer to the nativity scene than we might imagine.

Paul tells the Galatians today, "When the designated time had come, God sent forth His Son born of a woman . . ." It is that delightful and faith-filled woman whom we honor on the first day of the new year. We find Jesus and Mary together and nothing can separate them.

SECOND SUNDAY AFTER CHRISTMAS (B)
Si 24:1-4, 8-12   Ep 1:3-6, 15-18   Jn 1:1-18

Jesus' human genealogy is found in the Gospels of Matthew and Luke. John's Gospel presents His divine genealogy in its famous opening words: "In the beginning was the Word; the Word was in God's presence, and the Word was God." Fourteen verses later John adds: "The Word became flesh, and made His dwelling among us . . ." Fr. Bruce Vawter calls this passage "one of the most serious and sobering statements in the gospels . . ." The literal meaning is "He pitched His tent among us." It is a magnificent poetic expression of the intimate reality of God's presence in our midst.

Notice that in the first reading from Sirach today, the invaluable gift of wisdom has been personified and sent to earth to dwell among us also in a tent and to minister before the Lord. The Church is teaching us a unique kind of tent theology.

The Bible makes about 150 references to tents, with the first being in Genesis 4:20 — a statement that Jubal is the father of those who dwell in tents. The tent concept denotes not only the style and material stability of a dwelling but more importantly, the overall view of life itself.

A tent is for the pilgrim and the shepherd — a person on the move and traveling lightly. It stands in sharp contrast to a house, which is not for the pilgrim but the settler — the person who is established and intends to remain in one place.

Referring to the permanency of heaven, Jesus used the word "house" to tell of His Father's dwelling, where He will prepare a lasting place for us, although He personally had "no place to lay His head." The lasting stability of the Father's house with its many mansions is both our beacon and magnet.

Wisdom tells us that someday we will fold up our tents and move on to the everlasting Kingdom. If we travel lightly, we will be able to calmly pack and depart like the freed captives leaving Egypt under Moses. Our solid comfortable homes and mansions may suggest that we have here a lasting kingdom, but from wisdom's tent comes a timely warning that we are only passing through.

Jesus too is passing through as wisdom, light and love — none of which can stand still or be hidden. Wisdom must speak, light must shine, and love must reach out. His tent is still pitched among us in our brothers and sisters, each of whom is a tent containing the precious gift of His sacred presence. Although we may long for permanent stability, it is certain that we shall not find it here. Some never experience any security in this world. Those who find some, must acknowledge that it won't last.

We who are flesh, strive to become spiritualized and glow with His enduring love. The Lord is not a remote stranger who sends bizarre messages from outer space. He has become one of us, living on our human level. He has pitched His tent among us.

EPIPHANY (B)
Is 60:1-6   Ep 3:2-3, 5-6   Mt 2:1-12

Three different kinds of people with their particular ways of relating to Jesus are presented in today's Gospel reading.

1. *The Travelers from the East*, popularly known as the Magi or Wise Men, sought Jesus consistently through hardships and the fatiguing miles of desert journeying. Their star-bright faith led them through the darkness of uncertainty to the fulfillment of the deep hope which inspired them to begin their remarkable adventure. They were willing to leave home and those who loved them in order to find a greater and everlasting love.

2. *King Herod* sought Jesus for a different reason. He wanted to destroy Him. Herod could not bother himself to personally search for Jesus, so he commanded others to find Him and report back. His motives were hate and jealousy. In reality, Herod was seeking only himself. Jesus was an obstacle to be removed from his political and social path.

3. *The Local Citizens of Bethlehem* were indifferent to the whole event, with the exception of the shepherds. Although it had been foretold that the Messiah was to be born in their town, they were unconcerned. They refused the Holy Family a place at the inn and sent Mary off into the hills to give birth to the world's awaited baby.

These same attitudes are present in the world today. For our annual remembrance of the first Epiphany, let's consider them.

A. Many are deeply dedicated to the cause of Jesus and travel many treacherous miles. They have abandoned family, friends and even personal gain to find Him. They seek and find Him in their hearts, their homes and in their work. They discover Him in the liturgies of the Church and in the persons they meet.

B. There likewise are the selfish ones, like Herod. They use religion only for their personal gain. It helps them in politics and in business and gives them social standing, if they belong to the right church and are seen at the proper religious gatherings. They do not allow God to stand in their way.

C. Finally we have the vast numbers of the unconcerned, who know some of Jesus' marvelous history, have heard the prophecies and promises and yet just don't care about God, religion or church.

What's your position? Is Jesus a threat who hampers your style of operation? Are you perhaps indifferent to it all and simply don't care to be bothered? Or are you one of the modern day Wise Men, willing to sacrifice until you find your Lord?

The loving Jesus calls His people from hatred, darkness and indifference into His own blessed light, where we can present our gifts and happily return home.

BAPTISM OF THE LORD (B)
Is 42:1-4, 6-7   Ac 10:34-38   Mk 1:7-11

If a person who never attended church asked us what takes place there each week, we could reply that each year the Church presents 52 unique Sunday worship experiences, centered around the birth, life, death and Resurrection of Jesus.

The worship is composed of scripture readings; a homily to apply the readings to everyday life; the reenactment of the Last Supper; other prayers and songs.

We concentrated on the birth of Jesus during Advent, Christmas and Epiphany. This phase has now been completed. Last Sunday (Epiphany) we honored Jesus as a small child visited by the Wise Men. This Sunday He is a 30 year old man beginning His public life.

In just a few weeks Lent will begin—the 40 days' penitential season culminating in Holy Week, when we commemorate Jesus' passion and death. Then will follow the highlight of the entire year —Easter, celebrating the Resurrection. Throughout the remainder of the year, we will marvel at Jesus' miracles and praise Him for His teachings and promises.

In today's liturgy, Jesus begins His public life by being baptized in the Jordan. John the Baptizer hesitantly performs the ceremony. Normally his voice is loud and bold, but today he's nervous as the Messiah steps into the water. Jesus didn't need baptism but He wanted it. We need it and should want it.

We might well pause this day to prayerfully appreciate the fact that in baptism we were born again in the original and true sense of the term. By our baptism we were spiritually incorporated into the permanent membership of the Church. We are now gracefully bound together with other believers around the world, accepting the basic rules and duties of this pious corporation and sharing in its glorious privileges.

Once baptized, we can now share the sentiment of John—we too have come into contact with One more powerful than ourselves. His sandals we are not worthy to untie, but in spite of that He has invited us to share His life.

In the creation story in Genesis, the world came out of the water. The baptismal encounter is a new and personal creation story for each recipient. Now we are accepted by the merciful Jesus, washed in the cleansing waters and incorporated into His Body. Baptism makes us a new creation. From then on (spiritually speaking), the sky's the limit.

FIRST SUNDAY OF LENT (B)
Gn 9:8-15   1 P 3:18-22   Mk 1:12-15

Today, it's off to the desert, for this is the first Sunday of Lent. It's time for the annual retelling of the forty days of temptation endured by Jesus. Matthew's account was read last year; Mark's this year, and Luke's the next.

The temptation stories told by Matthew and Luke have vivid details of Jesus and the devil bounding from mountain top to temple, hotly engaged in debate. Mark omits these activities and verbal battles. He calmly narrates Jesus' entrance into the desert (aided by angels) to combat the devil and concludes with His victorious emergence.

Mark's terseness reminds one of Flanigan, the legendary

newspaper reporter assigned to cover train derailments. Criticized several times by his editor for making his accounts too long and rambling, he reacted one day by describing a very serious accident: "Off again, on again, gone again, Flanigan." Mark also consistently says much in a few words, then moves swiftly to another point. It is no secret why his Gospel is the shortest of the four.

The complete drama of the forty day desert experience is veiled in mystery but we are given the heart of the story. There was a time in our Lord's life, before His public ministry, when He made a solitary retreat in the wilderness. There He was tested by the forces of evil (wild beasts and the devil) and found both consolation and courage outside Himself (angels ministered to Him). He emerged from His forty days of training as a wiry athlete, ready for the ultimate test of strength and skill against His opponents.

People will shatter His ears with insulting accusations, spit in His face, nail Him to a cross—but aided by the desert days, He'll hold His almighty power in check. A man who chooses not to retaliate when it's within his power to destroy his enemy, is much stronger that one who must "repay" every injury. Jesus' enemies did not appreciate the calibre of the man they were attacking; otherwise they would have fled in terror.

The desert experience gave Jesus time to recall the past and envision the future. We too can profit by thinking in both directions. Remember our excitement a few weeks ago when professional football had its final showdown in the gridiron ritual known as "Super Sunday"? We were caught up in an event which didn't benefit or touch our lives, jobs, families, or help us with our problems.

Think ahead a few weeks to the Church's version of "Super Sunday"—Easter. In the Resurrection, Jesus made good His prediction to be victorious. That event was accomplished for us, and we share in the victory, for Jesus took the *sting* out of death.

It's spring training time in the Super Star's camp and you're invited to tag along into the desert. It could be rewarding as you battle the devil and wild beasts in your lives, and emerge as stronger persons. Don't be afraid, for the angels will bear you up and the Lord will be nearby.

SECOND SUNDAY OF LENT (B)
Gn 22:1-2, 9, 10-13, 15-18   Rm 8:31-34   Mk 9:2-10

The story of the Transfiguration of Jesus is told each year on the second Sunday of Lent. This year it's Mark's version, which is very similar to the accounts of Matthew and Luke. The Gospel account has a curious beginning — "now after six days..." What happened six days earlier that was so important? Let's backtrack to the previous chapter for the answer.

Two significant episodes preceded the Transfiguration: Peter identified Jesus as the Messiah, and Jesus gave the first prediction of His suffering and death.

The Transfiguration therefore was a timely mental lift for the disciples, six days after the Master's prediction of His imminent death. Elijah the prophet and Moses the lawgiver appeared, then faded into the background, leaving only Jesus — the prophet and lawgiver of the New Testament. The voice from Heaven stamped on Him the seal of approval.

Moses heard the voice of God and saw His presence in the burning bush. Now the three key apostles heard God's voice and caught a glimpse of the brilliant, burning inner life of Jesus and were convinced of God's presence within Him. There would be days ahead when their patience and faith would be severely tried and the memory of the grace-glowing Lord would sustain them.

Jesus imposed silence about the theophany on the viewers, most likely to neutralize the popular false opinion that His discipleship meant one big glory trip. Mark especially emphasizes the hardships and agony which the true Christian must endure, and downplays the glory and reward which may result from discipleship. In spite of what many would like to believe, we know that the Lord never promised us a rose garden: what He did promise was a cross—seven days a week—and eternal glory in the life hereafter. The pains of life are necessary but not attractive, and we naturally shun them and advise others to do likewise, as Peter attempted to dissuade the Lord from death on the cross.

We know that in law, medicine, business, the arts—in fact, any worthwhile activity we can think of—success is predicated on long years of dedicated and difficult work. In sports it is well-known that before one can kiss the trophy, there must be many torturous days of monotonous training. Bruce Jenner would testify that Olympic medals are not won simply by eating Wheaties.

The Lord purchased our future glory at the cost of great personal anguish. Since no disciple is above his master, we must share the cost if we hope to inherit the glory. The Gospel moral is rather simple: "No Cross! No Crown!"

THIRD SUNDAY OF LENT (B)
Ex 20:1-17   1 Cor 1:22-25   Jn 2:13-25

Do you know about the two giants who were engaged in battle at the time of our Lord? They pushed and pressured each other with authoritative power and continually tried to dominate. One giant was the MARKETPLACE; the other was the FATHER'S HOUSE. It was the old war renewed between the natural and supernatural, the human and divine; the battle of the two kingdoms.

Jesus loved the Father's House and when He saw that the Marketplace had infiltrated the sacred precincts, His inborn pride triggered a violent reaction. His immediate targets were the money-changers, whose job it was to convert the Roman coins to

Jewish. It was business for the sake of business, not for religion. To the best of our knowledge, Jesus acted alone, without the assistance of His apostles. His moves were dramatic and decisive. There would be no compromise on this issue.

The giants continue to tussle in our day as the spirit of the world vies with the spirit of Christ. Many see Jesus' response as fanatical, others as dedication to principle. How do you see it? Was a little money in the temple all that bad?

The Marketplace and the Father's House lure and tug at every person and we follow one and then the other and often try to compromise on both. Take the issue of life. Can it be bought or sold, or is its value beyond all price? The Marketplace will deal, the Father's House will not. What is the current market value of truth and honesty? Is it OK to buy sex from the vendor if you have the money, or are some things non-negotiable? Can you kill a man for a price? If you're shrewd enough, is it permissible to steal a fur coat, an automobile or the neighbor's husband, or are these "deals" always immoral, as taught in the Father's House?

Cattle and sheep, hay and corn and a million other items can be brought into the Marketplace but the Father's House is reserved for people who want to find peace and a deeper, loving knowledge of their God.

We are wise in the ways of the world but how do we fare in church? Of the 168 hours we have to spend each week, one at best is spent in the sanctuary, the others in the business of the world. That may be our most telling commentary on the location of our treasure and our heart.

Lent is a fitting time to catch a spark from the fiery zeal of our Lord. It's an ideal season for values clarification. When you come to the Father's House, don't bring along the Marketplace. Don't view church as something to get finished with, so you can return to more important things. For too many, it is just a pause between duties and not even the pause that refreshes. When you come to pray, *drive out* distracting thoughts. This is sacred time, for we are in the Father's House.

FOURTH SUNDAY OF LENT (B)
2 Ch 36:14-17, 19-23   Ep 2:4-10   Jn 3:14-21

Jesus had many encounters throughout His life with Jewish rabbis. He questioned them in the temple when He was twelve years old and debated with others in His mature years. Most rejected Him but one who didn't was Nicodemus. He is not a major character of the New Testament and is mentioned only by John, but he does weave in and out of our Lord's life. He was the inquiring one who came at night to express his faith in Jesus and ask about eternal life. Later in his circle of fellow Israelites, he counseled against condemning Jesus without understanding Him. Finally he showed up at the grave site with spices for the body and helped Joseph of Arimathea with our Lord's burial.

Today's Gospel contains Jesus' response to a question asked by Nicodemus on their first meeting. He wanted information about baptism and the means to achieve eternal life.

Jesus responded openly to His newly made friend, explaining that He would be lifted up as the serpent was lifted by Moses in the desert to heal the people. Many will be healed by the cross in the same manner, Jesus told him. The rabbi, being an intelligent Pharisee, understood the cited passage from the Book of Numbers and no doubt long pondered the analogy.

To this day, a similar image—of a serpent or serpents entwined on a pole—remains a visible sign of physical healing. This symbol appears on hospitals, ambulances and the stationery of many health service organizations. We don't need reminding of the immense impact the cross of Jesus has for spiritual healing.

In John's Gospel, Jesus is shown as coming to earth to become fully human (the Word was made flesh). That was the first phase of His mission. The second phase was to lift that humanness to eternal glory. He does not view death as a going down, but a going up. It's a skyward sweep rather than a crumbling into dust. This bold faith-filled concept should challenge us to plot the direction of our death. Like Jesus, we are born human and now we try to lift that humanness to glory through the rebirth of baptism and the eternal tug from the Savior on the cross.

In this Gospel, Jesus says that faith leads to eternal life. The Hebrew word for faith is *emeth*. It means strength, but a strength based on God, not on human security. This was really good news for Nicodemus and for us. Perhaps death for us means only defeat. Jesus smiles and reemphasizes that we are to think of it as a step up. The deeper our faith—our *emeth*—the better foundation we have for being lifted up by the healing from above to the glory of the Kingdom.

FIFTH SUNDAY OF LENT (B)
Jr 31:31-34   Heb 5:7-9   Jn 12:20-33

On July 18, 1938, an inexperienced pilot, Douglas Corrigan, attempted to fly from New York to California but ended up in Dublin, Ireland. The press dubbed him "Wrong Way Corrigan." I don't know how he became so confused but I do know that we all do plenty of things the wrong way.

We exhibit a very narrow view if we think, just because people don't do things our way, they're being done the wrong way. Hebrew and Chinese for example are written and read from right to left. That's different but not wrong. When our former President Carter and his folks from Georgia came to the White House, they found it difficult to get accustomed to the "strange accent" of northern people, and vice versa. There are many innocent and humorous instances where we set ourselves up as the standard.

Jesus told us that His ways are not our ways. He did many things backwards—to our thinking—for He was the paradox man. A paradox is a contrary view, something that seems to be untrue but is really true in a different way. It would seem, for example, that the following statement would be true. "I can be very happy if I live only for myself." Jesus says, "False." If you live for yourself only, you will be unhappy and sorry. If you want to be happy, live for others and die to yourself. This is the lesson taught in today's Gospel. The grain of wheat must die in the ground before it can grow and produce more wheat.

Jesus may have disillusioned the "intelligent" Greeks who came to talk with Him in this Gospel. They were often too sure of themselves, possessing reputations for great wisdom. He said that those who are foolish for God are really the wisest of people. God's chosen people, the privileged Jews, also heard Jesus say that the real chosen people are those who have their faith in Him. The proud and power-conscious Romans jeeringly snickered at the paradox, "only when you're weak are you strong." The Lord appeared to contradict most things people stood for and believed in. He would be a poor public relations man, for He was not trying to please but lead.

We have to admit He's not doing and saying things backwards; we are. If we think we're doing something the right way but it's not working and we feel discouraged, it would be well to turn around and look at Him. We may be going precisely in the wrong direction.

The standards of the world are very different than His. He is "The Way." Some think He's just in the way. The Christian will often be at odds with the world, as he tries to live the teachings of Jesus, for we appear often to have it all backwards—like Wrong Way Corrigan. The Lord, however, not only pointed in the right direction but invited His followers with the bold pronouncement: "I am the Way, the Truth, and the Life."

PALM SUNDAY (B)
Mk 11:1-10   Is 50:4-7   Ph 2:6-11   Mk 14:1-15:47

The liturgical celebration on the Sunday before Easter is very curious. Its two Gospel readings proclaim radically different sentiments.

We begin with a joyful bouncy *palm parade* with Jesus on the back of a donkey, entering Jerusalem. He's extremely popular with the citizens who hail Him as their king. He gets the "red carpet" treatment with cloaks and palms jubilantly strewn in His path. Our own parade and our prayers and resounding hosannas help make a joyful atmosphere.

Suddenly, with the abruptness of spring lightning, the mood changes. The second Gospel reading announces that the king is degraded to the level of a criminal. The victory confetti is replaced with whips, spit and choking dust. His donkey has disappeared and on His own back He carries a torturously heavy and awkward cross. The crowd is leaving Jerusalem and it's no celebration—it's an *execution march.*

The liturgy has done a complete about-face, just as the original crowd turned 180 degrees from "long live the king" to the defiant chant, "crucify Him." If we want an example of fleeting popularity, we have an excellent one at hand. Jesus is king for a day. Gradually the initial joy shrinks into the distance and we closely follow the death march to Calvary.

The sensitive celebrant of the Mass, reading the part of Jesus, hears his parishioners shouting, "crucify Him." Although he realizes most of them don't mean it personally, he still can feel a faint pang of the agony of Jesus, who realized His former "friends" now called for Him to suffer a most cruel death.

The Lord, who is the same yesterday, today and forever, is twisted by fickle human nature that can't be consistent two days in a row. This divided and dramatic message, which runs the complete gamut of the emotional spectrum, introduces us to the greatest week of the entire year. The various highs and lows of Holy Week will be explained and enacted by the Church as the week progresses. Everyone who cares about the Savior will want to follow Him through these momentous days ahead.

To show the particular kind of suffering Jesus endured, the Church has always employed the word, *Passion*. It's a deliberately selected term, meaning deep suffering which involves severe physical pain, keen emotional stress and acute depression. The seven days preceding Easter have a way of making one's personal hurts become very small.

EASTER SUNDAY (B)
Ac 10:34, 37-43   Col 3:1-4 or 1 Cor 5:6-8   Jn 20:1-9

Christ's return from the dead was a surprise, to say the least. Who expected Him to reappear? Even though He had predicted it, there was great lack of belief. People may have thought He meant it in a figurative sense — like rising up to live in memory, but not in real life.

On Easter Sunday, Jesus introduced a new glorified-body existence to the world. It was not a mere restoration like He had granted the daughter of Jairus, the son of the widow of Naim, or His friend Lazarus. These people had received back their lives in their former earthly bodies, and would die again. Jesus displayed a new kind of resurrected body that would never die.

There is a natural and enduring mystery associated with death, tombs and future existence. The American Indians buried food and supplies for the journey to the happy hunting ground. In 1922 golden treasures were discovered in the tomb of the 14th century B.C. Egyptian king, Tutankhamon, which continue to attract droves of fascinated visitors. Imagine the surprise when these treasures were first discovered in his tomb. But there was a much greater and lasting discovery in the tomb of Jesus. The priceless find was the empty tomb. Of all the treasures ever found, none can even begin to compare with the discovery of the empty tomb.

Between earthly and eternal life there once was a heavy barrier and a deep chasm, called death. Jesus rolled back the boulder and bridged the canyon. The tomb could not hold Him. Jesus is among the living.

The Lord promised to remain with us always — during earthly life, at death and for eternity. He died and rose, never to die again, and offered us an open-ended invitation into the future. We run to the grave with the two apostles each Easter and discover anew the priceless gift of the Risen Christ.

The word "Easter" is not a biblical term but one of Anglo-Saxon origin, which worked its way into our liturgy and theology at a later date. It well reflects the spring celebration when nature is reawakened from the winter sleep to grow, bloom and make the world beautiful. Jesus rose in conjunction with nature. The great event can never be silenced, for it speaks intimately to our deepest fears and hopes. As long as time shall last, the story of the Risen Christ will resoundingly echo from one generation to another and its hope-filled joy will reverberate from one century to the next.

SECOND SUNDAY OF EASTER (B)
Ac 4:32-35   1 Jn 5:1-6   Jn 20:19-31

Today's Gospel reading contains what scripture scholar Bruce Vawter calls "the most complete affirmation of Christ's nature to be found on the lips of anyone in the gospel." This precious affirmation is uttered by the apostle Thomas, who ironically is more remembered for his doubts than his faith. He never deserved the title of "doubting Thomas," which has shadowed him through the ages. He should be known as "courageous Thomas," with the uncanny habit of speaking clearly his opposing views, regardless of the pressures to agree or remain silent.

His calm heroic strength is completely ignored by the Synoptic Gospels (Matthew, Mark and Luke). John only highlights a few incidents where Thomas' inward bravery shines forth. In Jn 11:16, when Christ's life is feared to be in jeopardy, Thomas exhorts the others, "let us go along and die with him." In Jn 14:5, Jesus is telling the Twelve about eternal life and adds parenthetically, "You know the way that leads where I go." In reality they didn't know what Jesus meant and, lest they appear stupid, no one asked except Thomas. He broke into the Lord's dialogue with the query, "Lord, we don't know where you are going, how can we know the way?" Had he remained silent like the rest, we never would have heard the great summary of the Lord's mission. "I am the way, the truth and the life." Thanks, Thomas. We needed to hear that.

Today, John says the apostles are huddled in the upper room, hiding behind locked doors for fear of their enemies, finding courage and protection in numbers. Strange, isn't it, that Thomas isn't with them? Did he need the security of numbers and bolted doors? Apparently not. He was somewhere on the outside, all on his own. He was just that kind of guy.

The Lord makes His unscheduled visit, and the apostles are hysterical with sheer joy. When Thomas returns they shout in unison: "We've seen the Lord." Thomas calmly seems unimpressed and simply says that he wants to see the wounds before he shares their ecstasy. When Jesus invited him a week later to see and touch the convincing wounds, he offered no apologies and did not try to "explain" his need for further proof. He saw no need for any mental squirming. The truth was now present and typically he said what he felt: "My Lord and my God." That's the great statement that should be remembered rather than his previous lingering doubts.

Thomas encourages us to think, probe and question. Our faith must be real and sensible to us. If it is not, we have a good example for direct and vocal inquiry. To just sit back and nod our heads in agreement to confusing presentations is being very "unthomistic."

Try to catch the contagious spirit of the faith-filled apostle Thomas. You, like millions of others, might want to whisper his famous words at the elevation of the living bread, during the celebration of today's Mass.

THIRD SUNDAY OF EASTER (B)
Ac 3:13-15, 17-19   1 Jn 2:1-5   Lk 24:35-48

Today's Gospel reminds me of a true story. About the time Columbus was discovering America (1492), two young friends in Germany, Albrecht Durer and Franz Knigstein, were struggling to become artists. With much raw talent but few funds for attending the university, they decided one of them should find a job and support the other until he completed school. Then he could sell his paintings and finance the other's education.

To decide which should attend the university first, they drew lots. Durer went to school and Knigstein went to work. After a number of years the genius Durer was selling his beautiful paintings and he returned home to uphold his part of the bargain. Only then did he painfully realize the great price his friend had paid. Knigstein's delicate and sensitive fingers, necessary for fine painting, had been ruined by his years of rugged manual labor. Although he had to abandon his artistic dream, he was not embittered but rejoiced in his friend's success.

One day Albrecht, unnoticed, saw Franz kneeling with his gnarled hands intertwined in prayer and quickly he sketched them and completed what we now call the "Praying Hands."

Today art galleries feature many works of the famous painter, Albrecht Durer, but the people's favorite is the "Praying Hands." That painting has been copied millions of times the world over, telling its tender, eloquent story of love, sacrifice, labor and gratitude.

The hands of Jesus tell a greater story. "Look at my hands..." He says in today's reading from St. Luke, and "as He said this He showed them His hands..." The apostles thought they were seeing a ghost but the outstretched hands of the Savior were proof beyond any doubt, that He was no ghost. Vivid in their minds was the meaning of the scars and the memory of the cross. There was no doubt about the identity of this man. Luke records this touching scene in the last chapter of his Gospel. He wants us to remember what a friend we have in Jesus.

We easily give great honor to people in important positions. But we too seldom think of whose hands were gnarled and hardened so that they could attain their success.

Can we think of someone's hands that are scarred, twisted and bruised because of years of loving help offered to us? Perhaps those hands are now folded in death and they can only be seen in some time-worn photograph. Whose hands upheld and supported us when we were unable to stand on our own? We are not self-made people. The glories of the future are also gifts, handed to each of us by the One with the identifiable scars.

FOURTH SUNDAY OF EASTER (B)
Ac 4:8-12   1 Jn 3:1-2   Jn 10:11-18

I've heard many discussions about images of Jesus. It's often asked that if He walked the streets of modern day America, would He be wearing His flowing robe, sandals and long hair? Or would his garb be a suit and tie? A Roman collar? Sport clothes? I think the traditional robe would not be worn.

Some object to the whole image of the shepherd and sheep. "I resent," a man once told me, "being referred to as a dumb sheep." Touché! But don't read more into the statement than Jesus intended. I've never thought of myself as a sheep and I'm pretty sure the Lord doesn't view me as one either. Furthermore, He's not even a shepherd. We have not one incident in the Bible or tradition, where Jesus so much as touched a live sheep.

We are not to interpret all biblical passages literally. But we must see the basic lesson being taught. Jesus is like a shepherd and we are like sheep. That's a great compliment to us, for the shepherd loves his sheep and risks his life for them. Jesus is saying that His relationship to us is very close. We should feel honored, not insulted. The Lord used many different examples to convey His intimate union with humanity. He is our Teacher and we are His students. He is our Master and we are His disciples. He is our Savior and we are the saved. He is our God and we are His people.

Jesus is so complex that no one image can express all His qualities, so He used many. Like St. Paul tried to be, Jesus is "all things to all people, in order to win all." He is like a campaigner wearing a miner's cap and lamp in coal country, or appearing in a chief's headdress to impress the Indians. It's an attempt to identify with the people to win their confidence and their souls. In today's first reading He's referred to as a rejected stone that became the cornerstone. Again, said by way of analogy.

"That there be one flock and one shepherd" is also a figure of speech. Taken literally, it would mean that a time would come when there would be only one world religion. That is highly unlikely. Can you envision the various branches of Lutherans united in themselves or the different divisions of Methodists becoming one? Then picture all the 300 or so Protestant Churches in complete agreement. Merge in the Catholics and Orthodox and that's only the Christian religion united. Add next the Jews, who don't accept Jesus as Messiah. Impossible? Yet that's just getting started, for now we must bring together the Moslems, Hindus,

Confucianists, etc. and continue adding until we have all religious people believing and professing in unison, "Jesus is Lord."

Practically speaking, there can be an elementary unity of all humanity and, if not a basic worship of God, at least a common esteem for His moral principles. We can be one in love of our God and each other. We can be united in sincerity and honest dealing and living according to our own consciences. The Creator loves His flock composed of many kinds of sheep, whose different natures and ways He understands. He has provided space for all in the green pastures. Each one of us can feel safe and accepted under His watchful eye, for He is the Good Shepherd.

FIFTH SUNDAY OF EASTER (B)
Ac 9:26-31   1 Jn 3:18-24   Jn 15:1-8

A kindergarten teacher says that her five year olds have the delicate mysteries of mothers and babies all figured out. This is how it works. Women go to the hospital and have babies, which are placed in a warm room with a big window in the front, like a display window in a store. At different times during the day, the mothers stand in front of the window and look at all the newborn babies to see which they like best. The first mother to "get well" and be able to go home, gets to pick the baby she wants; the next mother to get well chooses second, etc. The last mother takes the one left.

Presume for a moment that such a procedure were possible. What mother would look at an infant and say "That baby is prettier than mine. I wish it belonged to me instead of the one I have"? None! Every mother thinks her baby is the nicest; even if the child is deformed, crippled or retarded. The natural bond between mother and child causes her to overlook all its deficiencies and see only its precious beauty. So regardless of the order in which they "got well" and went home, they would all choose their own.

In trying to explain God's intense love for His people, Isaiah uses the impressive example of the boundless love of a mother for her child. "Can a mother forget her child . . .?" No! Never! "But even if she could," says our Creator, "I will never forget you" (Is 49:15). Our mother gives us birth and God gives us daily rebirth and sustenance. Without His constant care, we would be fruitless, helpless; we would disintegrate into nothingness. The Gospel today speaks of this great dependency. "I am the vine and you are the branches. He who lives in me and I in him will produce abundantly, for apart from me you can do nothing."

We often pray to God our Father, but not to God our Mother. Yet if we analyze the divine qualities, God is as much or more Mother as Father. He is tender, faithful, loving, kind, constantly watching over us to pick us up when we fall.

Wouldn't it be true to say that your mother has loved you more unselfishly than anyone other than God Himself? Mother's Day is always on the Lord's Day, for between them there is a perfect harmony. The first to know of our conception was our Lord and the next was our mother. They've shared a lot with each other and us, and neither of their loves will ever die.

Whether it's child to mother or branch to vine, it's a close and necessary dependency. God is love and so is a mother.

SIXTH SUNDAY OF EASTER (B)
Ac 10:25-26, 34-35, 44-48   1 Jn 4:7-10   Jn 15:9-17

Some mighty powerful thoughts can be expressed in very tiny sentences. I would like to cite two examples on the subject of love. Both sentences have only three words. The first is: "I love you." When those words are spoken sincerely and intelligently, they are about the three nicest words you could ever hope to hear. But if said thoughtlessly or worst, deceptively, they have no beauty and become bearers of serious harm. This sentence is one of the most used and abused, producing both happiness and pain. Whether saying it or hearing it, be sure you understand it. Remember the old adage, "You can be kissed by a fool and fooled by a kiss."

Love is one of those mysteriously fundamental words whose full meaning is difficult to understand and explain, for it has many meanings. St. Paul struggled to define love. The best he could do was to supply adjectives explaining what love is and what it is not. He said love is patient and kind. He said it is not jealous, nor snobbish, never rude nor self-seeking.

In the second reading of today's Mass, St. John, the apostle of love with his deep searching mind, gives a beautiful definition which is the second powerful little sentence: "God is love." John develops his thought: "He who abides in love, abides in God and God in him." This profound passage has been set to music and is often sung as a refrain at liturgical celebrations, especially at penance services. When sung well the lyrics and melody evoke noble sentiments in us.

That "God is love," is a thought that could well dominate this Sunday's liturgy. There is a strong modern feeling that sex is love, without which there can be no complete love. What do you think? Some brag triumphantly, "We went all the way." That statement indicates that there's no further one can go. Not true. Sex is obviously a good and necessary part of human existence, and without it we would be one generation from the end of humanity. However, sex is not love but the *expression* of love. Sex is an occasional union; love is a constant one. Sex can grow weak, even die; genuine love does not. Love alone can take you all the way.

We also hear about free love. Now what in the world is that? Love is many things, but it's not free. True love is very demanding. It causes each lover to make many personal sacrifices for the sake of the other. Love, like the invisible yet irresistible force of gravity, pulls one into the world of another. It is neither free nor carefree. It has a million strings attached.

Various books, magazines and movies cheaply splash the word "love" across their titles and in their stories. These could be called exhibitions, orgies or sensationalisms, but all fair-minded people should shout, "Don't call it love."

In our efforts to purify the environment by promoting clean air and water, we should not forget that love also needs to be purified for it's a thing of beauty, blessed with lasting intrinsic value. Too long have we dragged it through the gutters of society. "There remain these three, faith, hope and love and the greatest of these is love" (1 Cor 13:13).

THE ASCENSION (B)
Ac 1:1-11   Ep 1:17-23   Mk 16:15-20

A key description of today's liturgy is found in the reading from the Acts of the Apostles: "He was lifted up before their eyes, in a cloud, which took Him from their sight."

Seven weeks previously, Jesus had died and was buried. Easter saw Him raised from the grave, and today He ascends from the earth to the right hand of the Father.

The venerated spot where this spectacular event took place is on top of a mountain populated by many ancient olive trees. It is aptly named the Mount of Olives. This lofty area which offers a magnificent view overlooking the city of Jerusalem, was frequented by Jesus as a place of prayer. It was here that He had taught the apostles to pray the Our Father. His terrible agony in the garden occurred nearby — in Gethsemane at the base of the mountain.

Today a small chapel stands on top of the Mount of Olives with a single narrow door which causes most people to bow when entering. The roof is a large white dome that immediately pulls one's attention toward the heavens. An indented footprint in solid rock is clearly evident, which tradition says is the exact spot where

Jesus stood before ascending back to His Father. Two footprints were present formerly, but one was removed to be relocated in another sacred shrine.

The Mount of Olives is a sacred place of lingering glory, for the Ascension is Jesus' victory celebration over sin and death. It's another convincing proof of the legitimacy of His title, "Lord." Ascension day commemorates a victory for Jesus and a promise for us that we too can eventually triumph over all that binds us to earth.

It is significant how the Bible describes Jesus in the presence of the apostles, just before the Ascension. He gave His everlasting blessing and reminded them that His farewell gift was a message of peace. Jesus also encouraged them to have enduring faith, to spread His sacred Kingdom and told them to let their lives be ruled by the Holy Spirit, Whom He promised soon to send.

Today may be called a farewell to His terrestrial friends and His way of life on this earth. Although good-byes are normally difficult to face, this one was certainly lightened by their collective hope of a future reunion with the Lord in His eternal Kingdom. In the meantime they would keep in touch through faith and prayer.

We too believe that the ascended Lord still continues to keep in touch with us as we meditate on His precious words in scripture, receive His life-renewing sacraments and try to discern His will in our daily lives. We can especially find Him in our sisters and brothers. In loving and serving them we are doing the same for Him, just as truly as if He were visibly present to us.

SEVENTH SUNDAY OF EASTER (B)
Ac 1:15-17, 20-26 1 Jn 4:11-16 Jn 17:11-19

Some people think they see God's presence clearly in spectacular calamitous events. The memory of a near accident usually triggers the statement, "God was with me." A California forest fire, a flood in Pennsylvania or a Minnesota blizzard provoke a barrage of dogmatic observations, in essence: "the good Lord is trying to tell us something."

Why don't we see His presence more in the calm, uneventful happenings of each day? Can't we find Him in the summer song of a bright little canary; a peaceful night's sleep; the rising of the sun (if you prefer, the turning of the earth — not so trifling, when you think about it); a strong heartbeat or your car's engine starting when you turn the key? For me, the floods, fires and blizzards hide rather then reveal Him. The severe storm at sea frightened the apostles, so they awakened Jesus and He quieted things down. His presence was in the calm, not the storm. (Mt 8:24)

Our prayer life also can be very private and quiet yet extremely effective, as we kneel or sit peacefully, offering up unvoiced thoughts to God. Patience and wisdom tell us not to expect immediate answers to prayer in the form of personal visions and wonders, but in the ordinary unfoldings of daily life.

The election in today's reading from the Acts of the Apostles disappoints those who only like dramatic religion. It's too simple. The story tells how the eleven apostles were seeking a replacement for Judas, and Matthias and Joseph consented to be candidates. The Eleven offered a short common prayer and drew lots — the choice was Matthias.

Now is that any way to choose an apostle? The whole thing is embarrassing, reminding one of the state lottery or of drawing raffle tickets at the parish festival. Sorry! Had God wanted to be dramatic, Paul would have been chosen as the new number twelve, not the unknown Matthias. That would have been a story full of action, power and holy symbolism. Imagine how it would read.

God personally and publicly appeared to Paul in the middle of the road at high noon. The fiery, intelligent persecutor of Christians squirmed helplessly in the dust, having been struck blind by the Almighty. On the spot he was born again, accepted the Lord, had his sight restored, and joined the very group he was trying to destroy, not only as a member but as a leader — one of the Twelve. How unfortunate was Judas' defection but how marvelous of God to send Paul to take his place. It reminds one of the fall of Adam occasioning the coming of Christ. Speculation could run wild with all the divine lessons the good Lord was trying to tell us.

Luke, however, tells the real story. The famous St. Paul did not receive the appointment as one of the Twelve, but Matthias did — all without flare or excitement. Did God miss a teachable moment? No! But we might! He is teaching us to see the genuine value of common people and ordinary events. Not many are blessed with the superior qualities of St. Paul. Most are of the calibre of Matthias — simple, quiet people who work hard and don't make the headlines. Regardless of how we would like the script to read, it's God's story to tell, not ours. Whether knocked to the ground or chosen by lot, He'll pick apostles His way.

My ears have never heard the Master's voice. I've neither seen my name in the clouds nor been blinded by His glory; but by God, I have been chosen as truly as Paul and so have you. Like St. Matthias, we should be proud of it.

PENTECOST SUNDAY (B)
Ac 2:1-11   1 Cor 12:3-7, 12-13   Jn 20:19-23

In the Acts of the Apostles, Luke pens a small but significant sentence about the Pentecost story. "All were filled with the Holy Spirit." Those seven words summarize that sensational event. This was the day the apostles individually and the Church collectively became instantly rich with internal spiritual endowments directly from God.

The sevenfold gifts were bestowed on this frightened group of believers, calling them to sudden maturity. Their new-found Wisdom, Understanding, Counsel, Fortitude, Knowledge, Piety and Fear of the Lord gave the recipients both incentive and ability to unlock the doors and face the world.

A number of years ago, Dr. William Menninger listed seven qualities one should possess to qualify as an adult person. It is surprising how closely his list coincides with the seven gifts of the Holy Spirit. Menninger said that to be emotionally mature, one should:

1. *Have the ability to deal constructively with reality.*
   The gift of WISDOM enables us to distinguish reality from fantasy and live accordingly.
2. *Have the capacity to adapt to change.*
   UNDERSTANDING helps one to accept changes, seeing them as being for the common good. Most don't like change but favor progress. There can be no progress without change.
3. *Have relative freedom from symptoms that are produced by tensions and anxieties.*
   COUNSEL leads us to delve beyond the visible to discover the hidden causes and symptoms of tensions and fears.
4. *Have the capacity to find more happiness in giving than receiving.*
   PIETY warns us against selfishness. The Acts of the Apostles, which describes the coming of the Spirit, also contains Jesus' adage, "There is more happiness in giving than in receiving" (Ac 20:35).
5. *Have the capacity to relate to people in a consistent manner, with mutual satisfaction and helpfulness.*
   KNOWLEDGE gives consistent direction to our lives, lest we be shattered by every passing emotion.
6. *Have the capacity to direct our instinctive hostile energy into creative and constructive outlets.*
   FEAR OF THE LORD is beneficial and prods us to accomplish good deeds which otherwise may be left undone. This fear is reverential, as a child fears (or respects) his loving father.

7. *Have the capacity to love.*
FORTITUDE is necessary for true love, for it gives us courage to make a solemn commitment in spite of the risk of being rejected.

The sacrament of Confirmation is often called our personal Pentecost. It's both a call to and a sign of spiritual maturity. Pentecost summons the apostles and us to the fullness of life. Living is so much more than just the passage of time. Suppose science could make us live 150 years. What would it profit if our ignorance, fear and hate kept us from enjoying and truly living those years? What use is a few extra years to the person who "kills" what time he has?

The Spirit of Pentecost moves us from fear to courage; from weakness to strength; from grabbing to giving. It dares us to live a faith-filled, love-inspired life each day. Pentecost launched a handful of scared people on the voyage of world conversion.

Come Holy Spirit, fill our lives with your precious gifts!

TRINITY SUNDAY (B)
Dt 4:32-34, 39-40   Rm 8:14-17   Mt 28:16-20

The Sign of the Cross is more than a routine procedure to begin and end a prayer. It is a prayer; a very profound one. This visible sign is a powerful profession of our faith in the existence of the Holy Trinity. In fact it's a mini-liturgy, doing and saying something that is distinctively religious.

One of the ways to augment today's celebration of the Feast of the Holy Trinity is to concentrate on the reverent use of this sacred sign.

We touch our heads showing our assent of faith, as we pronounce the name of the Father, our divine Creator. It's a dedication of our minds to God. Our fingertips next come to rest at the base of our hearts, symbols of love. We speak the name of the great Lover, the Second Person of the Blessed Trinity, God-Man and Savior. The sign is concluded as the fingers move from one shoulder to the other, signifying eagerness to give our arms and hands to good works under the guidance of the Holy Spirit. Finally the hands interlock, showing we are united and single-minded in our efforts. With this conclusive gesture we say "Amen"—so be it.

In the name of the Trinity we were signed in baptism, have had our sins forgiven and received many blessings. Although basic to our faith, the Trinity is not to be understood but professed and admired. Some people, desirous of solving every mystery, overly simplify God and claim to know His intimate nature and thoughts. They "interpret" the Bible avoiding scholarly assistance, which they say only complicates matters. This approach may be attractive but is not honest, for God is not simple, nor is religion.

We believe God is one nature but three persons, but the full meaning of those words is far beyond our poor comprehension. However, the Trinity is a unique model and sign of harmonious unity—a unity God expects to see in the daily lives of His children.

Every blessing of the Church flows from the Trinity, traced out through the Sign of the Cross. Under that sign you sealed your wedding vows, and that same familiar sign will bid you safe passage to the eternal Kingdom. May Trinity Sunday inspire each of us to manifest faith with our minds, love with our hearts, service with our hands, in the name of the Father, the Son, and the Holy Spirit. Amen.

CORPUS CHRISTI (B)
Ex 24:3-8   Heb 9:11-15   Mk 14:12-16, 22-26

Let's suppose that we had the privilege of spending ten days as pilgrims in the Holy Land. We visit most of the historical sites made sacred and famous by Jesus: the manger in Bethlehem, His home in Nazareth, the tomb in Jerusalem, the scene of the Visitation, the location of the Sermon on the Mount and Cana in Galilee. At each place, we sit down to meditate while one of our group reads the scripture passages relative to the scene. At the conclusion of our trip, we all agree that the sacred scriptures had come alive for us and that henceforth we would read them with deeper meaning and appreciation.

As I read the Gospel of today's Mass, the sights and sounds of the Holy Land come to my mind. St. Mark says that Jesus sent two disciples to prepare for the Last Supper. He did not give them any street address but simply told them to follow a man carrying a water jar. Water jars were normally carried by women, so the sight of a man carrying one would be unusual and easily recognizable. Jesus may have been deliberately vague about identifying the location so Judas would not know the meeting place and bring the soldiers to arrest Him. Jesus wanted this meal in security and peace, for it would have world-wide and lasting significance.

In our imaginations, let us walk through those same streets of Jerusalem to the place of the Last Supper, the holy cenacle or dining room. It is a large upper room located in the Mt. Zion section of the old city, unfurnished now and open-sided. Rebuilt many times through the centuries, it still retains a basic similarity to the original room where the Lord offered the first Mass with His apostles.

You may never travel to Jerusalem to see where the first Mass was offered but that, of course, is not necessary. The Mass has come to you. In your local parish church today, you can be present at the sacred meal. The essence of the liturgy is not where it happens but what happens.

The body and blood of Jesus were given to us on Good Friday eve. Before the following day would end, Jesus would be dead. Soon He would rise and ascend from the earth. Yet He would remain. He promised His presence in the bread and wine at the first Mass and each Mass that follows.

FEAST OF PETERS AND PAUL (B)
(see p. 40)

THE ASSUMPTION OF THE BLESSED VIRGIN MARY (B)
Rv 11:19; 12:1-6, 10   1 Cor 15:20-26   Lk 1:39-56

A visitor to the Holy Land today can, like Mary, "proceed into the hill country to a town of Judah" to visit the site of Zechariah's house, where she greeted Elizabeth. The outlying town of Ain Karim where Elizabeth lived, is nestled high in the mountains, overlooking the west side of Jerusalem. The winding upward climb makes one admire the physical strength of the Virgin Mary, who went, according to Luke, "in haste."

A large frescoed Church of The Visitation, now erected on the mountain, is ornamented with biblical scenes, commemorating that friendly meeting. The famous Magnificat prayer, uttered by Mary on this spot, is written at the church entrance in many languages.

Only a few of Mary's words have been preserved in the Bible, and these are mostly short statements such as "they have no wine" or "do whatever He tells you." But here on the mountain she prayed her longest recorded prayer. It gives us a clear insight into her life of faith, proclaiming the greatness of God and her own smallness, which she says is so deeply sanctified that "all ages to come shall call me blessed."

Mary received unique gifts from God. Her Immaculate Conception set her apart from us, who were conceived in sin. She is the

Mother of Jesus, a title, relationship and privilege granted to one person only. However, we can both applaud and hope to share the Assumption into heaven. She, a human like us, was taken to her Eternal Father. We believe that by His grace, the same reward can be ours.

Elizabeth praises Mary's trust in God's word, sentiments Jesus would also voice in later years. When the people in His presence called her blessed because she was His mother, Jesus replied that she's blessed not because she's My mother but because she heard God's word and kept it.

For Mary, living the word of God meant assisting her debilitated cousin through the final stages of pregnancy, even though she herself was with child. Envisioned as a small and quiet person, Mary moved in the midst of the action, fighting for the values in which she believed. She likewise walked near her famous Son in joy and pain, inheriting an immortal title — The World's Greatest Woman.

She is the pride of humanity, the blessed of the ages, the inspiration of artists, poets and theologians. Her *aves* are prayed by the learned and simple, the young and old. In our admiring love we have heaped upon her every praise and honor we have to offer. But no one has honored her more than God Himself. She is His own virtuous and beautiful Miss Universe. Chosen to be His mother, she is our perfect model. Because she did His will, she is blessed; a reward the Lord will bestow on all who hear His words and keep them.

ALL SAINTS (B)
Rv 7:2-4, 9-14   1 Jn 3:1-3   Mt 5:1-12

In the National Catholic Directory I noticed a church in San Francisco named "All Hallows." The title seemed a bit strange when I first read it. But having thought about it, I think it's very fitting for a community of Christian people. "Hallow" is from the Old English meaning "to make holy or consecrate." We say it often in the Lord's Prayer, "Hallowed be Thy name." In the Gettysburg Address, Lincoln used it: "We cannot dedicate, we cannot consecrate, we cannot hallow this ground." The title Halloween, of course, comes from it, meaning All Hallow's Eve, the evening before All Saints Day.

Today's Mass could be called the celebration of All Hallows, honoring those women and men who wear their ST. degrees in front of their names. Many of them are the famous saints who have been canonized by an official decree of the Church. We revere them as role models, people who spiritually made good and are now at home in heaven with their God. They come from every country, every walk of life and every economic level imaginable. They are men and women, old and young, rich and poor. Some were highly educated, and others never went to school. The recognized saints of the Church are different in hundreds of ways, but are similar in some basic ways.

Two common denominators especially are found present in the lives of these holy people. First, they all led disciplined lives. They had a divine model to follow and faithfully did so, often at the price of terrible sufferings and hardships. They were dedicated to their cause of holiness and were determined to see it through at all costs.

Secondly, they had an unusual capacity for loving God and other people. This enabled them to persevere and to rejoice that they could serve such a noble cause with their lives. In this way they lived for a reason far beyond their own wants and comforts, and thus found their lives to be extremely productive.

Many canonized saints left us written accounts of their anxieties and temptations. Although they appear heroic, in their own views they were weak and insignificant. Nonetheless, they are the spiritual celebrities in the Church's hall of fame.

Then there are the multitudes of "small time" saints whose names we'll never know, but who are happily home from a life of love and service. Finally we salute those millions of good people living today, the future population of heaven. They're in our homes, offices, supermarkets and schools. Hopefully, we are part of their number.

If we live by the Gospel standards, we are holy people. We are God's children, as John calls us in the second reading. Anyone who observes the beatitudes of Jesus in this Gospel, should delight in the last sentence: "Be glad and rejoice for your reward in heaven is great."

To one and all, great and small, well known and unknown: Happy Feast day and hallowed be your name.

THE IMMACULATE CONCEPTION (B)
Gn 3:9-15, 20   Ep 1:3-6, 11-12   Lk 1:26-38

Suppose a list of names was being drawn up in heaven and scheduled for release on earth in the near future, entitled: "My 100 All Time Favorite People," composed personally by God. Imagine the intense human speculation which would be generated by such a roster.

There would be a million questions as we waited to read it. Will it contain any people living today? Will most of them have lived in the ancient past? Which nationalities will predominate? Will there be more men than women? How many will be Catholic, Protestant, Jewish, Hindu or some other religion? Will some have no formal religion? How many names will there be of those not yet born? Perhaps most would be people we never heard of, for the Lord would choose by internal qualities rather than external notoriety. One name for sure would be present and no doubt written first: Mary, the Immaculate Mother of Jesus.

In the Bible God has already spoken glowingly about Mary. He has called her (through Gabriel) "Blessed among women, highly favored daughter." Besides being his "Most Favorite" she would also be chosen as "the fairest of them all"—no offense to Snow White. God convincingly demonstrated His concept of beauty with the creation of His mother. She was without any stain, even the inherited one from Adam, for she was preserved from that which the rest of us need to be purified.

Mary possessed an additional attractiveness—for, just like her Son, she did not consider her privileged position something to cling to. She was not a spoiled prima donna, but a gutsy and practical woman who campaigned for justice and peace, as did her famous Son.

The glory of this celebration of Mary's freedom from sin is found not only in what it meant to her but what it means to us today. We also have been favored by our God. We are grateful for the personal protection He has granted to us and for His sufferings in our behalf. To respond thankfully, the Church encourages us to imitate this totally human mother perfectly at ease with her God and carrying out His saving plans.

Jesus' mother lived the curious paradoxes which He would later preach. Although magnificent, she preferred to move silently in the background. Although we have many opportunities to be humble like Mary, how often do we parade under the banners of glory and pride? We need to re-echo her theme song in our hearts, proclaiming that the proud will be humbled and the lowly exalted.

This day we liturgically reaffirm our belief that Mary was born without sin into a sinful race, to give birth to Jesus who would take away our sins.

"Hail Mary, full of grace; the Lord is with thee; blessed art thou among women . . ."

SECOND SUNDAY OF THE YEAR (B)
1 S 3:3-10, 19   1 Cor 6:13-15, 17-20   Jn 1:35-42

Felix Pedro lived in the frigid wilderness of Alaska. One day while hunting moose he saw a golden nugget in one of the animal's snowy hoof prints. He realized that the nugget had become dislodged from between the moose's toes, so he back-tracked to the spot where it had crossed a shallow creek. There he discovered many more shiny nuggets and that started the Alaskan gold rush.

The same desire for hidden wealth brought the Forty-Niners rushing to California. From that remarkable event the state fashioned its one word motto—Eureka! It's a Greek word, meaning "I found it," or "I have made a great discovery."

It's a common sight today, along the beaches or in parks where crowds have been, to see someone with a Geiger Counter searching for lost coins or valuables. If we are looking for something valuable, we will go to a great deal of trouble to find it.

Today's Gospel reading is the story of two men's diligent search and thrilling discovery. They found Jesus. Along with many others, they had been waiting for the Messiah. When He was pointed out to them by John the Baptizer, they knew immediately that they were in the presence of an outstanding person.

When asked by Jesus, "What are you looking for?" they didn't reply "pearls," or "gold" or "buried treasure." Instead, they replied that they were looking for Him. If we are truly looking for Jesus there will be many occasions to meet Him, for He still passes by and invites us to Himself. Our God loves us and when we find Him we are welcome to stay for a day, a lifetime or an eternity.

It's nearly impossible to keep from telling others of our discovered treasures. Good news of every kind needs to be shared with others. The same is true in the case of Jesus.

Andrew, one of the two, was not content only to run and tell his brother Simon that he had found the Messiah. He personally took him to meet Jesus. Andrew could not act otherwise in the face of such overpowering goodness. He gave his brother the most precious gift anyone could ever give another — Jesus. The Lord was also waiting to be found by Simon — for as we know, He had a major job for him. This dramatic incident was the beginning of the first chapter of Church history.

The thrill of finding Jesus has been repeated millions of times with as much excitement as that encounter in the streets of Bethany. He still lives and walks our streets and country roads. We run to Him and ask where He lives. "I live," He replies, "within your very self, and in your neighbors; My glorified body is in the Eucharistic bread of the altar and My presence is in the words of scripture. I can be found in the beauty, power and order of My creation."

Which of life's values occupy our time and attention? "Where your treasure is, there also is your heart."

THIRD SUNDAY OF THE YEAR (B)
Jon 3:1-5, 10   1 Cor 7:29-31   Mk 1:14-20

The first priests were called from fishing boats and Jesus realized their difficulties in changing professions. He therefore assured them that their backgrounds would be useful in their new work. "I will make you fishers of men," He told them, with perhaps an encouraging smile.

Later He could have told Matthew that he would be made a tax collector for the eternal King; or Paul, the tent maker, that he would now be making spiritual shelters in place of cloth ones. Luke the doctor would have been told that he would be concentrating on the healing of souls. Each person had been prepared for the religious ministry in a uniquely different way, so that each could effectively contribute a slightly different nuance to the good news of Jesus.

Priests today have these same varied backgrounds which are equally valuable for their work. One priest may have been a professional singer; what a marvelous minister of religious music he could be. Another could have been a former entertainer; he can now lead people to Jesus with smiles on their faces. The same is true of those experienced in law, government, education, communications and nearly any profession we can imagine. There is no one ideal way to prepare for priesthood.

Happily, our modern seminaries no longer expect candidates all to fit into the same mold — in the "cookie-cutter" style of priestly formation. Priestly holiness does not exist in textbooks but in the real, warm-blooded person who has a unique past, an individual personality and abilities distinctively his own. We are not interchangeable parts to be shuffled into any church position and expected to operate in the exact same manner. Our skills vary and that is a blessing, for the Church is a many-faceted organization.

"We don't want every parish to be the same, like another McDonald's restaurant and we don't want people having their creativity dulled," said Bishop Kenneth Untener of Saginaw, at the University of Dayton in June, 1984. He said that many ideas and programs for the Church should come from the parishes, with those at the diocesan level cheering them on. "The chancery," he emphasized, "should be a resource center to help creative minds."

From where will come the Simons, Andrews and the sons of Zebedee for tomorrow and what will be their talents and styles of ministry? The Church has seen society move from fishing boats to space ships and during that period she too has made thousands of changes. But today as in the beginning, we still need quality people to be ordained to approach the altar, pulpit and marketplace with genuine talents and graces to minister to people.

Have you ever thought of responding? Jesus is calling in today's Gospel reading for the 20th century "fishers of men"!

FOURTH SUNDAY OF THE YEAR (B)
Dt 18:15-20   1 Cor 7:32-35   Mk 1:21-28

Many people think Beethoven was the greatest of all music composers. It was said of him that he lifted up mortals to heaven. Others believe that Mozart was superior to Beethoven. They say he brought the angels down from heaven.

What these brilliant composers did through their music, Jesus did through His eloquent preaching. He brought heaven down to earth and lifted earth to heaven. He, a native of heaven, came to live in our land and became a citizen of earth. He taught us His gentle ways and invited us to join Him back home when we leave here.

Today's Gospel passage from Mark vividly portrays the mighty power that radiated from the amazing words of Jesus. Mark says that He held the people spellbound in the synagogue of Capernaum for His teaching was radically different from what they had been accustomed to. He not only moved people, but evil spirits as well. They shrieked and instantly disappeared before Him like ice cubes in a hot furnace.

It was not only His personal magnetism and the strength of His convictions which profoundly impressed others but also the exciting freshness of His inner wisdom. The hungering people heard a "completely new teaching" which stood in contrast to the worn-out phrases of the uninspiring scribes.

Jesus demonstrated in Capernaum, what a recent Gallup poll revealed. People admire a leader who speaks in a definite and clear manner even though they don't accept his views. Such a speaker is more respected than one who gives his audience a lot of double talk. The Lord spoke clearly and taught what He believed, without trying to tiptoe around everyone's delicate sensitivities.

If we are to be faithful to His spirit and to the nature of our Christian faith, our message must be clear, convincing and filled with challenge. We cannot repeat by rote the old worn-out jargon words.

We normally welcome new approaches and discoveries in medicine, psychology and science, for they rejuvenate the lingering hopes of struggling humanity. Yet when that same newness surfaces in religion, many feel obliged to reject it as something suspicious or even harmful. Why is that the case?

Jesus' eternal message is aptly called the good *news*, which means that new ideas are good and we should not fear them. May we all share the excitement of the Lord's teachings and gain deeper insights into our wonderful world and mysterious selves, as His hidden truths gradually unfold before us.

FIFTH SUNDAY OF THE YEAR (B)
Jb 7:1-4, 6-7   1 Cor 9:16-19, 22-23   Mk 1:29-39

The drama-like nature of the Sunday liturgy is highlighted today with themes and feelings to move us from one point to another.

We see the terrible depression and misery of Job in the first reading. Who cannot identify with this suffering man? He feels that life is drudgery, like a slave in the hot sun wishing for a little rest under a shade tree. Even his resting times are troubled and sleepless as "the night drags on." We probably at one time or another have felt with him: "I shall not see happiness again."

If we read Job only, we would go home with a generous dose of negativism, but the liturgy quickly swings to a higher level with the chanting of the responsorial psalm. Here is confidence and uplifting hope. The goodness of God is affirmed and we are told that He "heals the brokenhearted."

Paul then reflects Christian encouragement by telling the Corinthians that he has voluntarily made himself a slave for Jesus and for the preaching of the Gospel. He does not view his hardships as depressing like Job, for he is working from a deeper hope and a higher motive. If we can share Paul's incentives, they can help to lighten our burden and lift our spirit.

Then Mark shows Jesus destroying impending evils as night draws on — that time of day which often invites fears and demons. The Lord is the light shining in the dark for His people. When darkness seems to be closing in, we can run to Him in prayer to scatter any destructive forces and make the night much brighter.

Jesus underlines the secret of His success as He breaks out of the darkness again. Before dawn, in the early morning, He goes to the desert to pray. This is the prolific source of His unconquerable power.

Where Job's day was filled with depressive drudgery, Jesus made His time more profitable by His good deeds to be accomplished for the benefit of others. Sorrow, pain and depression can be turned either inward or outward. They can easily control us, but with God's grace we can triumph over them.

Job's sleep was restless as he disgustedly awaited the dawn of another fear-filled day. Jesus had a peaceful night and welcomed the dawn of a new day with glorious opportunities. The rising sun found Him out in the desert, "absorbed in prayer." With what attitude do we cope with the days and nights of life?

Have we ever been "absorbed in prayer"? This means that all noises and distractions are cancelled out — so intense is our concentration and communication with our God. We no doubt have been absorbed in movies, books or ballgames — but what about prayer?

The Church sincerely hopes that this Sunday liturgy will uplift your spirits today and through the week. Certainly each day would improve if we could, like Jesus, end the one in contented sleep and begin the next absorbed in prayer.

SIXTH SUNDAY OF THE YEAR (B)
Lv 13:1-2, 44-46   1 Cor 10:31-11:1   Mk 1:40-45

How are you? Fine! And you? OK. These common greetings show concern for the health and wellbeing of others, and acknowledge that all are subject to hurts and sicknesses. Even the happiest of us live with fears of accidents and diseases which can suddenly place us on the sidelines. So it's natural to ask about the health of those we haven't seen for awhile.

Today's Gospel reading shows Jesus' concern for a diseased man who came to Him — a leper. Leprosy inflicts ugly scabs and ulcers on the body and face of its victim, and also attacks the muscles and nervous system. This contagious disease not only deprived its victim of good health but of personal dignity, for such a one had to be isolated. If others came near him, he was obliged to call out "leper! leper!" to keep the "clean" people at a safe distance.

It is coincidental that "leper" written backwards spells "repel" — for that truly was the effect, both because of fear of contracting the dreaded disease and of the unsightly appearance. A person today with cancer or heart disease can be treated with continuing dignity, and loyal friends and family can compassionately minister at close range — but the poor leper (at least in the past) had to suffer all alone.

Both the readings from Leviticus and Mark today discuss this dreaded illness. The Church's primary concern, however, is not from the medical viewpoint but from that of faith. Leprosy does to the face what sin does to the soul — it makes one ugly and repelling. By the blood of Christ, however, we have been cleansed of that ugliness. So the story is really not about a leper who was cured once upon a time. Rather, it's about you and me — right here and now — who have been healed of sin and eternal death by our gentle Savior.

It is with pride that we watch Jesus the Lover of outcasts to step up to this diseased man, alienated from society, and with His loving power send him back to his community — healed and sound. Sin, like leprosy, is fatal unless treated. We happily acknowledge that Jesus the divine Physician is still on call any time of the day or night.

This is a story of a conversion, a turning toward instead of a turning way. Everyone has inner beauty and value, and although we are divided from each other and appear to be ugly we can be brought back together through His healing.

Have we made lepers of some people by refusing to associate with them? They may be a family member, neighbor, former friend, business associate, or possibly a parent, child or spouse. It is now uniquely within our power to cure the leper, just as Jesus did. The question is not whether we can do it, but whether we choose to. No one else could cure the leper in the Gospel except Jesus, and he chose to do it. We are the only persons who can cure our self-made lepers.

We start by making contact with them; from there the curing process can flow both gradually and naturally. Perhaps we don't fully appreciate our power to heal, but we truly have it. Why not cure a leper today?

SEVENTH SUNDAY OF THE YEAR (B)
Is 43:18-19, 21-22, 24-25   2 Cor 1:18-22   Mk 2:1-12

In 1939, Fr. Walter Ciszek, S.J. who had left the U.S.A. to serve in Poland, was arrested by the invading Russians and exiled to Siberia. He stayed there 23 years, 15 of them spent in prisons and labor camps. Through all these long years, he always retained at least a glimmer of hope that someday he would return to his beloved country, the United States. Finally, when he stepped from a plane in New York in 1963, his joy was beyond words. His faith in God and in his priestly calling had sustained him in his long exile.*

For a person held against his will in a foreign and hostile country, there is no joy quite similar to returning home. This was vividly shown when our hostages in Iran (and more recently, those in Lebanon) were released.

The first reading from Isaiah in today's Mass is addressed to Israelite exiles in Babylon. The captives heard the exciting rumors, based on good authority that their sentence of exile was drawing to a close. They dared to believe in a speedy departure from the plains of Babylon to view again the setting sun, glistening over the restless Mediterranean, where the gentle waves caress the western shores of their native land. Their God has ordered the release, the prophet says, for they have paid enough in time and pain for their unfaithfulness. Yahweh has cancelled the remainder of the debt, only stipulating that they be a thankful people, loyal to His directives. These homesick people ecstatically realized that their God was doing for them what He did for their ancestors seven hundred years before when under Moses He led them from slavery in Egypt.

The message goes forth in the liturgy: all the listless and wayward exiles are invited to return to the familiar and friendly surroundings of the Church they left, and learn anew to trust their community and worship their God. Each of us in fact can ponder the question: Am I an exile from my God?

Isaiah's message is complemented by Mark's Gospel today, as the man exiled by pain, sin and paralysis is carried to Jesus. His trusting faith brought him to the Lord, and when they blocked the doors, he came through the roof. Jesus loved that man's perseverance (and especially of his friends who carried him) and welcomed him, cancelling on the spot both sin and paralysis.

Spiritual honors and gifts will flow abundantly during the coming season, and the welcome mat is on the Church's door step.

---

* Fr. Ciszek's autobiography, *With God In Russia* (America Press, 1964; Doubleday Image Books, 1966) describes his fascinating adventures.

It's an ideal time to effect a personal reformation. The uplifted open hand of Jesus will sign away our guilt, so we can again pick up our lives and walk to our promised home.

Hear ye, hear ye. There's good news in the wind. The balmy springtime will soon subdue the winter cold. The season of Lent is at hand and the Lord stands ready with His blessings.

EIGHTH SUNDAY OF THE YEAR (B)
Ho 2:16-17, 21-22   2 Cor 3:1-6   Mk 2:18-22

One day a young man and woman were married and like any other newlywed couple looked forward with excitement to a long and happy life together. To all appearances it seemed that they loved each other and were deeply committed to their mutual life. It soon became apparent to them and eventually to their families and neighbors that their marriage was a tragic mismatch.

The husband was a faithful, kind and considerate man, but his wife was unfaithful. She left him to spend her time in the company of many different men. Obviously her husband was tragically hurt yet he offered to take her back, which in fact he did several times. Life for this couple and their three children was not a happy experience.

Later he wrote a book about his marriage. We might think the pages would be filled with bitterness and pessimistic views, but instead they contain positive thoughts and show enduring patience and understanding. His book encourages those who face similar marital setbacks not to lose heart but rather to forgive and make a concerted effort to start over again. The name of this rejected husband is Hosea and we read a few lines from his book in today's Mass.

Besides being a husband and an author, he was also a prophet. Hosea preached in Northern Israel, which had undergone a type of divorce itself. The North had separated from the South and they became bitter enemies, to the point of trying to destroy each other.

The North especially had broken promises on its conscience, for it had abandoned the sacred covenant with Yahweh in favor of false pagan gods.

Hosea preached to these cheerless people in 750 B.C. and he spoke with convincing authority because he related his own sad experiences. He knew from practical living what Socrates would later tell the people of Athens about marriage. "If you marry well, you can become very happy; if poorly, you can become a philosopher."

The Church uses Hosea's insights to encourage us to be faithful to our God with the continual loyalty we promised Him in our baptismal vows. We all, in spite of our best efforts, break our sacred covenant with Jesus. But like Hosea, the Lord is always ready to forgive and take us back again — even though we continue to stray. Our union with Jesus, therefore, is also a mismatch — for He is ever faithful and we are not.

We approach each springtime of the year with new thoughts of beginning again. Especially in the penitential season of Lent, there is a welcomed opportunity to repair past failures. Jesus the tender Lover continually invites us to return home to His faithful intimacy. His lasting love for each of us is genuine, and our relationship is not "until death do us part" but is never ending.

NINTH SUNDAY OF THE YEAR (B)
Dt 5:12-15   2 Cor 4:6-11   Mk 2:23-3:6

It's very important (in one sense of the word) to be a fundamentalist — i.e., to analyze words, concepts and situations with the intention of discovering their origins and root meanings in order to gain a better understanding. A true fundamentalist, therefore, is one who believes in knowing the basics and building on them.

When it comes to religious "fundamentalism" as commonly understood today, the "fundamentalist" is really not what the word implies. The basic meaning of a Bible passage is often not found by simply echoing the literal definitions of the words. The true meaning is found in the intended concepts beneath the words.

The modern "fundamentalist" does not take adequate note of poetic expressions, exaggerations, ironic statements and various native idioms. He slavishly interprets each word in its modern meaning, which usually results in something very different from what the original author intended.

In a dramatic way, Jesus came to grips with this same type of scriptural confusion in His dealings with the Pharisees. They insisted on the literal "letter of the law" interpretation of a passage while the Lord insisted on the sense of the passage, the "spirit of the law."

Today's confrontation between Jesus and the Pharisees is over the question of how to interpret the law of the Sabbath rest. The Pharisees said that the law was definite; no work could be done on the Sabbath. Jesus said that the spirit of the law permitted, even encouraged a good work on the Sabbath. He emphasized that the good of people is superior to a strict legal observance. He taught that circumstances come into play when we try to arrive at the correct answer in any given situation.

Jesus defended His disciples' eating of the grain on the Sabbath by appealing to the common sense of King David. Technically David broke the Sabbath observance to feed his hungry men, but he did the right thing. Jesus like David, therefore, was more of a fundamentalist than the literal-minded Pharisees. Their interpretation of the law stopped at the surface meaning of the words, while His penetrated to the underlying sense and intent of the passage.

Jesus also cured the crippled man in the synagogue and again technically broke the Sabbath rest. His logic was that a person's physical integrity in this instance was of far greater importance than the mere external observance of the Sabbath. It is the question of placing people in a higher priority than the legal system. As Jesus said bluntly, "the Sabbath was made for man, not man for the Sabbath."

This passage involves more than simply what is permitted on the Sabbath. It pertains to our personal judgments and deeds each day of the week. It also serves as a warning that the literal meaning is often not the correct meaning. The true and honest fundamentalist is the one who stops not at the surface level of the Bible but probes to its deepest levels to truly understand the correct meaning of God's words.

TENTH SUNDAY OF THE YEAR (B)
Gn 3:9-15   2 Cor 4:13-5:1   Mk 3:20-35

"That man is out of his mind and possessed by the devil." Those vicious charges were hurled against the person who is the very essence of wisdom and holiness—Jesus. It is absolutely frightening how some people can mercilessly condemn others and destroy reputations in such a reckless manner.

Innocent people have pitifully little control over various false charges and suspicions which might be brought against them. Even if they attempt to refute evil accusations, they are still powerless to force others to change their views and reject slanderous lies. It's fortunate that the innocent don't hear all the negative comments unjustly directed against them, for the discouragement would weigh them down.

This Gospel reading should make us aware that there is no way to adequately defend ourselves against slurs and lies if someone is determined to spread them. Neither the saints nor Jesus Himself were spared. In this passage, Jesus the exorcist is accused of being possessed. He tried to refute the lie by saying that He was not under the devil's power—for if He were, how could He expel the devil? He said that it was by God's power that He cast out Satan.

It is this same driving strength of Jesus which we invite to break through our fear-fashioned barriers, like the Gospel's strong man, and free our spirits from the evils and superstitions which have held us captive. Our faith can enable us to be inwardly free even in the midst of external pains and confusion.

That curious biblical verse about the unforgivable sin is found in this reading. What is it? It is often called the sin against the Holy Spirit — that is, the continual profession of a lie when one knows the truth. The unforgivable sin is calling God, Satan; light, darkness; and good works, evil. This adamant refusal to acknowledge truth is a complete distortion, in fact, a total reversal of recognized reality. In such a bizarre self-made world of reversals where God is evil and sin is virtue, forgiveness has lost its reality and cannot be given or accepted. "Only he can be forgiven," writes Fr. John L. McKenzie, "who confesses that he has something to be forgiven."

In our lives we acknowledge Jesus as the Risen Lord, the universal Savior, the Light of the world and the wounded Healer, whose saving forgiveness flows easily — almost spontaneously — to those who want to sincerely know and love Him. If we retain this attitude, we need never worry about any unforgivable sin in our lives.

Our faith in the Lord and our love for Him makes us spiritual brothers and sisters. It binds us into a family of faith which is more intimate than a family united only by blood ties. We know that there was a deep abiding love which existed between Jesus and his mother. That same quality of love can be the basis of our friendship with the Lord. When we acknowledge His words and follow His ways, we are building an everlasting bond of unity with the Savior. "Whoever does the will of God is brother and sister and mother to Me."

ELEVENTH SUNDAY OF THE YEAR (B)
Ezk 17:22-24 2 Cor 5:6-10 Mk 4:26-34

We may consider ourselves expert in many different areas, but if really pushed for detailed explanations we would no doubt flounder. We know how to run a car — i.e., which keys fit the door and ignition, how to put it in gear, what to do if it stalls — but it's still probably a mystery to us how the car really works. The same is more or less true for articles like radios, televisions, calculators, etc. Anyone can strike a match, but who can explain the mystery of fire? We see millions of living organisms — blades of grass, trees, birds, animals and people — but who can truly explain life?

The mysterious nature of the "reign of God" is featured in today's Gospel reading. Jesus compares it to a grain of wheat which is first planted, then "dies" or germinates and finally matures into a full-grown plant. Even the tiny mustard seed, He says, is able to increase itself thousands of times to become a large bush. Think of a solid oak towering into the heavens, and then remember that it came from an acorn no larger than the tip of your thumb. The acorn has something special within, that, when planted in the soil allows it to become an oak tree. But both seed and soil are essential.

The Lord says that the same is true of His word and our response. The kingdom is not established by His words only nor solely by our efforts, but by the synthesis of the two. The farmer doesn't understand why or how the seed grows, for that happens automatically, according to a set of instructions which have been programmed into it by God. Thus the farmer can sleep while much of the maturation is happening.

The word of God — the seed of the Christian life — has been implanted at baptism, unknown to the infant but nonetheless growing within even during the sleeping hours. If the soil of our soul resists and expels the seed, there can be no new life. It is in our personal and conscious power to either accept or reject what has been planted within.

Since the clock of nature moves slowly, we must not try to force our maturity ahead of schedule. Before we can fully develop, we must first allow the seeds plenty of time to dig their roots of faith, hope, love, perseverance and justice into our supporting ground. The higher and taller we rise, the deeper our roots must be.

God's word will produce a bountiful harvest within us if we let it. What we need to do is simply provide a fitting atmosphere for the planting, growth and eventual harvest.

TWELFTH SUNDAY OF THE YEAR (B)
Jb 38:1, 8-11   2 Cor 5:14-17   Mk 4:35-41

A good crew in a rowboat could easily cross the Sea of Galilee in less than an hour. It's only eight miles wide at its broadest point.

Today's Gospel finds Jesus and his seaworthy apostles caught in the raging waters of this normally calm lake. At their emotional request, Jesus subdues wind and sea in dramatic fashion, but one wonders why they set sail in such adverse conditions. The Lord surely knew the danger in store and the apostles, being keen fishermen, must have had some indication of a brewing storm. Mark gives the reason for their launching in the first sentence of the reading: Jesus said to his disciples, "Let us cross over to the farther shore."

Remember that our Lord had only three years to proclaim His teaching, accomplish His healing and found the Church. He could not afford to sit in safe havens waiting for fair weather. His work this present day with a particular crowd was finished, and it was time to move to another, on the distant shore. He knew the gathering storm would not sink the boat, so He ordered the departure. He was also providing an opportunity for the apostles to solidify their faith in His decisions.

Jesus showed His trust in their ability to handle the boat by taking the helmsman's cushion and going to sleep. It appears the voyage was in opposition to the better judgment of the apostles, yet it must have hurt their pride to admit their inability to sustain faith in a safe arrival. "Don't you care if we drown?" they shouted, awakening Him. He calmed the wind and sea and turned to the frightened crew asking, "Why are you lacking in faith?" Very likely he went back to sleep, leaving the naval experts filled with awe mumbling, "We should have trusted Him."

For every follower of Jesus there will be many occasions to launch out over troubled waters for some distant shore, at his invitation. If we always wait for perfect conditions, we'll accomplish little. A fair weather Christian will dally, while one with a burning desire to accomplish a mission will risk all in faith. The pilgrim must expect storms of ridicule, severe criticism, even threatened violence, yet he goes forth. The secret of survival is not a bigger boat but deeper faith.

If the cause is good and faith is strong, the storm will not sink you for the Lord will be aboard and the farthest shore will be reached. When the Master is silent (or sleeping) it's a sign He has deep trust in you. Give Him your complete faith and sail on. Bon Voyage.

THIRTEENTH SUNDAY OF THE YEAR (B)
Ws 1:13-15, 2:23-24   2 Cor 8:7, 9, 13-15   Mk 5:21-43

In the early 1900's, Dr. William Mayo opened a small medical center in Rochester, Minn. Since that humble beginning, the now world famous Mayo Clinic has treated over three million people, who have come seeking cures for their illness. The possession of good health is so vital, that we hold in high esteem the medical profession and those with special talents for effecting cures.

Jesus spent many days of His ministry healing the sick and crippled. He didn't practice medicine but did perform genuine cures. His reputation spread and people flocked to Him.

A man in today's Gospel begs Jesus to come and "lay His hands" on his little daughter, "so that she may get well." On the way a woman, sick for twelve years, pushes through the crowd to merely touch His cloak, convinced a cure will result. She is healed on the spot, because of her faith in His curative powers.

When news arrives that the little girl has died, Jesus never breaks His stride but continues to the house and gives her a new lease on life. True religion and good medicine are joined in the person of Jesus. Today they continue to work together for the benefit of society.

Through the sacraments, the Church reaches out to heal. Reconciliation is meant to leave a person feeling better and stronger, ready to begin anew with a good outlook. The sacrament of the sick, approached with faith, consoles, strengthens and cures the recipient of many hurts and fears. It's an example of faith healing at its best.

In the Church we pray for the sick, interceding in behalf of others. Much depends not only on the disposition of the sick person but on the faith of the one asking. Jairus' daughter did not ask Jesus for the cure; her father did. Possibly the little girl herself had no knowledge of Jesus, but her dad believed and Jesus came and worked a miracle because of his faith.

We should not think that all religious healings happen on the center stage of a large auditorium or on television. I believe the genuine healings are private and hidden. Notice in the Gospel, how no one knew the woman was cured except the woman herself. Before He blessed the little girl with new life, Jesus put out the crowd. He was not seeking public applause.

The cures of Jesus were neither magical nor automatic. They flowed directly from religious conviction. Therefore faith must be present before every prayer we pray; before every sacrament we receive; before every healing we seek.

FOURTEENTH SUNDAY OF THE YEAR (B)
Ezk 2:2-5 2 Cor 12:7-10 Mk 6:1-6

St. Mark relates in today's Gospel the confusion caused in Galilee the day Nazareth's most famous citizen returned home. The residents of that small inland village hastened through the winding streets to hear Him at the local synagogue, for His reputation had preceded Him. His Sabbath sermon amazed the curious crowd, but left them more concerned with the source of His knowledge than His luminous message.

These Nazareth people were not the easiest to cope with, and their unsavory reputation had long been rumored through the neighboring towns. When Philip informed Nathanael that he had found the Messiah, who was from Nazareth, Nathanael quipped, "Can anything good come from Nazareth?" (Jn 1:46). In fact, true to their pathetic image, Luke says the natives expelled Jesus from the village and intended to hurl Him over a cliff but He disappeared (Lk 4:28-30). We can understand why He didn't say much for the first thirty years of His life. It's likewise easy to comprehend why He adopted Capernaum as His "new hometown" during His public years. So all the Rodney Dangerfields of the world can take heart. In his own hometown even Jesus Christ got no respect.

The 10,000 inhabitants of Nazareth today still walk with lingering pride through the dusty, sometimes smelly streets of the old city, leading their donkeys and camels. Since the day He returned with His apostles, Jesus has brought numerous disciples to this Galilean village, supplying the natives with food and clothing from the profits of tourism.

The town is now at ease with Jesus, evidenced by the 1968 construction of a magnificent church over the site of the Annunciation — one of the largest Christian churches in the Middle East. They likewise proudly point to Mary's Well, which still supplies the city — explaining that Jesus and His mother came there for water, as do the women and children today.

The rejection of our Lord by His hometown people is a warning to us not to reject or underrate a person because of our prejudices. It's easy to see our neighbors as being inferior to those in far-off exotic places. An expert has been defined as "one from at least 100 miles away." These experts appear superior because we know of their degrees and virtues, but not of their weaknesses. The flaws of the local people are more exposed to us and often obscure their good qualities.

We too have grown up with Jesus, meeting Him at a very tender age and remaining life long companions. We must be careful not to imagine we know Him entirely and take Him lightly. He is the expert in every sense, and has come from more than 100 miles away.

Nazareth asked if He was not the carpenter. Yes, and so much more. "Where did He get His knowledge?" they asked. He always had it. What kind of wisdom does He have? Divine wisdom, Nazareth, Divine! The Son of God grew up in your town and walked your streets but you didn't know Him. In our neighbors He walks our streets, moving among us today. Do we know Him?

FIFTEENTH SUNDAY OF THE YEAR (B)
Am 7:12-15   Ep 1:3-14   Mk 6:7-13

In our day to day living, we become dependent on material securities, thought to be essential for our routine existence. This is especially noticeable when we get ready to go on a trip and try to decide what to take along. Usually we take too much, trying to anticipate imagined circumstances. Part of the reason for overpacking is that we are reluctant to break out of our established pattern.

Camping vacations are good examples. See how the modern Daniel Boone goes roughing it. He drives an air-conditioned camper with a built-in dishwasher, stereo and color television. He ventures into the "wilderness" with the comforts of home.

Jesus tells the apostles in today's Gospel what to take along for the journey. In essence He says to take the treasured message and skip the extras — even essentials like food and money. They were to live off the land, earning their keep by ministering to others.

Thousands through the centuries have taken His advice literally and abandoned all material securities to live for the Kingdom of God. The most famous was the 13th century Italian, Francis. He left behind the plush life for the simple, and thereby amassed a fortune in golden grace and divine love. Nor is the practice limited to Christians. The 20th century Hindu leader, Mahatma Gandhi, did the same and found rewarding peace of mind. Others, for merely practical reasons, have kept their lives uncluttered. While serving as a Union general in the Civil War, Grant took nothing extra on his campaigns, believing that to move quickly one must move lightly. It takes much faith to leave home without our accustomed supports, especially for U.S. citizens — who are 6% of the world's population using 50% of its goods and services. Jesus, a poor man Himself, usually catered to the poor, for they trusted in Him. The rich often trusted in their own power and wealth.

Like most Bible directives, this one must be pondered and used as each sees fit. However it is both an ideal and a challenge to our encumbered life style, which can rob us of needed freedom and mobility.

How did the apostles fare, out there on the road with no backup supplies? Quite well! It worked pretty much the way the Lord had predicted. None of them died from exposure, neglect or hunger. In fact, they achieved a high calibre ministry. The Gospel says they "expelled demons, anointed the sick and worked many cures."

SIXTEENTH SUNDAY OF THE YEAR (B)
Jr 23:1-6   Ep 2:13-18   Mk 6:30-34

The apostles had been sent, two by two, on their first religious mission by the authority of the Lord Himself. Bubbling with novice fervor, they returned highly excited about the impressive things they could do in the name of Jesus. Following this practical experience, they wanted and needed to be with the Master and compare notes with each other. Jesus understood their need for rest and suggested that they get away from the crowd for a private discussion.

Matthew gives another reason for their brief withdrawal from public view — the recent death of John the Baptist. Jesus had been close to John, His baptizer and herald; and some of the apostles had originally been John's disciples. They now needed to ponder the meaning of his life and death, share their profound sorrows and reflect on what awaited them in their own ministry.

Although their plans were frustrated when the impatient crowd intruded upon the private scene, the story clearly exemplifies the necessity for human support and the obligation to take time off from the constant routine of duties. This Gospel prerogative is currently carried out in our days off, times of recollection, annual retreats and sabbaticals. These change our pace and place that we might regroup our weakened energy, faith and commitment.

This is necessary not only for the clergy but for all people. Work six days and rest one day is the advice given in the first chapter of Genesis. We all know the body's demands for sleep and how sluggish we feel after a restless night. In Rome the siesta time is religiously observed each day between 2 and 4 P.M. Mondays are days of rest with most stores and shops closed. We might think these people are unbusiness-like or lazy, but they reply "we work to live; not live to work."

Leisure time is especially important for those who give advice and direction to others. The counsellor's mind needs time to put things together, build up a reserve of knowledge and give from his or her fullness, like a reservoir. He or she cannot race from one case to the next, like a rushing shallow river. The Rule of St. Benedict has advised society for 1500 years to live according to the threefold rhythm of prayer, work and recreation.

An occasional dinner out for a husband and wife can produce a continual bonding of their union. Obviously they would have food at home, which they could eat and save money, but that's not the point. There are greater things to save than money.

Maybe you're pressed for time with tons of work to do. You still have an obligation to take a break for a little while, as Jesus counseled His first recruits, who had a whole world to save. Remember, He made the blueprints of human nature and knows how we're meant to work.

SEVENTEENTH SUNDAY OF THE YEAR (B)
2 K 4:42-44   Ep 4:1-6   Jn 6:1-15

Today's Gospel story of the little boy who gave away his lunch occurred in Tiberias, the beautiful resort city on the west bank of the Sea of Galilee. It was during the Paschal season and Jesus saw a great crowd approaching. They reminded Him of the vast congregation that followed their God out of Egypt twelve centuries earlier, who were fed in the desert each morning with bread from heaven. Now looking at Philip, standing nearby, Jesus asked his opinion about feeding these tired people with bread. Philip replied that the idea was simply impractical.

Having overheard the conversation, a small boy, perhaps ten years old, told the apostle Andrew that Jesus could have his lunch if that would help. Andrew smiled politely at the youth's naivete, yet was impressed with his "foolish" generosity. He finally felt compelled to relate the boy's offer to Jesus. "But what good is that for so many?" he quickly added, lest he sound ridiculous. Surprisingly, Jesus was pleased with the offer. He accepted the gift and proceeded to use it to feed 5000 people.

The gift was insignificant, but what gift isn't, when offered to God, owner of the universe? It's not the size or value of the gift that's important, but the love and spontaneity with which it's given. Remember how Jesus was impressed by the widow's penny in the collection basket? He openly marvelled at the rich faith attached to her small gift.

The Lord does wonders with simple offerings, given in genuine love. Big gifts presented in His name — for tax deductions or to impress others — don't seem to capture His delicate attention. We all have many small but beautiful gifts we can offer. Who can't afford to give a few minutes of prayer to Him each day? Some possess talents for special services like reading at the Sunday liturgy, leading songs, playing the organ, teaching C.C.D., or assisting the crippled. There are hundreds of valuable voluntary services (gifts) we can offer. Your freewill donation in the collection envelope is another example of an offering to the Lord. Remember that no gift is too small or useless if given in the proper spirit.

Common bread is multiplied spiritually to feed a hungry soul. The Lord can change a simple jar of water to wine; a cup of wine to His own life-giving blood. Add His blessings to little gifts (a few loaves and fishes) and there's enough for all.

The small boy who because of his generosity gave up his lunch, now had more than he could eat. It's a minor miracle to fill a ten year old, but Jesus does not leave his friends hungry. I would like to think the Lord sent home his newly discovered young friend with a couple baskets of leftovers. What you give away, you'll get back many times, he said, "pressed down and running over, it will be poured into your lap." Jesus is never outdone in generosity.

EIGHTEENTH SUNDAY OF THE YEAR (B)
Ex 16:2-4, 12-15   Ep 4:17, 20-24   Jn 6:24-35

It is easy to understand why the early Hebrews desperately wanted to leave Egypt. The Egyptians had originally befriended the Hebrews, who came seeking food; but that was when Joseph, a Hebrew, was serving as "Vice President" of Egypt. Their privileged status died with Joseph, and they had to provide forced labor for building projects. Their lot was about the same as that of the Egyptian peasants. The Hebrews were given good food, shelter and some security, but their lives were barely tolerable, for they had no freedom. After generations of bondage, Moses, the freedom fighter, came forward to lead his people out of slavery, working extraordinary signs and wonders to accomplish it.

Today's first reading from Exodus picks up the story during their forty years' trek back home. Now they were responsible to Yahweh rather than Pharaoh, for at last they were free. No more whips to make them build brick walls. Liberty, however, has its price. They paid by marching in the desert, camping in the open and eating food far inferior to that of Egypt. Since freedom had not produced the total happiness envisioned, they blamed Moses for bringing them out to the desert to die. Loud requests echoed through their camp to return to Egypt, where although they would lose their freedom, they could at least settle down and have something decent to eat. Moses prayed to God, who in turn sent a daily ration of quail and manna to keep them from backtracking to Egypt.

There's a strong tendency in human nature to turn back in the face of difficulty. Often our objectives are far off, with many hurdles standing in the way. After an initial big effort, we simply get discouraged and want to turn back.

We may fail to find peace and fulfillment in religion, if we're afraid to move out of old patterns for new ones. It's important that we don't equate *new* with *wrong* (or *old* with *good*). Few things in this world are that cleanly cut. Most who don't like change, do like progress; but there can be no progress without change. Those Hebrew grumblers had only eaten the bread of Egypt and couldn't conceive of good or better bread in Israel. The return to Egypt would have been the wrong move, for soon they would again have lamented their lack of freedom.

To think that the best of life is in the past is foolish. It doesn't say much for the ingenuity of your kids. We should acknowledge and appreciate the past. But like the trailblazer Moses, we must push on, fully expecting better things ahead. Across the deserts, the mountains and years, we hope to attain our heavenly home. It's up ahead — not behind. The Eucharist, our manna from heaven, is strength for the long journey.

NINETEENTH SUNDAY OF THE YEAR (B)
1 K 19:4-8   Ep 4:30-5:2   Jn 6:41-51

Elijah, the fiery 9th century B.C. prophet, had proven his worth by correcting kings, triumphing over false prophets and raising the dead back to life. He was loved by the simple, feared by royalty and was a close friend of his God. Who more than Elijah had reason to be hopeful, optimistic and happy?

Today's reading from the First Book of Kings shows Elijah in a state of acute depression, for he was human and subject to every weakness that is our common lot. He feels abandoned by God and disgusted with people and life itself. Aimlessly, refusing to eat, he has wandered off into the desert. There the great burden of distress causes him to collapse under a broom tree, in a state of semi-consciousness.

Personal problems, worries and discouragements can reduce the strongest of people to bitter helplessness. It matters little whether one is a religious leader, like Elijah, or is without religion.

The pains of life touch both saints and sinners, rich and poor. There is no shot to immunize us against depression. Ah, but there is hope. An angel of the Lord sees the prophet in his pathetic state and ministers to him, bringing food and water. The angel returns a second time and helps him on his way.

We too can be a ministering angel to someone having a bad day, by bringing understanding and encouragement to them. It's also important to realize that someday we'll need compassion and care from another, for everyone takes a turn under the broom tree.

The Church tries to be a ministering angel to suffering humanity through the sacraments. Forgiveness lifts us to our feet while the food of the Eucharist revives our strength. Jesus shouts in today's Gospel, "I myself am the living bread," saying that if you eat it you will never die. The Eucharist is Jesus the living bread, going out as He did in Galilee, to renew the lives of the confused and lonely.

People come to church in many frames of mind. Some are happy, others empty and troubled. One has a hopeful vision for tomorrow; another is ridden with guilt and anxiety. The believing community therefore should be a friendly ministering angel by sharing, listening and accepting others, so that no one has to walk alone.

There are many aids along the way for those who stand in need. With a lot of grace from God and a little help from your friends, you can abandon the broom tree to climb the mountain of the Lord.

TWENTIETH SUNDAY OF THE YEAR (B)
Pr 9:1-6   Ep 5:15-20   Jn 6:51-58

"It's hard to believe everything the Catholic Church teaches," an 18 year old girl recently remarked. I knew she had something particular in mind, so I patiently waited for her to continue. "Like the bread, you know, the body of Christ. I realize it's Jesus but . . . well it's difficult to explain. You know what I mean?" I knew what she meant, for I have puzzled over the doctrine of the Real Presence for many years and still do. She was ready to listen, so I reflected out loud my thoughts on the holy Eucharist.

The body of Christ present in the host is His risen body — the post-Resurrection body or glorified body. Jesus is not present in the Eucharist with the body of bones, skin and flesh which He received from His mother. He's there in His RISEN BODY, glorified by His Father when He rose from the grave. It's that body which can move instantly from one place to another, which needs no food or sleep, which passed through the locked doors of the upper room without bothering to open them.

His risen body can take any form or shape and be present in any place and yet be invisible. His presence in the bread and wine is real but mystical; it is neither apparent to the senses nor obvious to the intellect.

Christ is present in other ways in the Mass: in the words of Sacred Scripture, in the moments of silence, in the hymns and prayers. He is present in the tiny hands of an infant, in the dim eyes of an old man and in the sign of peace. In the Holy Eucharist, however, He is present in a unique way. When we approach the altar to receive the body of Christ, we have our finest example of His abiding presence with us.

John's reading today, from his eucharistic 6th chapter, recounts the words of Jesus: "I myself am the living bread . . . the bread I give is My flesh for the life of the world." This passage is filled with references to new life. The new bread which Jesus promises is a clear reflection of His resurrected life. He now dies no more, and those who eat this bread of the risen Christ will, like Him, live forever. The same is true of the blood of Christ.

When body and blood are separated, we have death. The separation of Jesus' mystical body and blood on the altar is a reminder of His death. Our reception of the Eucharist is the full sign of the new life which Jesus promises us.

The first reading from Proverbs today sees Wisdom calling to her followers: "Come, eat of my food, and drink of the wine I have mixed." We have a similar invitation in the Holy Eucharist, and as we come to Communion we are called as well to "advance in the way of understanding."

Mass therefore is a commemoration of the value of life. It is the ritualistic reenactment of what the Savior did for us and continues to do.

We offer our thanks for His mystical presence among us in the bread of eternal life.

TWENTY-FIRST SUNDAY OF THE YEAR (B)
Jos 24:1-2, 15-17, 18   Ep 5:21-32   Jn 6:60-69

There will be fidgety, adverse reactions by many women in the pews today to St. Paul's matrimonial advice: "Wives be submissive to your husbands." This passage normally inspires husbands to nod reverently, displaying their great respect for the sacred scripture. Because of this and similar texts, St. Paul does not get high marks from many women.

Very conscious of the need for feminine equality and common human dignity, the Church maintains that this text should not be deleted or denied, but expanded. Women should be submissive to their husbands; but men should be equally submissive to their wives. Being submissive means to be humble or compliant to another. It also means to leave something to the discretion or judgment of another person. Marriage is a sharing union, a twofold consignment of love. It implies that husbands and wives, by the nature of their agreement, must be compliant to each other for the union to endure.

We can ignore Paul's advice and have a situation where the

wife rejects submissiveness and the husband does not yield to her wishes. Such a marriage will produce only division and provide another sad case to keep the divorce courts busy. But if each could be courteous and accommodating, then they would always mutually try to give as much love, submission and deference to each other as possible. Marriages like these would eventually put the divorce courts out of business.

Paul says something else in this reading to married men: "Husbands love your wives." This also implies that women should love their husbands. If the submissiveness in marriage is not of a loving nature, then the union is not a happy one.

Marriage was never intended as a clever way to make people hate each other. It is supposed to bring fullness of life and mutual respect. As the Church respects Christ and Christ loves the Church, so says St. Paul, wives and husbands are to comply with and love each other. It's not a question of who makes the rules and who observes them — each does both. Would Christ who died for the Church to make her "holy, immaculate without stain or wrinkle," want to make her into a slave? Can the Church which owes her life to Christ ever fail to give Him the greatest love? Christ and the Church are one in mind, heart and purpose. Paul, the Preacher to the Gentiles, says that's a superb model of what every marriage should be.

Husbands be submissive to your wives. Wives love your husbands. As the Bible says, you've left your father's house and now cling to your spouse. You once were two but now are one. If you continue to pull together, you'll never pull apart.

TWENTY-SECOND SUNDAY OF THE YEAR (B)
Dt 4:1-2, 6-8   Jm 1:17-18, 21-22, 27   Mk 7:1-8, 14-15, 21-23

If questioned why we gather in church on Sunday, most would answer, "to worship God." The questioner may still be confused, for there are numerous meanings to that phrase — "to worship God." Some think that it means singing religious songs; for others it's saying common prayers or silent ones. Worship for some may mean hearing a homily, or receiving Holy Communion, etc. There's a clear-cut definition of worship in the second reading today from the epistle of St. James. "Looking after orphans and widows in their distress and keeping oneself unspotted by the world make for pure worship . . ." This is a call to *do* worship rather than simply *pray* worship. A kind act offered for another is a gift to God, which is at the heart of any true definition of worship.

St. James gives us a threefold approach to pure worship. First and most important is to help the helpless. These are the orphans of the world, the abandoned babies, without mother and father, immature and frightened, able to do little except cry. There are so many hungry and hurting people in the world, and caring for them is pure worship. Mother Teresa, aiding the poorest of the poor, excels in this category. We extend our hands in worship when we reach out to the profoundly retarded, the acutely depressed, those burned out or drowned out by drugs and alcohol. The Church has programs for these and many other unfortunates. As part of the Church we support and share in this special worship.

The second way to worship is to care for widows in their distress. Widows are not as helpless as orphans, and they're not all in distress — but many are and need our help. Many widows and widowers need encouragement, advice, and temporary financial assistance. They need transportation to the store, doctor or to church. Widows have not only lost a spouse; they have lost youthful strength, clear eyesight, hearing, sharpness of mind and mobility of body. They might survive on their own but our outstretched hands can bring them many beautiful blessings. In doing so, we worship God.

Thirdly, we are to walk through life carefully so that we do not become entangled in the evils of the world. Here a warning is in order: Don't become so concerned about keeping yourself unspotted by the world that you forget about the orphans and the widows.

Whoever and wherever we are, there's opportunity to put the worship of good works into effect in our own neighborhood. We should never minimize the profound value of formal worship at church and private prayers at home. But according to St. James, our prayers will get a hearing before God only after we have tried to help the orphans and widows in their distress.

TWENTY-THIRD SUNDAY OF THE YEAR (B)
Is 35:4-7   Jm 2:1-5   Mk 7:31-37

In 1850, a Steubenville, Ohio lawyer, Edwin Stanton, and his associates requested the legal services of Abraham Lincoln, the competent lawyer from Springfield, Illinois to assist in an infringement of patent case in Cincinnati. When the two men were introduced, Stanton greeted him coldly and blatantly ignored him throughout the case. He even whispered to others in Lincoln's presence, "I won't associate with such a long-armed gawky ape as that." Twelve years later, Stanton was appointed Secretary of War by the President of the United States, Abraham Lincoln. Three years later, he stood at Lincoln's bedside during his dying hours, pitifully weeping at the loss of his dear friend. If we must judge others, it's wise to avoid bitter words; for like Stanton, we may later have to eat them.

St. James says in today's second reading, that it's so easy but so wrong to judge another by outward appearances. This passage is a vivid reminder to avoid both favoritism and discrimination.

Our country was founded on the principle of equality for all citizens. Violations of this law are against both the Constitution and the Gospel. Some thrive on favoritism as a way of life. You've heard the old line. "I know someone in an important position who owes me a favor. I'll tell him you're my friend and he'll get you the promotion." Such a procedure is unjust. No one should be given a promotion, honor or better position, simply because he's someone's friend or relative or because he looks nice, dresses well or is a certain color.

Could you imagine a judge in a courtroom condemning an alleged criminal on his looks, clothes or neighborhood? Each case should be judged in itself and of itself, here and now.

If you — like Lincoln — are judged unjustly, you shouldn't fret too much, for you're in good company. His neighbors thought that young Thomas Edison was insane. When Albert Einstein failed his college entrance exam, he was judged stupid and sent home. Even Jesus was called a fanatic and a lawbreaker.

Inspired by God who "judges the world with justice and governs the people with equity" (Ps 9:9), we must extend that same balanced treatment to all. Whether it's the fashionable clothes and gold rings of the rich, or the shabby garb of the poor, they're only externals worn by those for whom Jesus died. There was no favoritism or discrimination at Calvary.

TWENTY-FOURTH SUNDAY OF THE YEAR (B)
Is 50:4-9   Jm 2:14-18   Mk 8:27-35

The setting for today's Gospel narrative is the flower-covered foothills of misty snowcapped Mount Hermon. There Jesus and the twelve apostles discuss His identity. As they walk near the source of the Jordan River, he calmly asks, "Who do people say that I am?" After hearing their varied responses, the Master replies with another question: "Who do you say that I am?" First Jesus asked what they had heard about Him from others, now He wants to know what they think of Him.

The general public saw Him as the reincarnation of John the

Baptist, Elijah or some prophet. Jesus' close friends, however, acknowledged Him as the long-promised Messiah.

How do people see Jesus today? Many (like Christians) say He's God. Others (like Jews and Moslems) say He's a great man but not God. Some see Him as a friend and love Him. Others view Him as a judge and fear Him. Many try to imitate Jesus by praying much in church. Others say they act like Him when they're working for human rights and arms reduction. Some think His teachings are strict. Others say He's lenient.

As current disciples, how would we answer Jesus if He asked us what people say about Him? We would have to reply that they say almost everything imaginable — all the way from believing that He lives in each person and directs every thought and action, to the belief that He doesn't exist at all.

The first question about the public's view is intriguing, but the second one is more vital and personal. What do you think about Jesus? Don't quote some book or authority. Just answer from your own honest belief. Is He really God? Did He die for you? Does He know your name? Do you see Him in your neighbor; feel Him in yourself; hear Him in the words of scripture; sense His presence in the Eucharist? Can you relax with Him or does He scare you? Perhaps we feel like Pilate, who after a brief encounter with Him asked publicly, "What am I to do with Jesus?"

Peter triumphantly calls Him "Messiah," but rejects the thought of a suffering Messiah. Jesus dramatically corrects him. Today's Gospel concludes with Jesus calling together both the crowd and the twelve to remind them, "If a man wishes to come after Me, he must deny his very self, take up his cross and follow in My steps." I believe Jesus is demanding yet understanding. I believe He's a fair judge yet a personal friend. I believe He's a profound, unfolding mystery. What do you think?

TWENTY-FIFTH SUNDAY OF THE YEAR (B)
Ws 2:12, 17-20   Jm 3:16-4:3   Mk 9:30-37

There are two evil spirits who continually roam the world, traveling together into every country, city and home. Their names are Envy and Jealousy. We often speak of them in the same breath, since they normally work together. These twin forces of evil are powerful and greatly influence how we treat each other.

The Church recognizes their destructive power. All three readings of today's liturgy are alerting us to their insidious existence. In the Book of Wisdom, jealousy condemns the just man "to a shameful death." St. James states that these two vices produce "all kinds of vile behavior." The Gospel of Mark tells how jealousy had even infiltrated the minds of the apostles. They "had been arguing about who was the most important."

If we are discontented because of the good fortune of another, we are suffering an envy attack. We are led to hate another person because he or she possesses nice things which we don't. It's good to admire and desire material possessions, good looks, abundant finances, etc. But envy goes beyond this, causing us to hate the possessor and wish misfortune for them so the possessions would be lost.

The other half of the duo, Jealousy, is a suspicion within, caused by the mistrust of another. It is an unpleasant fear, intolerant of any rival. Envy and jealousy, like ants and termites, silently creep into the dark corners of our homes.

There is a story that jealousy first appeared in Eve, when she accused Adam of being with another woman. Adam laughed, saying there were no other women. But when he went to sleep, she counted his ribs just to be sure. Suspicious jealousy cannot trust the words and motives of another, and so the jealous heart can never rest.

As far back as 500 B.C. the Greek playwright Aeschylus said, "It is in the character of few men, to honor without envy, a friend who has prospered." How sad it is that we interpret another's success as our failure. The envious and jealous person imagines many enemies, but in reality is his or her own worst enemy.

The liturgy invites us to sincerely trust those people who are close to us and to rejoice at the good fortunes of others. If we hope to improve spiritually we must constantly be working to discard the evils within us. Envy and jealousy should be two of the first to go.

TWENTY-SIXTH SUNDAY OF THE YEAR (B)
Nb 11:25-29   Jm 5:1-6   Mk 9:38-43, 45, 47-48

Moses called a special meeting for his elders, where they were to receive a unique outpouring of God's spirit so that they could prophesy. Two of the elders, Eldad and Medad, missed the meeting but still got the spirit. At this Joshua, Moses' aide, complained and asked him to declare the spirit invalid. But Moses would not. He said he only wished more people had the spirit of God. He was not concerned with how they got it, but was simply glad they had it. In other words, he said, don't impose limitations on what God can do or how He must do it. This is the message of the first reading.

The Gospel is similar. John told Jesus that there was a man using His holy name to expel demons. Because "he is not of our company," John said, "we tried to stop him." Jesus, like Moses, did not want the man stopped. He said, "anyone who is not against us is with us."

We owe a reverent respect to our Church with its rules and ways of worship, and members should observe them. We are glad that God is present to us, but we should not say that He is absent to others just because they do not belong "to our company." Churches should not engage in this quarrel of who is right and who is wrong, but should acknowledge the differences and accept those who are not opposing us, as being for us. Both the Old and New Testaments

(Moses and Jesus) present this balanced style of ecumenism.

If various Christian denominations are to work together, it's vital that we live in unison with our own members. It would be wrong for Catholic charismatics therefore to think that they relate to God in a more perfect way than other Catholics. It is likewise wrong for "Council of Trent" traditionalists to envision their way as the only way for Catholic worship. If we are truly Spirit people, we'll have the spirit of love and peaceful cooperation. If we are really traditionalists, we'll go to the source of tradition where Jesus taught us to be accepting of others.

We must be skeptical of those who say there is but one way to do anything — especially in religion. There are thousands of ways to live, work, find God and worship Him. There are many roads to heaven with various "companies" along the way providing needed help and good directions. We are to worship as we see fit and respect others who believe and worship differently. Such is commanded by Jesus (and Moses). The many diversities on earth have not been produced only by men and women. God has created, by His own free choice, a world full of varieties; demonstrating that He doesn't think in terms of only one way.

TWENTY-SEVENTH SUNDAY OF THE YEAR (B)
Gn 2:18-24   Heb 2:9-11   Mk 10:2-16

The Book of Genesis presents two stories of the Creation. Chapter one tells of the famous six days and emphasizes the making of the material world. Another scenario explaining the origin of human life appears in the second chapter. The two stories, with differing points of view and vocabulary, come from separate sources. The Bible was assembled from various oral and written traditions, and the biblical writers were more editors than authors. They placed these two stories side by side, rather than unifying them into one single account. Today's initial reading from the second chapter describes, in a figurative way, the origins and union of man and woman.

This passage emphasizes the unity of marriage, with statements like "bone of my bone and flesh of my flesh," bespeaking a loving intimacy and togetherness. If we are of the same bone and flesh as another, then our bodies and minds are compatible and each can freely give and receive without rejection. Compatible love and respect in marriage is the best basis for a lasting union.

The story portrays the first couple being introduced by God in person and joined with His blessing. Each man and woman planning a life-long marriage should proceed slowly, trying to be certain they are joined by God and not pushed together by immaturity, a desire to leave home, or physical attraction. The rising divorce rate is a bewildering religious and social problem which injures good people and often permanently scars innocent children.

Being "two in one" has many connotations, but nowhere is it more clearly seen than in the life of a child. Regardless of the separation, divorce or death of the spouses, they will always be "two in one" in their children. Since marriage produces the profound, irreversible consequence of human life, it was intended by the Creator to be a permanent union. Jesus reaffirms, in today's Gospel, the ancient ideal of the unbreakable bond.

How do we know if love is true and if it will endure? We don't. Like most ventures in life, each person must intelligently make the best judgment possible, have faith in God's original plan and try to bring it to a happy fulfillment. If love is true on both sides, nothing can sidetrack it. Like God its author, true love goes on and on.

TWENTY-EIGHTH SUNDAY OF THE YEAR (B)
Ws 7:7-11   Heb 4:12-13   Mk 10:17-30

A religious sister surprised her community several years ago when she requested a full-time ministry to help rich people.

Mother Superior was not impressed with her proposal, and stated that she should serve the poor rather than the rich who possess "everything they need." I never heard if sister's wish was granted or rejected. I hope she got permission, for whether a person is rich or poor, the key word is not *rich* or *poor*, but *person*. Rich people are fortunate in some respects, but in other ways they can be hurting, lonely and more hungry than the poor.

We meet an unhappy rich man in the Gospel of today's Mass. This young person is very sad and needs encouragement to be less attached to his wealth so that he can better follow the Lord. Many rich people are despair-prone, for they experience no pleasure in the simple things of life. Acquiring a new appliance, car or house is an important event for the poor, but for the wealthy, these usually mean little.

When one of the world's richest men died some years ago, the minister told the 20 people attending his eight minute funeral, "We bring nothing into the world and take nothing out." At a casino he owned, they observed a minute of silence in his honor the day of the funeral. But one impatient gambler shouted, when the dealer lingered a few extra seconds, "He's had his minute, cut the cards!" That may be a typical commentary on our appreciation of the rich — especially when dead.

The rich man in the Gospel was invited by Jesus to be a close friend, perhaps one of His disciples. Maybe he would have been selected to replace Judas. Only the Lord knows what had been in store, but his riches would not release him for he could not release them.

If you are wealthy, you should have a Christian outlook on your possessions. If you're poor, you also need some guidelines about monetary values in life. You might note these four suggestions. 1. *Remember you must let go sometime.* 2. *Find joy in giving rather than grabbing.* 3. *Live by the cross sign (†), not the dollar sign ($).* 4. *Be assured that material wealth is fleeting security. You need lasting security.*

TWENTY-NINTH SUNDAY OF THE YEAR (B)
Is 53:10-11   Heb 4:14-16   Mk 10:35-45

It was His last trip to Jerusalem and Jesus was openly preparing the Twelve for the momentous events of His last days on earth. He predicted that His enemies would "mock Him, spit upon Him, scourge Him and put Him to death and on the third day He would rise again." The Lord now was ready to answer any questions they might have about His tragic plight. At this sensitive moment He was also seeking the tender support of these, His closest friends.

The tense silence was broken by the two brothers, James and John, who showed that they had missed the message of the suffering Messiah and were thinking only of Him as triumphant conqueror. They requested places of honor in His Kingdom to be established — at his immediate right and left. Their abrupt and selfish request must have been discouraging to Jesus, who had placed Himself in the role of a servant but was being asked to grant His disciples positions of honor and dignity. The other ten were likewise horrified at the brashness of James and John. It seems no accident that Luke omits this incident from his Gospel and that Matthew attributes the inappropriate petition to their mother.

Regardless of what exactly happened and who made the request, one thing is clear. Jesus informed James and John and the other apostles that they would all be called to suffer with Him.

Jesus taught that the Kingdom is different from earthly kingdoms. "Great men exercise authority" in the civic circle, He says, but in the Church the great people are those who serve others. "Whoever wishes to be first among you shall be the slave of all." The only way we can share in Jesus' glory is to first share in His suffering.

Contrary to some modern opinions, pain and suffering are not punishments, nor are honors necessarily gifts of God. We must constantly keep clarifying which standards we follow. Like James and John, we might be insensitive to God's ways by trying to be very important in worldly ways. Do we sometimes chant, "I'm number one" at least secretly? Where do we find the Lord's "number ones"? They're not necessarily sitting in high positions of authority, but they're the hard working servants of society.

THIRTIETH SUNDAY OF THE YEAR (B)
Jr 31:7-9   Heb 5:1-6   Mk 10:46-52

There is a high hill on the west side of Jericho which offers a panoramic view of the ancient city. The splendid colors of flowers, mingling with the orange blossoms and palm trees, are a delightful sight. It was in this fertile Jordan River Valley town that Bartimaeus lived, smelled the fragrant blossoms and heard the leaves rustled by the gentle wind. But he never saw its beauty, for he was blind.

Through the pen of St. Mark, Bartimaeus finds his way into today's Gospel, sitting in the right place at the right time — when Jesus just happened to be passing by. He had heard of the famous Miracle Worker and when told He was right here in Jericho, Bartimaeus suddenly decided to make the biggest gamble of his life. He would call out for Jesus to work one more miracle in Jericho — for him.

He was afraid that perhaps Jesus wouldn't even hear his call, that people would laugh at him. Yet the thought of being able to see, capable of finding a job and being independent, strengthened his courage. When the crowd grew louder (meaning Jesus was very near), Bartimaeus out-shouted them with eight well-chosen words: "Jesus, Son of David, have pity on me." It was this forceful prayer which reached the ears of the Lord, causing Him to stop and ask the bystanders to bring to Him the man who prayed that beautiful faith-filled prayer. Bartimaeus began to tremble, causing someone to offer reassurance, "You have nothing to fear from Him." To the question, "What do you want Me to do for you?" the frightened but expectant blind man cried out, "I want to see!" His world of darkness continued a few moments more as he heard the words, "Your faith has saved you." Suddenly he saw the sunshine, colors danced before his eyes and the most breath-taking sight of all was the celestial face of Jesus.

We could make the words of Bartimaeus our own prayer for mercy, entreating the Savior to relieve our sufferings with His healing blessings. Try the prayer if you have spiritual blindness and can't accept others or find any good in them. Pray those words if you're blind to your faults, have lost your way through life or have no hope for a glorious future. Pray with courage and shout twice if you must, even if others tell you to be quiet.

You may feel helpless, sitting on some dark back road of society, but Jesus still passes by. He wants to lift you from your gloomy shadows of despair. Regardless of how far from Him you may be, trust His mercy and ask His help for He will hear you. Someday you will behold Him face to face, like Bartimaeus. Just you wait, you'll see!

THIRTY-FIRST SUNDAY OF THE YEAR (B)
Dt 6:2-6   Heb 7:23-28   Mk 12:28-34

We show devotion to our country through the Pledge of Allegiance to the Flag, expressing our feelings in patriotic words and gestures. The hand of strength is placed over the heart of love as we demonstrate support for our beloved land. We also make the pledge while standing as a further sign of respect.

In the Gospel of Mark, read at today's liturgy, we have a pledge of allegiance to our God. When Jesus was asked to identify the primary commandment, he replied by quoting the passage from Deuteronomy known to the Jews as the Shema. This Old Testament text — the first reading today — acknowledged the

Lord our God and bids each of us to love Him with all of our heart, soul, mind and strength. Jesus joins this to Leviticus 19:18, "You shall love your neighbor as yourself." That's it, He told his questioner, there is no greater law by which to live.

If we would read the next four verses in Deuteronomy, we would hear the author giving further advice about the use of the Shema. He says to drill these thoughts into your children, speak them at home and away from home, say them whether busy or at rest, bind them to your wrists and foreheads and even paint them on your doorposts and gates. In other words, keep the law of love continually before your eyes.

We can lose sight of God's words just as we are often confused about our country's doctrines and Constitution. Several years ago 2300 federal employees in 12 Washington agencies were asked to sign their names to a document if they could accept it. 68% refused to sign. When asked where they thought the statement was from, some said "The Christian Science Monitor," others "The National Catholic Observer," still others "The Communist Manifesto." In reality it was a quotation from the Declaration of Independence.

It's easy to blame the ills of our country on the president or other leaders and absolve ourselves of any responsibility. But the best leaders in the world could not make a good country if the citizens failed to cooperate. Christianity is not totally successful in our society because of our half-hearted love and efforts, even though we have the best of leaders in Jesus.

During the reading of today's Gospel let us stand and pledge our allegiance to our God with all our hearts, all our souls, all our minds and all our strengths and resolve to extend more genuine love to others. It's an invitation to be a full-time citizen and Christian. Jesus says "there is no greater commandment than these." Those who follow them "are not far from the reign of God."

THIRTY-SECOND SUNDAY OF THE YEAR (B)
1 K 17:10-16   Heb 9:24-28   Mk 12:38-44

The worshipers calmly entered the Temple, depositing their donations into the venerable-looking container near the door. Sitting in a chair nearby, Jesus noted the amounts of money each dropped into the treasury. Then He called the Twelve over to share His insights about the wealthy and the poor, the big checks and the small coins.

One person had deeply impressed him — a poor widow, who had given a mere pittance, compared to most of the others. No doubt, He prefaced His remarks with the reminder that He was not condemning the big gifts by praising the small ones. That would have been foolish, for the Temple needed large donations to continue as a place of worship.

Although the widow gave only two paltry coins, worth but a few cents, Jesus was impressed. He praised her because it was a high percentage gift. The others, He said, "gave from their surplus wealth, but she gave from her want . . ." The wealthy gave a tiny fraction of what they possessed, but she gave nearly everything she had. The value of the gift was practically nothing but Jesus saw the value of the giver.

Today, many people feel that money is a forbidden topic in the pulpit, that it is unspiritual and unworthy to be associated with worship. Some even say that's why they avoid church. However, Jesus apparently saw no conflict between scrutinizing the collection basket and preaching the Kingdom.

Granted that "money sermons" are overdone by some preachers, generosity is still a valuable virtue. Furthermore, if religion is to speak to our needs, hopes and worries, we must talk of money — which is at the heart of many of our dilemmas. "How much does it cost?" is a phrase continually on our minds and lips. The cost of "running the church" is a heavy burden for all pastors.

I don't see this Gospel as trying to embarrass the rich to

donate more to church and charity but as a call for *all* to be generous. Being poor does not absolve one from this. "Two small copper coins" are very pleasing to God if that's all we can afford. Regardless of the amount, each should make *some* offering, and it will be valuable if it flows from a spirit of sincere generosity.

THIRTY-THIRD SUNDAY OF THE YEAR (B)
Dn 12:1-3   Heb 10:11-14, 18   Mk 13:24-32

"Glory be to the Father, the Son and the Holy Spirit. As it was in the beginning, is now and ever shall be, *world without end."* Each time we say this familiar prayer, we express our belief that the world will never end. However both the Book of Daniel and the Gospel of Mark, read today, forecast the end of the world. We of course are speaking of two different worlds.

The world without end is the state of eternity — also without a beginning. The world designated in today's reading is the one where we, at the present, live. The origin of our world is wrapped in mystery, as are the beginnings of human life. Equally debated and even more obscure is the time and manner of the world's demise.

People throughout the ages have frequently predicted its imminent end, but the rugged old world keeps spinning merrily on its way.

The biblical writers, having lived thousands of years ago, envisioned a much simpler world than we now know. They thought it rested on pillars, with openings in the sky to let in the sun and the rain. The earth was considered to be only a few thousand years old, and to be much larger than the sun or the moon.

Today we know that the earth has been here for billions of years and is a tiny fraction of the size of the sun. We now realize, through modern science, that the size, age and complexity of the universe are absolutely staggering. Neither Bible nor religion were ever meant to scientifically explain the time and manner of the world's origin or ending. It is enough that they tell us that God is responsible for the universe and for us.

We are obliged to ignore the contrived blueprints of the end of the world churned out by the false prophets of today. This same type of pseudo-speculation was common just before the year 1000 A.D., triggered by a text in the Book of Revelation stating that Satan would be unchained after 1000 years (Rv 20:7). With the year 2000 approaching, ending the second millennium, predictions of world destruction are increasing again.

When Jesus was questioned by His apostles about when the world would end, He replied that no one knows, not the angels, "nor even the Son, but only the Father" (Mk 13:32). He was saying politely, it's beyond your competence — don't worry about it. Today the Church simply reaffirms that we have here no lasting kingdom, but seek one that is beyond.

THIRTY-FOURTH SUNDAY OF THE YEAR (B) SOLEMNITY OF CHRIST THE KING
Dn 7:13-14   Rv 1:5-8   Jn 18:33-37

Billions of words have been spoken and written to explain Jesus to the world, but still we fail to understand His profound meaning. By contrast, we sometimes discover one small sentence which is tremendously enlightening about the nature of our Lord. Such a sentence opens today's passage from the Book of Revelation. "JESUS CHRIST IS THE FAITHFUL WITNESS, THE FIRST BORN FROM THE DEAD AND RULER OF THE KINGS OF EARTH." This statement presents three basic truths in less than twenty words, which we are invited to joyfully contemplate on the Feast of Christ The King.

1. *Faithful Witness*   Jesus tells of realities He has seen and

we haven't. He has witnessed to the Holy Trinity, proclaimed the Kingdom of Heaven and told of a glorified life without end. Through His death, He has testified to the transcendent reality of love and forgiveness. Unable to comprehend these and other spiritual teachings, we yet believe them because of the Faithful Witness.

2. *First Born of the Dead*   In His victory over the grave, Jesus proclaimed the truth of the resurrection. By this remarkable event He shows how life continues from this world to the next, where death can no longer touch us. As each of us approaches death, we can do so with buoyant confidence. The Lord has overpowered the desolate grave and promised the same for those who believe in Him. The First Born is the inspired model for all of us born into time and eternity. He has walked down life's uncertain road, uprooted the dead-end signs and built a bridge, opening the way to the eternal Kingdom.

3. *Ruler of Kings of the Earth*   He ruled before any king, and when all kings will have vanished Christ the King will continue to stand firm forever. Some kings are weak and some are mighty, but no king except Jesus is Almighty. He is king-sized in love, patience, forgiveness and moderation.

Christ the King is meant to rule our lives and have first place. Do we hold Him in that elevated position of honor? Must we confess to being ruled by inferior powers, such as greed, lust, revenge, anger, etc.? If so, what have we done with Jesus? Like the people at His trial, our lives may be crying out to the world, "We have no king but Caesar."

The Church's celebration in honor of Christ The King is reserved for the last Sunday of the liturgical year, so that we can again publicly pledge our allegiance and follow Him into the new season of Advent. As Christians, we are invited to anchor our hopes and dreams in Jesus. He is the Way to victory over death; the Truth, our credible witness; and the Life, both now and forever.

Cycle C

FIRST SUNDAY OF ADVENT (C)
Jr 33:14-16   1 Th 3:12-4:2   Lk 21:25-28, 34-36

A thought-provoking article was published in the "Catholic Exponent" (Youngstown, Ohio) several years ago entitled: "Mass Lasted Twelve Hours At Marquette University." It told how some college students and campus ministers spent a weekend at a retreat house, leisurely offering the Mass at a meaningful, reflective pace.

Before breakfast they sang the opening song and had the penitential rite and initial prayer. The Gloria, scripture readings, responses and homily took place before lunch, which was a simple meal to express solidarity with the hungry of the world.

Following lunch, they spoke of the meaning of grapes and wine, of oil, flour and water, and then mixed dough into loaves for the oven. While the bread baked, some prepared supper and others rested. Later, the freshly baked bread was offered at the altar, followed by the eucharistic prayer, the Our Father and Holy Communion.

After supper, the group prayed the concluding prayer, received a blessing and all sang the recessional song. The article stated that it may have been the longest Mass in history.

Many of us don't see the Mass as something to get caught up in, but as something to get through. No matter how good the quality of worship, if it extends over an hour, many parishioners become impatient.

The Advent season, which we begin today and continue until Christmas, is the celebration of patience. During this season of four weeks, we reflect on the long centuries of waiting for the coming of Jesus into the world.

A spirit of patience and a slower pace would be helpful to those of us who rush into most things, including worship. Remember, we serve a God who dwells in eternity, where life is unhurried. We, by contrast, are creatures of another world, born and schooled to keep pace with fleet-footed time. To better know

God (and ourselves), we must think of and pray to Him in a calm, unrushed manner. In heaven, all are caught up in the eternal contemplation of divine beauty. Our goal is to someday become immortalized dwellers of this eternity. For now, we leisurely recall the Lord's coming into our world and try to make Him more present in our lives during this Advent time. 'Tis the season to be thoughtful and walk slowly. After all, the Lord did not rush into the First Christmas.

SECOND SUNDAY OF ADVENT (C)
Bar 5:1-9   Ph 1:4-6, 8-11   Lk 3:1-6

Bridge the valleys, cut through the mountains, straighten out the sharp curves and smooth the surface! American ingenuity has responded admirably to this advice of John the Baptist. Our country can display approximately 42,500 miles of four-lane National Interstate Highways, carrying 25% of the nation's total traffic. This well planned cross-country network was eagerly promoted by President Eisenhower, basically for military purposes. The road system, identified by the familiar red, white and blue signs, can quickly deploy troops to any part of the country.

The primitive roads and nameless paths traveled by the Baptist were a great contrast — winding, rough and mountainous. John understands, like the present-day highway builders, that the more hazards removed, the better the road.

Poetically, John uses the image of the road to show how we can either encourage or impede God's entrance into our lives. We have a duty to level off our sharp peaks of pride, selfishness and blind ambitions, which become mountain-sized obstacles between God and ourselves.

Valleys also slow the journey to our Savior. These are the low, cold areas of depression, fear and despair. They obscure the warming sun and keep us wandering along the dark edge of night.

Advent is the "coming toward God" season, when each of us is challenged to examine his or her way to the Lord. If you are lost and going in circles, ask for advice or call a counsellor to help lift your spirits from the depths or to bring you down from fantasy to reality.

John wants us to straighten out our dead ends and hairpin curves of double standards, lying, cheating and crookedness.

Our rough ways of acting and speaking can become more gentle; our former violence can be paved with compassion. The Herald of the Messiah continues to shout. "Prepare the way of the Lord." With barriers removed, God is not far from us. If the obstacles remain on our way of life, we make contact or even communication with Him nearly impossible. God comes to us on the roads we make. If He doesn't come, we have not prepared the way.

THIRD SUNDAY OF ADVENT (C)
Zp 3:14-18   Ph 4:4-7   Lk 3:10-18

The Christmas season, forecasting peacefulness, often brings the opposite. How can sadness crowd out the pleasant thoughts of His birth, and the gifts, good food and warmth generated by our annual circle of family and friends? Some psychologists attribute Christmas depression to our carefree childhood emotions, which we will never be able to recapture. Others say that holiday sorrow is triggered at this sentimental time by a keen sense of our many unfulfilled dreams. Even if we don't understand the causes, we have all to some degree experienced this Christmas despondency.

The Church demonstrates her ancient wisdom today by celebrating a Sunday of Joy, two weeks before Christmas, to counteract our negative gloominess. The prophet Zephaniah sets the desired mood in the first reading: "Shout for joy, O daughter Zion, sing joyfully, O Israel."

The second reading today also helps set the mood, with St. Paul cheering the Philippians: "Rejoice in the Lord, always . . . Dismiss all anxiety from your minds." This is good news for everyone. The world in general stands in need of all the joyful thoughts available during this season.

If we are more joyful and less pessimistic in mind, perhaps our bodies will respond favorably, helping us to achieve a fuller degree of health and holiness. Modern wholistic health care tells us that a joyful mind promotes a healthy body.

You have probably heard or read of how the magazine editor Norman Cousins came down with a terrible sickness and was not responding to medicine. He decided to buy a small piece of equipment, which he positioned in his room, and it helped him regain his health. That equipment was a projector with which he watched the Marx Brothers' movies, and he laughed and laughed his way to health.

There are many reasons to be happy. This liturgy challenges us to smile, hoping for good things in the future and being glad that Jesus was born into the world as Savior of all. His presence continues to warm our cold world and make a hostile environment peaceful. "Rejoice in the Lord always. I say it again. Rejoice!"

FOURTH SUNDAY OF ADVENT (C)
Mi 5:1-4   Heb 10: 5-10   Lk 1:39-45

A man told me once that he stopped sending Christmas cards, going to holiday parties, and buying gifts. It was becoming too expensive and didn't make sense anymore. We can all appreciate this feeling, when we're stuck in pre-holiday mall traffic, or are crowding to the checkout counters and see the cash register totaling up large figures. But the expenses and inconveniences are soon forgotten in the hope of making someone happy with a gift purchased just for them.

Gift giving, card sending and visits are obviously things we don't have to do. But these kind and thoughtful deeds strengthen our ties of family and friendship. The Scrooges may seem to be more happy since they don't spend money on others or try to be friendly, but most likely they're very sad and lonely people. The tragedy is that this is their own doing. They don't realize that there's more joy in giving than receiving.

We have an excellent example of the true spirit of Christmas in today's Gospel, in the kindly deed of the Blessed Virgin Mary. She, being pregnant, could have easily chosen not to visit her cousin Elizabeth. But precisely because she was pregnant with Jesus, she could not remain aloof.

It was "with haste" that she climbed the long steep hill to her cousin's home in Ain Karim, to willingly assist her. Her greeting was so divinely inspired and powerful, that it moved Elizabeth to spontaneous prayer and uplifted the spirit of her unborn child John.

When we visit friends and family we should carry with us that same joy-filled attitude, which in itself is a tremendous gift to offer another. Using Mary as our model, we might try to worry less about being entertained and concentrate more on helping and uplifting. Jesus told the world that He came to serve, not be served. I wonder if He learned that from His mother.

Happiness can be found in the most unusual places. Mary discovered it in the hill country, in the stable and even in exile, for Jesus was with her. Since He promised to be with us, our finest gift to others is to live and give His love.

CHRISTMAS MIDNIGHT MASS (C)
Is 9:1-6   Tt 2:11-14   Lk 2:1-14

In a neighborhood school, a class of children with learning disabilities was presenting a Christmas play for the PTA. The production had three acts. The opening scene was at Nazareth, with the decree of Caesar Augustus; the next was at Bethlehem with the refusal of the innkeeper; and finally, the manger site in the hill country. The faculty and parents were anxious about the children's abilities to perform properly, but the first act went just fine.

In the second act Joseph and Mary knocked on the door of the inn and were quickly refused by the little innkeeper, with the words: "There is no room." They pleaded again very sorrowfully and he hesitated a bit but then said his lines: "There is no room." The script called for one more plea and refusal and this time the dejected couple begged for a room with all their hearts. The little innkeeper began his refusal but could not continue. He broke down and sobbed: "You can have my room." The teacher quickly got the play back on track, but the audience was visibly touched by the innocent spontaneity of this caring little child. In him, they saw demonstrated the true meaning of Christmas.

All of us to some degree play the role of innkeeper. We accept or reject others. Are we more like the original innkeeper who turned them out into the lonely night or the small child who welcomed them in? Perhaps we hang "no vacancy" signs around us by our rude words, gestures or tones of voice — telling others we don't want to be bothered; we're too busy or tired. If we are the exclusive type, catering only to the better class of people, the chances are that we would have turned away Joseph and Mary — and in doing that we would have also rejected Jesus, hidden within.

Some people are strictly unbending, while others believe that there's always room for one more. Can we make an exception in an exceptional situation, like that of Jesus, Mary and Joseph?

It is said of Mother Teresa of Calcutta, who has helped perhaps a half million people die with a bit of dignity, that she always makes room for one more. Don't you wonder what Jesus was thinking of in later life when He said, "Whatsoever you do for others you do for Me"? Could He have been reflecting back to the day of His birth and the rejection scene at the Bethlehem Inn?

Christmas is the traditional season of giving, but the better gifts are not the material ones. A true and beautiful present for another is a bit of our time when we think there's none to spare; a little advice and direction if we are so blessed and another is in need. We can give a simple smile of friendliness to one hurting silently, whose life may be filled with confusion and pain.

Jesus left His secure home in heaven and came to earth as a little child, like the innkeeper in the Christmas play. He also invited us to His house not for one night but forever.

SUNDAY IN THE OCTAVE OF CHRISTMAS
FEAST OF THE HOLY FAMILY (C)
Si 3:2-6, 12-14   Col 3:12-21   Lk 2:41-52

A long time ago in the city of Jerusalem, there lived a man by the name of Sirach. He was well educated and possessed considerable wealth. During his younger years, he had served as a diplomatic emissary to foreign courts. Later in life he established a school in Jerusalem, where he taught on religion and culture.

He wrote an inspiring book about 180 B.C., filled with the practical wisdom he had acquired over the years. Eventually his book found its way into the Bible. Today we know it as the Book of Ecclesiasticus — the church book. Sometimes it is simply called the Book of Sirach. Its fifty-one chapters touch all areas of life, love and the pursuit of happiness, with particular emphasis on the nature and objectives of family life.

For the celebration of Holy Family Sunday, the Church has selected a passage from Sirach for the first lesson. His views today are addressed primarily to young people. He says, in essence: Children, remember that the Lord has bestowed on your parents both honor and authority. You remember the fourth commandment—Honor your father and mother. Well, that's excellent advice and I heartily agree. God loves you very much when you love your parents because that's a sign you love Him, for your parents are His representatives. If you give respect to them, God promises to forgive your sins, even the most embarrassing. If you want God to hear your prayers, then you must hear and obey the voice of your parents. Furthermore, the blessings of a long life are extended to those young people who respect their parents. Don't forget that honor to father and mother does not cease when you become 18 or 21. It continues when they grow old and weak in mind and body—even when they die.

Sirach's teaching is perpetuated in the prayer over the couple on their wedding day. "May your children bring you happiness, and may the love you bestow upon them, be returned to you a hundredfold."

Finally the Gospel according to Luke reaffirms that a holy family is not necessarily a tension-free family. Not even Mary and Joseph enjoyed that luxury. The twelve year old Jesus was lost. His parents were upset, and when they found Him the words of Mary carried a bit of fire: "Son, why have you done this to us?" Like the Holy Family, we should solve our misunderstandings quickly, as both children and parents continue to grow in wisdom, age and grace.

OCTAVE OF CHRISTMAS
SOLEMNITY OF MARY, MOTHER OF GOD (C)
Nb 6:22-27   Gal 4:4-7   Lk 2:16-21

The first official reading in the liturgy of the word for the new year is from the Old Testament Book of Numbers. The Lord is giving Moses the particular words of a blessing, which he in turn is to tell his brother Aaron to bestow upon the people. Through the centuries, these hallowed words have been repeated by the Hebrews millions of times and this biblical benediction is still popular today. This brief but beautiful blessing is included in the sacramentaries on our Christian altars, as a recommended dismissal at the conclusion of the liturgy.

These divine words were no doubt prayed over the head of Mary as she attended the worship services with her family when she was growing up. The Church now finds it appropriate to read the priestly blessing of Aaron on this day when we honor Mary as the Mother of God. The text is deeply meaningful when applied to her, for the Lord did "bless and keep" her. We still call Mary blessed, and it's so commonly applied to her that the word has become part of her title: the Blessed Virgin. God likewise kept her free from sin and keeps her memory and honor very much in the forefront of our faith.

Mary has spiritually inherited the second line of this well-wishing prayer: "let His face shine upon you." The Lord's face glows with grace and beauty. He smiled at her, and she at Him. That warm smile will forever live in the heart of the holy Virgin "full of grace."

The concluding thought in the third line: "The Lord . . . give you peace," applies in a unique way to the woman who conceived, developed and physically gave birth to the world's most outstanding Peacemaker. She could rightfully be called the "Mother of peace."

Notice that the perceptive liturgists who assembled the readings for this feast, picked Psalm 67 as the responsorial to serve as a commentary on the first reading. This psalm is the same priestly blessing turned into a sublime prayer of praise and supplication. It reflects similar thoughts and even repeats some of the exact words of the ancient blessing.

Peaceful thoughts and intentions are always recommended,

and especially so at the beginning of a new year. But whether we say a specific Mass for peace or for the Solemnity of Mary, the ultimate purposes are intertwined and unified. Both Mary and her famous Son are models of peace in their personal lives and teachers of peace in their words.

If everyone in the world would pray Psalm 67 with and for each other, we would not need to spend 40% of our taxes for a defense budget to protect us from being killed by our neighbors. We must somehow learn to have faith not only in God but in humanity. Our task is to conceive, develop and give birth to a better world on this earth.

"The Lord bless you and keep you!
The Lord let His face shine upon you and be gracious to you!
The Lord look upon you kindly and give you peace!"

SECOND SUNDAY AFTER CHRISTMAS (C)
Si 24:1-4, 8-12   Ep 1:3-6, 15-18   Jn 1:1-18

The Church today presents the same Gospel which is read for the Christmas Mass of the Day. In former years, this passage was read at every Mass as the "Last Gospel," and that is a commentary in itself of the profound importance the Church attaches to it.

Conceived in the probing mind of John, it carries the reader far back into the beginning of time, before human life or even the creation of the world. It's the New Testament representation of the Genesis story, opening with the same words: "In the beginning..."

Our search into the past is every bit as exciting as our attempts to see into the future. John is able to carry our minds back to the point of reality when there was only God, existing in His mysterious oneness of nature and trinity of Persons.

The Word, whom we now know and love as Jesus, was born in human flesh (which we celebrate on Christmas), but His birth was not His beginning. The Word is of the nature of God and as such existed forever, but we are incapable of grasping the concept of "no beginning." This passage of John therefore makes us bow in complete humility and wonderment before the Infant born at Bethlehem, as we try to fathom the depth of His eternal nature. Of all the Christmas gifts ever mystified by wrappings and ribbons and presented to others with love, none was ever disguised so completely as the inner life of the Lord Himself.

This Gospel is one that we could open and read on a cold and dark winter night and it would cause our minds to soar across a million light years, like a well-directed missile on flight to probe the origins of light, time and life. It can only leave us with the deepest respect and admiration for the promised and delivered Messiah, who came out of the formless past, with complete knowledge of it. Jesus is spiritual Being, bearing the fullness of light, sound and love, and in that primordial thrust He brought it to fallen humanity on this small planet of earth.

We have here a profound meditation not only on mysterious beginnings but also on man's God-given dignity. Since "the Word was made flesh and made His dwelling among us," we stand in awe at the unexplainable love which God has for the sons and daughters of Adam.

Our respect for all people regardless of their physical or moral conditions should be enhanced by this reading, for "of His *fullness* we have *all* had a share." Notice that the share was not of a mere fraction of His goodness — we have shared *His fullness*, and that's staggering. We are Godly.

No one is a self-made independent. Our most basic gifts and privileges flow from the Word — the inner nature of God. We unite in collective gratitude, offering a community response of praise and thanksgiving.

The beauty of Christmas is really not to be laid aside for another year. Rather, it is with us each moment of every day, through the years of life and for eternity.

EPIPHANY (C)
Is 60:1-6   Ep 3:2-3, 5-6   Mt 2:1-12

Twinkle, twinkle, little star
How I wonder what you are,
Up above the world so high
Like a diamond in the sky.

Long before Jane Taylor composed her famous nursery rhyme, "The Star," St. Matthew had written of another friendly light which twinkled across the heavens, enticing Wise Men from the Orient, all the way to Bethlehem. With wonderment, like the little boy in the movie "Close Encounters," they followed its magnetic brilliance until it stopped over the house of Jesus.

Annually on this Sunday, we read the fascinating story of the star in Matthew, with Magi, gold, frankincense and myrrh. Separated in time but closely associated with the Nativity, Epiphany is sometimes called "Little Christmas."

The majority of Bible experts teach that this particular section of the New Testament belongs to a Hebrew style of literature known as Midrash. It is highly symbolic and its literalness is to be taken with the proverbial "grain of salt." Matthew uses this literary style to demonstrate Jesus' fulfillment of Old Testament prophecy. Later Christian tradition has continued to read these chapters in a "Midrashic" way. Note that Matthew does not say that the Magi were kings or that there were only three of them. Those details were added by later folklore and tradition.

Matthew intends to show in this passage that Jesus did not come only for the descendants of Abraham, but is the Man for all nations. The Magi traveled as proxies for the Gentile people, and their gifts were donated remotely in our names.

The Epiphany celebration furthermore presents jarring contrasts between wise and foolish people and how they search for Jesus and what they expect of Him. With faith, these king-sized men searched the heavens and were granted a vision of light. With a dream to fulfill, they began their spiritual pilgrimage. Each of us also has a dream to dream and a star to follow.

The evil Herod, however, with no faith in the spiritual world, was a fearful man with only insincere questions about Jesus. He saw no guiding star, for he didn't look skyward. His world was beneath him. He lived by manipulating people with money and force. He was afraid to dream a happy dream. Unlike the Wise Men, he offered no gifts to Jesus, but rather viewed Him as a rival to be destroyed. Herod caused Jesus and his family to flee and hide from him.

Good people (Magi) love the light of truth and seek it. Evil people (Herod) banish it from their sight. Have you seen the Light? Does it direct your journey through life?

BAPTISM OF THE LORD (C)
Is 42:1-4, 6-7   Ac 10:34-38   Lk 3:15-16, 21-22

Thirty quiet years had passed. Now it was time to go to work. His first step was to seek out His cousin John, daily growing in popularity because of his famous Jordan River baptisms. Jesus also received the "baptism of repentance," not because He was a sinner but to identify Himself and His imminent mission with and for sinful humanity.

Tradition says that this took place on the west side of the Jordan, approximately four and one half miles north of the Dead Sea. As the cool river water flowed over His head and body, and He heard the voice from heaven, Jesus knew He was now a public figure. He was moving swiftly toward center stage, from where he would never retreat. John likewise would change, for his public stature would soon be dwarfed by the increasing popularity of Jesus.

Immediately afterward, the Lord hurried into the mountains near Jericho to finalize His plans, pray to His Father and be tested by the forces of evil. Then, He began His three year non-stop mission of preaching, curing, counseling, building for the future and dying for the liberation of humanity. Yet the first public step had been baptism, and He saw His entire mission as its fulfillment. "I have a baptism to receive and what anguish I feel until it is over" (Lk 12:50).

That same Spirit-filled water at one time flowed over our heads. Regardless of our ages, it was our first step in faith. Even though most of us do not remember the event, it charted our course toward Christ.

The Church continually tries to impress on us the dignity of this sacrament of initiation. Parents requesting baptism for their children are expected to faithfully attend Mass as a sign of their Christian sincerity. Adults asking for this beginning sacrament must first devote much time to prayer and study.

Baptism is the foundation of the sacramental system. It is so basic to our spiritual life that it is a kind of second birthday. Jesus explained it to Nicodemus as being born again (Jn 3:3).

Do you know when and where you were baptized? If not, why not find out and celebrate it as your birthday in faith? You might attend Mass that day, say a rosary, make a holy hour, or reread the baptismal promises and meditate on their meaning.

"This is my beloved, in whom I am well pleased," can be applied to anyone who lives his or her baptismal promises faithfully throughout life.

FIRST SUNDAY OF LENT (C)
Dt 26:4-10   Rm 10:8-13   Lk 4:1-13

Adam, tempted in the garden, fell by eating the fruit; but Jesus, when enticed by the lure of food, triumphed. In Him we have removal of original sin and a fresh beginning. He is the New Adam. The fact that Jesus was tempted proves He is human. That He didn't succumb is a sign of His divinity.

In today's Gospel, it seems that the devil wanted to know Jesus' identity and tried to trick Him into working a miracle that would prove He was God, for only God could turn rocks into bread. If the local baker happened to turn bread into rocks, it is a sign of human weakness; but turning rocks to bread requires a greater power.

This whole temptation scene shows the strength of Jesus, who could control His great hunger. If we were famished, we would probably do almost anything to get food and would feel justified in doing so. When it concerns food, some of us fall very easily. The devil knows how to handle a hungry man, but he never learned how to handle a hungry God.

Jesus did not turn rocks into bread — but later, at the Last Supper, He turned bread into His Body. This holy Bread, received with earnest faith, can effect yet another change — that of a weak soul into a strong one. The Bread of the altar is the staff of eternal life, and to that mystic Bread we should be enticed.

Jesus was tempted by the devil to other foolish deeds, such as bowing down to worship him — which He didn't do, of course, but which we might do if the payoff is big enough. Then there was the invitation to leap off a tall building — the corner of the Temple overlooking the deep Kidron valley. It would have been a show-off stunt to impress the people. Here again, Jesus didn't jump for glory; just as He didn't jump off the cross, in spite of His agonizing pain. Instead, we do the jumping, to gain approval or applause and to avoid little inconveniences or difficulties. We manifest a severe spiritual weakness when we jump to false conclusions about others and misjudge their motives. That's sinful.

Jesus must have endured numerous temptations during His life, especially in those unsheltered public years. We believe He emerged completely victorious — a 4. average, summa cum laude.

As for the rest of us who fail our many temptations, we realize that the power of Christ has not yet really taken hold of our lives. As we read the story of the temptations, let's acknowledge some basic truths. We are weak. Jesus is strong. We need Him.

SECOND SUNDAY OF LENT (C)
Gn 15:1-12, 17-18   Ph 3:17-4:1   Lk 9:28-36

Rising abruptly from the cultivated plains of northern Israel is the famed Mount Tabor — Galilee's most picturesque mountain. This majestic, tree-covered elevation is six miles east of Nazareth. Honored in Jewish history as the site of a decisive victory over the Canaanites, it is hallowed by Christians as the sacred scene of the transfiguration of Jesus.

Atop this 1600 foot mountain, tradition says the three privileged apostles witnessed an astonishing change in the appearance of their Master. Bathed in glorious light, Jesus accepted approval from the Father as His "Beloved Son." He also received support from two of the most outstanding names in Hebrew history — Moses and Elijah. The Lord's radiant splendor, previously disguised, here stood revealed.

It was a sneak preview of the Resurrection and was the closest glimpse of heaven that Peter, James and John had ever seen. Mesmerized by all of this, Peter expressed a strong desire to remain. Speaking in behalf of the other two apostles, he offered to pitch tents for Jesus, Moses and Elijah. He, James and John would be content to sleep in the open, if only they could stay.

Gradually the two Old Testament celebrities faded into the thin mountain air, as did the emphatic request of Peter. Sufficient would be the memory, since it was not God's plan for the Redeemer and His apostles to settle on the mountain, basking in carefree glory.

"This is My beloved Son," had been proclaimed at Jesus' baptism, and now again these words were repeated with the Father's additional advice, "hear Him." This event moved Jesus to begin speaking openly of His coming death and Resurrection. He said, "Tell the vision to no one until the Son of Man has risen from the dead."

There's goodness and glory in all of us — often unseen and unappreciated by others and even by ourselves. God sees more than meets the human eye and it's His grace that makes us truly beautiful. It's good to remember that, especially in hard times. Jesus must have recalled Mount Tabor when he climbed his next mount — Calvary. The memory helped Him to know that the Father had not forsaken Him.

Lent is our transfiguration time, to be achieved through reconciliation, the Eucharist, good works and prayers. During this season of reform, we are encouraged to deepen our internal attractiveness. There's hidden beauty in all, but especially in those souls approved by God. They are gradually being transfigured into everlasting glory.

THIRD SUNDAY OF LENT (C)
Ex 3:1-8, 13-15   1 Cor 10:1-6, 10-12   Lk 13:1-9

If you swing and miss the baseball three times, you're on your way back to the dugout. Three failures to clear the bar in pole vaulting or high jumping and you're automatically out of the competition. Three is often our limit in forgiving injuries or tolerating failures.

The owner of the fig tree in today's Gospel feels the same way. He wants the tree chopped down because it has failed to produce any fruit for three years. Jesus, playing the part of the gardener, intercedes in behalf of the faltering tree. Let's give it another chance, he reasons; I'll offer it my personal attention and encouragement, and maybe it will produce figs. The Lord is thinking of fulfillment, not destruction — and it's not about trees He's speaking but struggling humanity.

Our demanding society can coldly scream, "three strikes and you're out." Jesus, displaying bold mercy, calmly adds, "make it four." He constantly envisions improvement, and blesses our clumsy efforts. Mercy in action is a strong positive virtue, which should not be interpreted as soft-hearted weakness.

I remember many occasions when neighborhood kids of various ages would be engaged in a softball game and a little batter would strike out. Often some sensitive player on the other team would shout, "give him another swing." Imagine the loving peacefulness if that same attitude would prevail in all areas of life.

Peter denied Jesus three times, yet was given another chance and never denied Him again. He went on to become the Pope and died a martyr's death. Without that gratuitous fourth swing, the entire history of Christianity would have been written differently. Judas was also offered another chance but refused it.

Forgiveness is an integral part of God's nature, not to be abused or presumed but used by weak struggling people like us. Since the Creator knows our proneness to failure, He ministers to us not in terms of "three" or "four" but extends His mercy to "seven times" and even "seventy times seven."

In this little parable, failing humanity plays the role of the fig tree, with demanding society as the boss and Jesus as the gardener. Holy mercy wins the argument and the story has a happy ending, for the tree is spared and figs are expected next year. The tree should never forget Who caused the owner to change his mind and spare its life. The Gardener did it.

FOURTH SUNDAY OF LENT (C)
Jos 5:9, 10-12   2 Cor 5:17-21   Lk 15:1-3, 11-32

Among his many talents, Jesus was a superb story-teller. It would be difficult to identify His best story, but today's would rank near the top. It's the parable of the Prodigal Son.

The central figure is an attentive father, who is a very good man — perhaps too good, when it comes to catering to the whims of his two ungracious sons with their radically opposing views of life. He is generous, permissive and forgiving to the younger, and self-effacing, patient and consoling to the elder. Although the one is prodigal and the other paranoid, the caring father is understanding and supportive to both.

Many applications can be and have been made of this time-honored story, but in its current mid-lenten context, it invites us to confidently approach our forgiving Heavenly Father, who understands and loves us dearly.

We may be like the younger brother, dissatisfied with home life, carefree and irresponsible. He wasn't a bad kid — just restless and adventurous. He did, however, insult his father grievously by asking for his share of the inheritance — which customarily was divided up only after the father's death. Perhaps he didn't intend the insult, but asking for his portion of the estate was like telling his dad to drop dead. The father, no doubt shattered by this impulsive brashness, still gave him the money.

Are we not like the insulting prodigal sometimes — insensitively sinful toward God and others, while considering ourselves clever and cool? Often those we offend suffer in silence — like Jesus on the cross. Lent calls us to a deeper appreciation of others by looking beyond our own selfish attitudes.

Maybe we identify more closely with the older brother — being withdrawn, unpopular, bitter and afraid to mix with others. Perhaps, like him, we find security in excessive devotion to duty and saving our money. We may be critical of civil and church leaders and mistrusting of people in general; thinking that those who act friendly are only trying to take advantage of us. Lent in this case invites is to open up, communicate and share with our brothers and sisters, realizing that they love us for our own sakes and that the Father loves us even more.

Whether prodigal or paranoid or whatever, we need not feel rejected. Although our sins have told Jesus to drop dead — which He did, but not for long — He still invites us to return home any time we're ready. There's more to life than we find in the pig pen. The Father offers us a robe, a ring and a roast beef dinner, with family and friends around His table. Come on home!

FIFTH SUNDAY OF LENT (C)
Is 43:16-21   Ph 3:8-14   Jn 8:1-11

The *Accused*, a young woman, was forced in front of the crowd. The *Accusers*, the Scribes and Pharisees, experts of and devotees to the ancient religious law, publicly announced her offense. The *Judge*, Jesus, also an expert lawyer (but more people-than law-centered), was challenged to pronounce the verdict.

This charade was orchestrated by the enemies of Jesus, not from a sense of justice but to publicly embarrass both Him and the woman. If He granted her freedom, He would be openly rejecting the law. If He observed the law and permitted her death for adultery, He would be contradicting His own previous teaching. The baited trap, deviously set, appeared inescapable.

Momentarily He studied the dust of the earth, the origin and destiny of the human body, then let it run mutely through His hands and doodled in it with His finger. Did He think of how human nature, like the dust, was so easily manipulated — pushed this way and that with little resistance, clinging to what it touches? Did He silently wonder why this woman, known to the Hebrews as the weaker sex, should be condemned to death when the man, presumably the stronger, should go free?

The woman's fate — to live or die — seemed to hang in the balance awaiting His decision, but in reality there was never any doubt concerning the verdict. She would live and He would tell her of God's love, which would kindly lead her to repentance.

Jesus challenged the self-justified accusers to judge their own hearts as they had this woman. Since all were guilty of sin, there was no move to execute the woman. This dramatic yet tender message of mercy, demonstrated by Jesus and told by John, is the story of *The Stone Not Thrown.*

Even today, many still believe in throwing stones which kill the good name of another — character assassination. Often those who smugly stand in judgment and hurl their condemnations are more guilty of the same sins than their accused victims.

Jesus doesn't snuff out the smoldering wick or break the bruised reed. He could trace the sins of any of us in the dust — not for others to see, but to show us that He knows. Jesus doesn't write them in rock to remain but in dust, to be blown away with His forgiving breath.

The story of *The Stone Not Thrown* summons us to judge our own hearts; to live and let live.

PALM SUNDAY (C)
Lk 19:28-40   Is 50:4-7   Ph 2:6-11   Lk 22:14-23:56

Today's Gospel reading, preparing us for the week ahead, is the passion account by St. Luke. Although similar to the other Gospels, it makes unique contributions to enrich our faith in the suffering of Jesus. The following, for example, are some unparalleled Lucan passages. He alone mentions the sweating of blood; the shuffling of Jesus between Pilate and Herod; the conversations of

Jesus and the two criminals as they hang on their crosses. Also peculiar to Luke is the discourse between Jesus and the women of Jerusalem, and the healing of the servant's ear which had been cut off by a sword in the garden.

It appears that Luke was trying to show the ministering mercy of Jesus to the very end, in spite of His own personal sufferings. He views Jesus as the man in the middle, serving, uniting and bringing peace to all who come into contact with Him. It's ironic how His trial brought a sense of unity to the country of Israel, by establishing friendship between the Roman, Pilate, ruler of the South and the Northern leader, Herod the Jew. Jesus too was in the midst of the Jerusalem women, giving them courage on His road to death.

Dying between two criminals, one jeering, the other supporting, He ministered with the promise of paradise. He hung between earth and sky, between God and humanity, with the rough wooden beams crossing between his head and heart. Both realistically and symbolically, Jesus was and is the center of salvation history — never faltering but manifesting courageous love under pressure.

One final unique contribution by Luke is the passage about the agony in the garden, where an angel came to minister to Jesus. The angel is unnamed and unknown and perhaps, we think, unnecessary — for what can one insignificant angel do for the Son of God? His visit does help Jesus, giving Him needed strength and support simply by his presence. The human fall in the Garden of Paradise had necessitated the Garden of Gethsemani, with a new Adam and a new beginning. Jesus was tempted to side-step the approaching agony, praying: "Father, if possible let this cup pass me by." But, perhaps aided by the presence of the unknown angel, He accepted the bitter choice.

Like angels, we can minister to others — even those more powerful and intelligent — simply by our presence in times of need. On Holy Thursday we recall the Last Supper, the First Mass, the institution of the Priesthood, and the washing of the feet, but don't forget that it's also the anniversary of the agony in the garden.

Can we, like the nameless angel, spend some quiet time with the Lord that night by our physical presence in church? Can we also stand near His cross the next day? We may hear Him whisper our name with a promise of paradise.

EASTER SUNDAY (C)
Ac 10:34, 37-43   Col 3:1-4   Jn 20:1-9

We come to church today knowing that the prayers, readings, homily and music will all tell of the Resurrection of Jesus from the grave. This is the good news of Easter Sunday, which we prepare for and celebrate each year. In this sense our annual celebration is very different from the first Easter. That day the apostles didn't know the victim would become the victor. They felt that the victim would remain a victim, and they would see no more of Jesus.

For the sake of speculation, suppose Jesus had not risen up bodily from the grave. Would Christianity have flourished to become the great world religion it is today? Founders of other major religions such as Abraham, Confucius, Buddha, Mohammed, etc. did not rise up bodily from the dead, yet their religious doctrines spread and continue to this day. Thus the Resurrection probably was not absolutely essential for Christianity's beginning and survival.

The Resurrection therefore should not be the sole criterion by which we judge the authenticity of Jesus and His teachings. Although our belief in and love of Jesus does not depend entirely on the Resurrection, it is nonetheless the best evidence we have for our belief that He is God and can do anything He wishes.

Notice that His major rejections took place before the Resurrection — Peter's denial; Judas' betrayal; Pilate's unjust sentence and the feisty opposition of the Scribes and Pharisees. Had these people witnessed the Resurrection, they could never have stood in opposition to Him. Therefore we, the post-Resurrection people, should be firm in our faith, for we have experienced His overpowering glory.

The reaction of the disciples on the first Easter Sunday was very curious — almost humorous. They ran directly to the spot where they were told Jesus wasn't. They did not know where He was, but for the time being they were more interested in precisely where He was not. Once they knew where He wasn't, then they remembered and understood what He had said about rising from the dead. They now knew that He was alive and well, just as He had said.

Dead men do talk, for after His death Jesus said, "Do not be afraid," and "I am with you all days even unto the end of the world." The Resurrection is God's stamp of approval on the words and deeds of Jesus. It is good news for all who must face the grave.

SECOND SUNDAY OF EASTER (C)
Ac 5:12-16   Rv 1:9-11, 12-13, 17-19   Jn 20:19-31

Each year on this Sunday following Easter, the same selection from John is read, telling how the apostles locked themselves in the upper room "for fear of the Jews." A modern commentator speculated that John doesn't tell the whole story; there was another reason why they bolted the doors — fear of Jesus.

There was increasing evidence that Jesus had risen from the dead, and soon would be paying them a visit. But they were not ready to face Him. The Eleven, whom He considered His most trusted friends, had failed Him miserably during His trial and death. They had been too terrified to support or even acknowledge Him. All had abandoned Him except John, who stood beside His mother. Now they were painfully ashamed of their cowardice and were fearful of encountering an angry Master. Locking themselves in their room showed their awkward immaturity; they were like little boys who had broken a window and were tensely awaiting punishment from their father.

As they pondered what He might say or do, and how they should react, He suddenly was standing in their midst. His first words were "Peace be with you." Whew! What a sigh of relief must have circulated the room. If the Lord had been disappointed or angry, He had now forgiven them and there was no mention of chastisement.

Following His peace-greetings and victory-smile, He showed them His scarred hands. His true identity was not doubted, for He also displayed the wound in His ribs where the spear had punctured his heart. John tells us this in an emotional and descriptive sentence: "At the sight of the Lord the disciples rejoiced." The first peace-message of His risen life was repeated a second time, and then He told them to do for others what He had done for them, by being merciful and harboring no grudges.

To be Christ-like can mean a variety of things, but perhaps being peaceful and forgiving comes as close as any. Had Jesus sought revenge, this would have been the ideal time and place, but that thought did not enter His mind. We are not only expected to retell the mercy of Jesus but to demonstrate it in our personal conduct by loving our "enemies" — those who have hurt us, been unfaithful and abandoned us in our times of urgent need.

Any of us could easily justify the "sweet revenge" approach against others and it may even be humanly satisfying — but it would mean that we were spiritually immature. Jesus uplifts us to a risen life above the old hurts — on the highway to exalted happiness.

THIRD SUNDAY OF EASTER (C)
Ac 5:27-32, 40-41   Rv 5:11-14   Jn 21:1-19

Jesus was raised in northern Palestine in Galilee, in the agricultural country far removed from the noisy imperial city of Jerusalem in the south. In recruiting His apostles, He chose Galileans, with the exception of Judas, who came from Kerioth in Judea.

Many of these young men were called from their fishing boats off the Sea of Galilee. During their three years of apprenticeship they learned to give speeches, manage huge crowds and adjust gradually to an entirely different mode of life. Each morning they would awaken expecting new and fascinating events, orchestrated by their miracle-working Leader.

Together they traveled the entire length of the country, and became familiar with Jerusalem and its massive Temple, protecting stone wall and winding streets. They learned the ways of the Scribes, Pharisees and Sadducees, with their varied political, legal and religious leanings. But always they walked in and were shielded by the lengthening shadow of their fearless Master.

When Jesus was captured, they suddenly found themselves frightened and weak. Fear of the volatile Jerusalem mob caused Peter to utter, "I swear, I don't know the man." Judas also, pulled more by avarice than loyalty, here decided to end his life in suicide. It was this same city with its vying tensions and frenzied crowds that brought Jesus to His painful death.

Now in today's Gospel that all seems to be far behind them. The young men from Galilee are back on their favorite lake, doing what they did three years earlier — fishing those blue, enchanted waters. It was almost as though they had never left, but the first chapter of Christianity had been written and they had witnessed every move.

Chapter two begins on this warm spring morning with the risen Jesus calling them from the fishing boats for the second time.

He invites them to breakfast on the beach with a calm pastoral setting as a background. Here they are asked to make their commitments as leaders of the newly founded Church. Their baptisms have been completed and confirmation day is only a few weeks away. They must decide, once and for all, between the Church and the fishing boat.

We see Peter making his triple profession of love and hear his future fate of crucifixion. The others also pledge their lifelong loyalty to Jesus and once again the abandoned fishing boats are left tied to the piers. Soon they will leave their beloved north country for their fiery Pentecostal confirmation in Jerusalem; then on to their mission — wise, Spirit-filled and beyond intimidation.

FOURTH SUNDAY OF EASTER (C)
Ac 13:14, 43-52   Rv 7:9, 14-17   Jn 10:27-30

"I'm a person not a sheep," exclaimed a lady attending a Bible class. She told how the biblical passages referring to people as sheep always made her cringe. Some others who said they "hadn't really thought about it before," agreed that she made a good point. I tried to explain that the sheep and shepherd expressions (and many other scriptural verses) are poetic — not meant to be taken literally.

As the shepherd and sheep theme runs through today's liturgy, please remember that there is no implication that we are dumb animals, blindly led by another. The Bible is truly a book of many literary styles. There is much poetry in it, meant to be interpreted by common poetic rules.

Take for example the verse, "I am the vine and you are the branches." It's not literally true, of course — but Jesus is like a vine as our source of life and strength; and we are like branches, being dependent on Him.

In another instance He called His apostles "fishers of men."

Literally this would be a crude image, especially if we are the fish dangling from a hook or entangled in a net. The expression simply means that they will bring many people to God, as a fisherman catches many fish. The analogy is not meant to be carried further. In similar fashion, Jesus literally is not a shepherd and we are not sheep. But poetically He knows, loves and cares for us like a shepherd, and we trust and follow Him like sheep. The Hebrews to whom these words were addressed thought and spoke in very concrete images, and the message was clear and powerful.

The shepherd symbol applied to God has long been a favorite, for unlike most other animals the sheep voluntarily follow the shepherd rather than being chased from behind. It is also said that in ancient times the shepherd would break one leg of an unruly sheep which constantly strayed, lest it get lost or killed by predators. The shepherd then would carry the injured sheep whenever the flock moved. When the leg finally healed, the sheep would never stray again for it was now the shepherd's pet.

Our Good Shepherd blesses us with guidance and discipline for our good, lest we stray and get lost. Jesus, in taking human flesh, accommodated Himself to our nature, language and ways. Whether it's leading, feeding or healing, the analogy of the shepherd and his sheep is fittingly applied to the spiritual bond between the Savior and His people.

FIFTH SUNDAY OF EASTER (C)
Ac 14:21-27   Rv 21:1-5   Jn 13:31-35

"I was never able to thank him personally, but we looked into each other's eyes before he was led away." That dramatic encounter was between a 40 year old political prisoner, arbitrarily condemned to death, and another man who volunteered to die in his place. Francizek Gajowniczek has now more than doubled his years of earthly life since that fateful day at Auschwitz in July 1941. The other man, Fr. Maximilian Kolbe, died two weeks later in his 47th year, but not in vain.

In Oct. 1982, 150,000 worshipers gathered in the Piazza of St. Peter's to witness Pope John Paul II (who says that his own vocation was inspired by Fr. Kolbe) pronounce his fellow countryman a canonized saint of the Church. "Greater love has no man than this," said the Pope, "that a man lay down his life for his friends." He was reading from the Gospel of John the words of Jesus, who knows all about laying down one's life for one's friends.

The world stands in awe of the heroic deed of Kolbe, but what he did was no more than is expected of any Christian who is serious about taking Jesus at His word. In today's Gospel, John is again proclaiming the boundless love taught by Jesus. "I give you a new commandment: Love one another. Such as my love has been for you, so must your love be for each other" (Jn 13:34).

The commandment was new in the sense that it called one to a universal love of the deepest intensity — the love with which He loves us. The old commandment: "Love your neighbor as yourself," found in Lv 19:18, is terribly challenging but not as much as the new commandment. For example, the word "neighbor" is somewhat limiting in scope and the Jews debated about who was included in the term. The new commandment to "love one another" is without any limiting borders. Also, the intensity is different. The old commandment expected us to love others as much as we love ourselves. The new commandment says to love others as much as Jesus has loved us. Our self-love is no doubt intense, but the Lord's love for us is more intense.

A sure proof of genuine love is giving your life for another, as the Savior did — and Fr. Kolbe. St. Peter talked about dying for Jesus before His crucifixion but that was empty talk, no more meaningful than a rooster crowing at daybreak. Later, when he had matured in faith, Peter fulfilled his promise and died a martyr's death.

In a cold and violent world, full of hatred, Fr. Kolbe demonstrated that he truly was a disciple of Jesus by his love for another.

SIXTH SUNDAY OF EASTER (C)
Ac 15:1-2, 22-29   Rv 21:10-14, 22-23   Jn 14:23-29

Before Jesus ascended into heaven, He demonstrated that His boundless love would be as true and constant when away as when present. Since we celebrate His spectacular Ascension soon, these timely reminders of divine intimacy are presented today.

The theme of enduring love which threads its way through the fabric of our Gospel can also be applied to the annual celebration of Mother's Day.

The affection of a mother for her children is perhaps our best analogy of God's love for us. The marital love of husband and wife may be more intense and expressive, but when it encounters tension, unfaithfulness and other hardships, we sadly know how easily it fails. The alarming divorce rate only too clearly shows how many marriages were based on short-lived attraction, and how they died bitter deaths with no hope of resurrection.

A mother's love, on the contrary, strikingly resembles God's love and can endure many dark days or even years of neglect, pain and confusion and still be ready to forgive and take back the erring one. We try to consciously recall the divine fondness for frail humanity by the deliberate use of the term, "Holy *Mother* Church."

It would seem logical to suppose that much of the spontaneous tenderness exhibited by Jesus in word and deed came from the gracious influence of His mother. Her amiable qualities perhaps likewise molded the fiery young John into the "Apostle of Love" during the years he cared for her, fulfilling the last wish of Jesus.

The observance of Mother's Day resonates with definite religious overtones as we acknowledge unfailing devotion, constant understanding, a kindness often abused, taken for granted and yet never withdrawn.

Several years ago Erma Bombeck wrote a column about God making the very first mother, which I will summarize. He gave her fascinating eyes to see through closed doors, knowing what the kids are doing before she asks. Those same gentle eyes can talk to a child who fails, saying: "I understand and love you." God was fashioning her beautifully soft but very tough, when a curious angel, watching the creation, ran his finger across her face and said, "Oh, there's a leak here." God quickly explained it was not a leak but a tear. The angel asked the meaning of a tear and God said it stood for "joy, sadness, disappointment, pain, loneliness and pride in her family." The angel smiled and told God He was a real genius to place a tear on her face. God looked puzzled and replied, "But I didn't put it there!"

Every mother's cheeks have had their share of tears. God didn't put them there, but He knows why they're there and so do we. Thanks for caring.

THE ASCENSION (C)
Ac 1:1-11   Ep 1:17-23   Lk 24:46-53

Jesus lived 30 quiet years, then 3 of intense activity, culminating in His death and resurrection. In His risen state he resided 40 more days on this earth and returned to heaven. The anxious apostles protested His departure, but the Lord said it was for the best. Before becoming outward bound from here to eternity, Jesus pledged to send the Holy Spirit as a vigorous Presence in His newborn congregation. Jesus is the energetic Leader of a pilgrim people and when His mission was fulfilled, His farewell was expected. According to His Father's will He had to let go of this world, and so do we.

Life is an unbroken series of letting go of one phase and moving on to the next. We are graduated from one class in school to the next in a rhythmic pattern until we reach our final graduation. We let go of the past and a familiar way of life when we move to a new neighborhood. Aging is a slow development from this first life to the second, requiring delicate adjustments along the way, by which we are positioned into the proper attitude for a new birth in the heavenly Kingdom. Death for some tolls the sounds of finality — the end of all; but for others it is the final graduation — a fresh beginning in the land to where Jesus ascended.

Many times we resent the persistent pace of reality, moving us from one stage of existence to the next. Some parents, for example, cannot accept the fact of their children growing up, accepting responsibility and leaving home. They prefer to acknowledge them only as little girls and boys. The problem is within themselves, for they don't want to face their own aging process.

If we rebel at every hint of change whether within ourselves, the Church or society, then the mere thought of leaving this world becomes for us very frightening. If we could always see life as a constant change from day to day and even from minute to minute, then our thoughts of death and departure would be far less upsetting.

Our religious development should also keep pace with our years. It should relate to Jesus as He was at different stages of His life. We first met Him as little children and identified with His role as a Child, for He appeared very similar to us. Some unfortunately have never moved beyond this cradle spirituality even in their mature years. The crib life was short-lived and the Infant in the manger doesn't answer the ambiguous questions adults ask. We must follow the grownup Jesus through His sermons and come to Gethsemani and Calvary, into death and back again, and finally to His return to heaven to be with the Father.

The Church herself must age and mature, just as people do. She has moved geographically from the tiny upper room, to the

Middle East, and then to Europe and the world over. From the small handful of believers described in the Acts of the Apostles, she now embraces millions of people of all races and conditions.

Our daily way of life should be dramatic, moving and constantly changing. It's a series of accomplishing the tasks at hand, then passing to the next level; then letting go and being lifted up all the way from here to eternity.

SEVENTH SUNDAY OF EASTER (C)
Ac 7:55-60 Rv 22:12-14, 16-17, 20 Jn 17:20-26

The first reading today presents an inspiring story of a courageous young man named Stephen. He was one of the seven deacons chosen from and by the community of first-generation Christians, and approved by the Apostles. They were deeply spiritual and prudent men chosen to preach in the name of Jesus and care for the needy. False charges were brought against Stephen, and he was tried before the Jewish general court — the Sanhedrin. There, he demonstrated his understanding of Jewish history and concluded by accusing his audience of opposing the Holy Spirit. The people were infuriated and dragged him out of the Temple and stoned him to death.

As he lay dying, his thoughts were on his Master, praying: "Lord Jesus, receive my spirit." Then, crying out in a loud voice, he said, "Lord, do not hold this sin against them." Then he died.

Stephen's death was very valiant and served as a morale builder for the early suffering Christians. His brief life and gallant martyrdom have continued to inspire following generations, and the Church presents him today as a role model of fearless courage and Christian conviction.

The Christians of the twentieth century need inspiration as much as those of the first century, especially the young who often see life as cold and empty. Several years ago a national study revealed that at least 35 young people in the U.S.A. commit suicide every day. This certainly must betray a lack of inspiration, with shattered dreams and goals too remote to be attained. There is a profound difference between taking your life and giving your life, as in the case of the young Stephen. There are many inspiring stories of stars, heroes and heroines, but few of them are in sports or the movies.

One such superstar is Mother Teresa of Calcutta. In 1946 she abandoned her "safe" position of geography teacher in a private girls' school and changed career, life style and religious order to minister to the poor, sick and dying. It's a type of total giving, like St. Stephen. The people who do such things are tremendously inspiring.

In his "Psalm Of Life," Longfellow wrote:

> *Lives of great men all remind us*
> *We can make our lives sublime,*
> *And departing, leave behind us*
> *Footprints on the sands of time.*

Life is boring, useless and without purpose only for those who wish to make it such. There are millions of models, past and present, whose lives can lift ours to a higher level. Remember that a better you makes a better world. Nobody was created just to be a nobody.

PENTECOST (C)
Ac 2:1-11   1 Cor 12:3-7, 12-13   Jn 20:19-23

Today is the celebration of *Wind and Fire*. The word "pentecost," per se, does not adequately describe this celebration. It is simply a Greek word meaning "50th day" — that is, the 50th day after Easter. On this day, however, the apostles and the other first

Christians truly got ecstatic about their mission of preaching Jesus. They were all inspired.

The dramatic story of Pentecost is told in the Acts of the Apostles, sometimes called the "Gospel of the Holy Spirit." It tells how God "put a tiger in the Church's tank," and how she started to move, expand and preach boldly to people everywhere. Some were willing, even anxious to die for Jesus, like young Stephen. Some did a complete turnabout with their lives, like Paul.

Others found themselves not only able to speak in unknown tongues but to work astonishing miracles. Peter cured a crippled man and Philip seemed to receive the gift of fleet-footedness, when he ran and overtook a chariot pulled by running horses. He heard the driver reading from Isaiah, and explained to him how this was a prophecy of Jesus. Philip baptized the driver in a roadside pond and disappeared, snatched away by the Holy Spirit. He had to be inspired. The leaders were no longer afraid to face the world, for they had the Spirit. They were going out and speaking out.

Like His death and Resurrection, the descent of the Holy Spirit was also predicted by Jesus. This crowning event of redemption confirmed and sealed the Church's confidence in the person of Jesus and His word.

Pentecost, we emphasize, is not just for Pentecostals — any more than baptism is only for Baptists. Although interpreted in various ways, Pentecost is for all Christian believers. To live Pentecost we need not pray in tongues, hold hands in the air, or punctuate statements with "amen," and "praise the Lord." These are praiseworthy if natural and sincere, but to be pentecostal is to be Spirit-filled.

To speak truthfully is to imitate the spirit of Pentecost. To live sincerely without dominating is to live Pentecost. We share the work of the Spirit when we speak to others of God, reflect Him in our actions and support with encouragement and donations those who sincerely tell of His love and mercy from the pulpit and through radio, TV and the press. It's all a part of modernizing the age-old message by making all come alive in the name of Jesus.

Today's liturgy is meant to move us in the flow of the Spirit and make it hard to sit still. Man alive! There's lots of good news to inspire us and enable others to see and feel the Wind and Fire.

TRINITY SUNDAY (C)
Pr 8:22-31   Rm 5:1-5   Jn 16:12-15

The people who ask the most questions about God are children and theologians — and their questions are surprisingly similar. Does God exist? Where does He live? What does He look like? Where did He come from and how does He spend His "time"? The search never stops. When one inquiry is answered, it usually triggers others.

Actually, the deep mysteries of religion are not answered but only commented on. Even Jesus didn't give direct responses most of the time. He replied with a story, a parable, or a comment. "What is the Kingdom?" they asked, and He responded, "It's a net full of fish." "How about the Church, what is it?" "A mustard seed." "How can you tell if a person is wise or foolish?" "One builds a house on rock, the other on sand." These are not complete answers but enlightening comments designed to make people think.

Trinity Sunday presents us with some real puzzlers. Can you explain the Holy Trinity? No! But we can make a comment: it's like a triangle, a shamrock or something that is three and yet one. The mystery deepens as we try to explain the perplexing ways in which our triune God relates to mankind. We simply don't know why good people suffer and sometimes die young, or why God permits serious accidents, personal violence, hatred and war.

Religion is well supplied with a multitude of unfolding mysteries of which the Trinity is only one — but the major one. It's no real accomplishment to ask a question which perplexes the experts, for we have millions more good questions than good answers. People often think that the priest, bishop or pope, is the "answer man." Not so. These persons are expected to have some penetrating insights, but basically they cannot answer religious mysteries. Their best response is to make an intelligent comment in the form of a symbol, story or perhaps a simple act of faith.

The mysteries of religion are not the kind which are waiting to be solved. Rather, they are to continue as mysteries and be acknowledged and appreciated. The Trinity is saying something to us about God's inmost nature. Although it is beyond human explanation, we will have our own "answers" but they will all be incomplete. God is too big and complicated for our little minds to grasp completely. But even though He cannot be fully explained, we can always admire and believe in Him.

It is an even deeper mystery why this infinitely intelligent and all-powerful Creator has freely chosen to love creatures like us. Another mysterious question is: How in the world did we ever get invited to His home, to live with Him forever? What a lovely mystery!

CORPUS CHRISTI (C)
Gn 14:18-20   1 Cor 11:23-26   Lk 9:11-17

Remember the old commercial: "Wonder bread builds strong bodies 12 ways"? It's a good example of the advertising technique called "implied uniqueness." The implication is that the other breads do not build strong bodies 12 ways — although probably they do, for they're all basically the same.

Today on the Feast of Corpus Christi, we proudly present the "Wonder Bread of the Altar," making mighty claims about what this sacred Bread is and does. The Church is not using the technique of "implied uniqueness" but is saying outright: this is the

Bread that came down from Heaven, and it is unique for it's the Body of Christ.

The Holy Eucharist is an honored memorial of the *Risen Christ*, who at the Last Supper both announced His departure from this world and promised to remain in the breaking of the Bread. The Church sees eucharistic overtones in other scriptural passages — in Jesus' multiplication of the loaves to feed the multitude, and even in the manna, the bread from heaven, that Moses and the Israelites gathered on the Exodus in the 12th century B.C.

This religious Wonder Bread has a rich and ancient history and is unique in its ability to fashion healthy Christian lives, in 12 ways and many more. Frequent reception of Holy Communion has long been advocated as a singular way to spiritual advancement. The tiny grains of wheat from which the Bread is made were buried in the teeming earth like Christ and then rose up to new life.

Precisely how Jesus is present in the Bread has been a centuries-old controversy, which unfortunately still divides the various Christian churches. Catholics profess a real and permanent presence; Presbyterians and Methodists understand it more in a figurative sense; some Lutherans follow a middle course and see the presence as real but temporary. Some see the presence in the Bread, others in the believers. In ecumenical pursuits most Protestants say that Communion is a "means" to achieve unity with a person of another denomination, and encourage intercommunion. Catholics see it as a "sign" of complete unity already achieved, and therefore do not favor intercommunion.

We could all improve unity between God and humanity and among people and religions in general if we could make Jesus more present in our daily lives especially after we have received Holy Communion. If we profess the Real Presence, and in Holy Communion accept the Lord into our lives, then Jesus should be visible in us to all we meet.

FEAST OF PETER AND PAUL
(see p. 40)

THE ASSUMPTION OF THE BLESSED VIRGIN MARY (C)
Rv 11:19, 12:1-6, 10   1 Cor 15:20-26   Lk 1:39-56

Today we celebrate Mary's personal fulfillment. Most people try to be fulfilled in this world, but many take the wrong approach and never find the peace they seek. The prayerful Magnificat of Mary in our Gospel reading refers to the various false ways that people try to find contentment on this earth. Some try to belong to the class of the mighty and dominate other people. Others are too proud and become instantly unhappy when they discover that someone else has possessions and honors which they lack. Mary also says that the rich are not inwardly contented and that the poor in many ways are more fortunate. The mother of Jesus, like her Son, is teaching the paradoxical mystery that things and people are often the exact opposite from what they appear.

There is no total or perfect fulfillment in this world, but those who are seriously preparing themselves for the eternal future do experience even here an inward contentment. Mary says that the way to ultimate happiness is the road of lowliness — in other words, having a true and honest picture of one's self. The humble and poor in spirit are not concerned about projecting any image except the one which is true. Mary is a grand example of the combination of indescribable dignity with matchless humility.

The Virgin Mary is taken to heaven and glorified not only as a woman but as a representative of the entire human race. She gave birth to only one Child but He has become the adopted Brother of millions. She, therefore, is called "mother" by Christians throughout the world. Mary is our best model of a gracious and peace-filled lady, for she found a way of life which worked for her and she faithfully lived it to the fullest. Her assumption into heaven was the eternal reward by her heavenly Father for her most beautiful and productive life.

One day, I asked a fourth grade class what event is celebrated on August 15th. One boy replied, "That's the day the Blessed Virgin Mary was zoomed into heaven." The class giggled but he had been serious, and I explained the need to both hear and see words in order to understand them. "Zoomed" and "assumed" not only sound alike, I thought later, but being "zoomed into heaven" is a graphic picture of this event in Mary's life.

The Magnificat-values are presented today to demonstrate the way this unique lady successfully lived them out. The feast also speaks to the sacredness of the human body, for God took it to Himself. It also presupposes and reinforces belief in eternal life on the other side of death.

Joyfully we celebrate the glories of Mary, sing her praises and participate in public worship with our brothers and sisters in faith, for we are all children of this dear and loving mother. Perhaps also at home today, we might find time to pray the 4th glorious mystery of the rosary. Collectively and individually we renew our hope and offer our prayers that when our days on earth are spent, we too will be "zoomed into heaven."

ALL SAINTS (C)
Rv 7:2-4, 9-14   1 Jn 3:1-3   Mt 5:1-12

Too often during presidential campaigns, political organizers discuss what kind of images they wish to create for their candidates. That terminology reminds me more of casting for a leading role in a movie than selecting a person to lead the nation. A good image is necessary to get elected, but are we satisfied only with the outward appearance? Don't we care to see the real person beneath the image, and don't we have a right to?

We all like to know what other people think of us and whether we are approved and accepted by them. As Christians, however, if we were as concerned about our image from God's point of view as we are about the way other people see us, we would be well on the way to sanctity. Just imagine our daily efforts if we always kept in mind that God reads our innermost hearts and we always tried to impress Him. It would make us genuine people, reflecting outwardly the true picture of our real selves.

The saints were and are those kinds of people and the Church presents them to us today for our adulation and imitation, in their ways of outstanding holiness. The past is filled with them and we have every reason to believe that the future will be likewise. We're well acquainted with the famous holy names of the past and some of the household names of our day, but who will be the saints of tomorrow? Where will they come from? Have you ever really thought of aspiring to be a future saint? Everyone has a chance, for there's no one way nor one type of person to become a saint.

A traveling portrait painter stopped in a small village hoping to get some business. The town drunk came along in his ragged and dirty clothes, unshaved and unbathed. In his state of partial intoxication, he wanted his portrait painted and the artist complied. He worked painstakingly for a long time, painting not what he saw but what he envisioned beneath that disheveled exterior. Finally he removed the painting from the easel and presented it to his customer. "That's not me," he shouted. The artist gently laid his hand on the man's shoulder and replied, "But that's the man you could be."

Everyone needs to be challenged to a higher and better style of life, and the invitation is especially vital for hurting and discouraged members of society. The important aspect is not where we've started but where we hope to end. God's graces and our encouragements can turn a tragic beginning into a brilliant success.

Regardless of what and who we are at present or have been in the past we can be better, virtuous, and saintly. Anyone can do it and millions have. Many have accomplished a nearly 100% change in their lives on the road to holiness. Today we offer our prayerful petitions that we continually change for the better and begin right now with stubborn determination to become the persons we really can be.

THE IMMACULATE CONCEPTION (C)
Gn 3:9-15, 20   Ep 1:3-6, 11-12   Lk 1:26-38

In 1792 a baby boy was born to the Ferretti family who lived in a small village in Italy. He was named John. As he grew into manhood, John realized and appreciated the many unique blessings which had been given to him. He was intelligent, very handsome and belonged to a noble family. Besides these many gifts, however, there was one particularly bitter sorrow in his young life. He had epilepsy.

He prayed fervently to be cured of his illness and miraculously the disease disappeared entirely. John attributed this to the intercession of the Blessed Virgin Mary, and with deep gratitude he vowed to spread her tender devotion and motherly love to all people. He even officially took for himself the middle name of Mary.

On December 8, 1854, the Pope published an encyclical, *Ineffabilis Deus*, where he proclaimed the Immaculate Conception to be a defined doctrine of the Catholic Church. How do you suppose John reacted to this honor conferred upon Mary by the Pope? He was deeply pleased for, you see, John Ferretti was the Pope.

He had been elected in 1846 and took the title of Pius IX. One of his first acts was to send letters to all the bishops of the world, soliciting their views about defining the Immaculate Conception as an article of faith. Three bishops replied negatively but over 600 answered with an enthusiastic yes. The teaching therefore which he proclaimed to the world was that Mary was preserved from all sin before and during her entire life.

Today we continue to teach and celebrate this unique Marian privilege as defined by Pius IX, and the Church still invites us to give praise and honor on her feast day, for we see her as the new Eve and the beginning of a renewed creation. Mary was a new creation in her own right, not subject to the inheritance of old sins and failings. Pius IX taught that she was preserved both from the sin itself and also the effects of it. She inherited the best of the old with none of its weaknesses; concerning sin, she never had to say she was sorry.

By baptism we too have been delivered from the original fall. Although we still struggle with personal weaknesses and unfaithfulness, we believe that holiness is obtainable, "for nothing is impossible with God." Holy Mary, preserved from sin, pray for us sinners, now and when we die. Amen.

SECOND SUNDAY OF THE YEAR (C)
Is 62:1-5 1 Cor 12:4-11 Jn 2:1-12

We normally would not expect to hear a Sunday Gospel about wine, women and song, but this is what John presents today. He tells of a wedding reception which Jesus, His mother and the apostles attended. The crowd was drinking wine, dancing and singing, with Jesus joining in the merriment.

Jesus' presence at the wedding feast at Cana makes some people feel uneasy. To remedy the dismaying situation, they say that it wasn't wine Jesus and the other guests were drinking, but grape juice. I agreed it was grape juice at one time, but that was long before the wedding reception. Isn't it ironic that many fundamentalists who advocate the literal meaning for every word of scripture, say in this case that *wine* means *grape juice*?

Well, back at the reception, they were having a good time because "at a certain point the wine ran out." The waiters filled six stone water jars with water, each holding about 20 gallons; and quicker than you could say "fermentation," Jesus produced 120 more gallons of "the bubbly stuff." Then the singing, dancing and drinking continued, with the groom being complimented on the quality of his wine. Whatever and whomever the Lord blesses, takes on genuine quality. He makes neither cheap people nor cheap wine.

This benevolent miracle in fact was not Jesus' original idea. He was practically "forced" into it by His mother. At first Jesus protested, stating that He would make no wine before His time. But the Virgin Mary convinced Him that this was the time. Thus, John is presenting a warm, humanistic view of Mary. She did not live her entire life with a sword of sorrow piercing her heart. She too could laugh, dance, sing and order 120 gallons of wine.

On several occasions people have told me that they would not be serving alcoholic beverages at their marriage reception, for they were having "a Christian wedding." I suppose they consider the whole Cana affair very un-Christian.

The key concept is *to use but not abuse*. Drinking wine, like eating food, spending money, using time, sex, sleep, work or whatever should be done with thoughtful intelligence. We can be foodoholics, talkoholics, sexoholics, workoholics or alcoholics but still we should not condemn something because people abuse it. "I'll drink to that," is an old and sacred expression for giving your word. It's an unwritten signature, a promise to keep your part of the bargain.

We know there was a heavy concentration of pain and sorrow in the lives of Jesus, Mary and the apostles — but here we meet them in one of their most joyful, relaxed times.

Our Lord proclaims the goodness of all creation. All things can add to the fullness of life. Jesus demonstrates at Cana how recreation and having fun go hand in hand with work and prayer.

THIRD SUNDAY OF THE YEAR (C)
Ne 8:2-10   1 Cor 12:12-30   Lk 1:1-4, 4:14-21

Today we are graciously invited by St. Luke to attend an ancient Jewish worship service, in the Nazareth synagogue. The guest rabbi is Jesus, briefly visiting His hometown. An attendant hands Him a scroll which he slowly unrolls. He then reads aloud Isaiah 61:1-2, "The spirit of the Lord is upon me; therefore He has anointed me. He has sent me to bring glad tidings to the poor, to proclaim liberty to captives, recovery of sight to the blind and release to prisoners. To announce a year of favor from the Lord."

He rolls up the scroll and sits down, while we ponder the meaning of the passage and the identity of the person of whom Isaiah is speaking. "Today this Scripture passage is fulfilled in your hearing," Jesus finally says. He is claiming to be the Messiah and declares that the prophet is referring to Him. Many of the congregation snicker in disgust; they don't believe Him.

Now it's twenty centuries later. We hear the very same words read at Mass and we question again His bold pronouncement. Is Jesus the Messiah? Has He fulfilled the promises He made?

We acknowledge Him as the Messiah, the One anointed by God. We address Him as Christ, which means "anointed." We likewise assert that He did and still does carry out His pledges to the poor, the captives, the blind and prisoners.

Notice that He didn't promise to make the poor rich, but to bring them glad tidings. The world today is full of poor people but because of the life and teachings of Jesus, they can better cope with poverty. Christianity has brought glad tidings to the poor in numerous ways — as in the example and deeds of St. Francis of Assisi, St. Vincent de Paul, Mother Teresa and in the works of Catholic charities and the like.

The blind, still physically without sight, have faith and hope in Jesus, which gives them clearer insight into the meaning of their deprivation and acceptance of their heavy crosses. Captives and prisoners too can experience much freedom in spirit, if they turn to Jesus asking forgiveness while attempting to reform their lives.

The Lord came to bring inner peace and freedom regardless of external circumstances. If we interpret His promises literally (externally), He would be a failure as long as there were poor, blind and captive people. In many ways the external world seems unaffected by Jesus. His words are addressed to the human spirit.

It is highly unlikely that the world can ever be free of crime, disease and pain, but the human mind can find hope, liberty and glad tidings by accepting the person and message of the Messiah. "The Kingdom of God," He said, "is within you."

FOURTH SUNDAY OF THE YEAR (C)
Jr 1:4-5, 17-19   1 Cor 12:31-13:13   Lk 4:21-30

Tell people they're attractive, intelligent and suave; they'll sing your praises and call you the greatest. Admonish them for imprudence or sinfulness; they'll lose composure and you'll lose their friendship. Most of us do not accept correction gracefully and usually tell our monitors to mind their own business.

It was, however, the sacred business of the biblical prophets to solicit reforms from society with avenging messages from God. Faithfulness to the demands of their office normally left them with few friends.

In the first reading today, we meet the outstanding prophet of the Old Testament — Jeremiah. For forty arduous years he exposed the national guilt of Judah and wrote the longest book of the entire Bible. He endured violent abuse from discontented people he tried to reform. Although God promised him personal protection like that bestowed on "a fortified city," he found his work perilous, displeasing and often revolting. Candidly he confessed his continual struggle between public commitment and personal doubt. So what motivated him to continue? It was the profound conviction that his prophetic vocation was genuine, conferred by God. Although tempted many times, he would not abandon it, lest he offend his beloved Yahweh.

Jeremiah's articulate words and unchanging pleas present a stimulating challenge for today's society which so easily "does its own thing," ignores the commandments and glibly terminates binding promises. Religious vocations, business commitments, marriage vows and personal obligations are daily forsaken in the face of whimsical conflicts. Even though his vocation was thrust upon him without choice, since he was appointed before birth as "a prophet to the nations," Jeremiah lived and died his calling. He would no doubt call our "burn-outs" "cop-outs" and term us a lax generation. Of course that would disturb us, but that was his profession.

Six hundred years later, the greatest Prophet of all times faced similar problems, as noted in today's Gospel. A mutinous and selfish crowd escorted Jesus from His hometown, intending to hurl Him over a cliff. He had dared to preach religious and social improvement to a very unreform-minded people.

The prophets continue to speak to us today, not only in scripture but in the souls and voices of those who promote the timeless values of love and honesty. Genuine prophets preach not their own words but God's, and they will suffer and even die for the message. If you can find a true prophet, you've found a real friend. He or she will lead you to God.

FIFTH SUNDAY OF THE YEAR (C)
Is 6:1-2, 3-8   1 Cor 15:1-11   Lk 5:1-11

"Holy, holy, holy . . ." is spoken to God and "Lower the nets," is spoken by God. These two brief proclamations merit bold print in today's liturgy. The author of the first, Isaiah, is recording a transitory vision he experienced while at prayer in the Temple. The angels huddled around the throne of the Almighty, and chanted in Hebrew the triple holy. This was the only way the language could express the superlative form of the adjective — by repeating the positive three times. We recognize this sublime prayer as the introduction to the canon of the Mass, still retained in the original Hebrew form.

In comparison to the vision, Isaiah saw himself as very unholy, and welcomed a lip-cleansing ceremony by the application of a burning coal. Following his searing purification, he could boldly proclaim readiness to serve God — "Here I am, send me." He is both attracted to God's adorable holiness and overjoyed that he can share in it.

The Church helps us appreciate the sacred nature of God through word and sacrament, encouraging us (like Isaiah) to imitation.

The second statement is found in the Gospel as a command of Jesus to Peter. The chief apostle was hesitant to comply, for the best time for fishing had passed with the cool hours before dawn. Being a professional fisherman, he protested what seemed bad advice. Like a seasoned fisherman Himself, Jesus patiently waited for Peter to lower the nets after he had exhausted all the reasons why he should not. Amazed at the abundant catch of fish, Peter "the expert" learned a lasting lesson about trusting the sacred word of the Lord.

It's difficult for us to follow faith's advice in daily life, especially when we feel competent and well informed. Whatever the case may be, we must humbly learn with St. Peter that our knowledge of catching fish is nothing when compared to His, Who made the fish.

These two statements originated centuries apart. Fortunately for us they are now united in the same liturgy, since they complement each other. This is the connection: if we can truly proclaim the holiness of God, believe in His profound love for us and appreciate his smiling wisdom, then with full confidence we can lower the nets at any time or to any depth He requests.

The events of life will continue to puzzle us, with accidents and diseases sidelining some, while others are blessed with good fortune. God's ways are not our ways, but His ways are best. We're on the road to holiness when at His gentle invitation we can lower the nets willingly and say to the Master, "have it your way."

SIXTH SUNDAY OF THE YEAR (C)
Jr 17:5-8   1 Cor 15:12, 16-20   Lk 6:17, 20-26

The first sentence of the Bible tells of God's loving power, creating and embracing the virgin waters of the earth. A few verses later (Gn 1:20) He calmly says, "let the water abound with life." And so it did, not only with fishes and other creatures of the deep but with the energetic life of its Maker. His presence is still manifested today, shouting from the surging ocean waves and gently reflected in the noiseless rivers. We see His life-giving graces in a cool, refreshing drink of water and there are memories of His suffering in our warm salty tears.

Having inherited His tempered power and balanced wisdom, the waters faithfully serve their Master. The same great flood both destroyed life and also saved the faith-built ark of Noah. The Red Sea drowned the charging Egyptians only after it had protected the fleeing Hebrews. In baptism, also poured with the water over the infant's head are the demanding commitment to Christian integrity and the grace to accomplish it.

In the first reading of today's Mass, Jeremiah proclaims water to be the symbol of God, speaking of divine blessings under the image of the flowing streams. Any person, he warns, who tries to live without God's blessings will become an isolated barren bush in the desert, dwelling in "a lava waste, a salt and empty earth."

The season of Lent gives a clear call to those engaged in empty or sinful pursuits, to revisit the stream of renewal and find again their true source of strength. "Blessed is the man who trusts in the Lord," says Jeremiah, for he "is like a tree planted beside the waters." Shall I be a barren, dying bush or a green, growing tree? That is the question. It's my decision — the choice of the two ways.

We should not view this season of reform as a heavy imposition, but as a joyful invitation to work in and with the Church for personal and community improvement. If we stay near our life-giving source, Jeremiah assures us that we will not wither from the deadly heat or the lure of sin.

We should note how Psalm 1, used as the responsorial for this liturgy, resonates the same scriptural overtures as Jeremiah. Both prophet and psalmist testify that life without God is like trying to live without water. These voices of the Old Testament prepare hurting humanity to hear the call of Jesus: "Come . . . I will refresh you."

SEVENTH SUNDAY OF THE YEAR (C)
1 S 26:2, 7-9, 12-13, 22-23   1 Cor 15:45-49   Lk 6:27-38

The world famous industrialist and philanthropist, Andrew Carnegie was once asked how to be happy. Carnegie said that he would prefer to answer the question, how to be unhappy. He said that to be miserable, you should grab every possession possible, think only of your own interests, and be dominating and revengeful so others won't take advantage of you.

Happiness is a very tricky thing, but it certainly will never be found solely in the acquisition of material goods. The poor will never believe that, and the rich will never forget it. Nor can happiness be found in selfishness, domination, revenge or in trying to subdue any rival that may appear on the horizon.

In our Gospel reading today, Jesus presents a positive program for pursuing happiness which includes being kind and compassionate to the very people we would expect to fight and conquer. He wants us to be non-retaliatory people because that's the way our Father in heaven treats us. If God would apply all the rigors of justice that we deserve, none of us would be left standing. So since He is kind to us, is it really too much to ask that we be forgiving to others? It's an invitation to think divinely instead of humanly. That's difficult, but just because something is difficult doesn't mean that it's not right. The right decision is often the difficult one, which the strong will follow but the weak will avoid.

The challenge to "be compassionate as your heavenly Father is compassionate" does remain the Gospel ideal. Just imagine what kind of a peaceful and fear-free world we would have if everyone observed that rule.

We seriously question if such an ideal arrangement could ever exist. Most would probably place it in the realm of fantasy. Yet, it is better to strive for this ideal and fall short than never to have tried at all. It would be worst of all to pursue this ideal, reject it and end by demanding violence and revenge.

Happiness is found in the midst of hardships and troubles. It's found not by trying to escape but by living through and accepting adversities with good grace. You are a better and happier person if you neither judge nor condemn. Your God will note your conduct, and He is the One who wrote the rule: "The measure you measure with, will be measured back to you."

EIGHTH SUNDAY OF THE YEAR (C)
Si 27:4-7   1 Cor 15:54-58   Lk 6:39-45

Jesus has many titles: Son of God, Savior, Messiah, etc. These biblical names are well known but somewhat confusing, since they all pertain only to Him. He has another title which we can certainly understand much better — Teacher. Nicodemus called Him "a teacher from God," and other passages refer to this as well: "He began to teach them . . . by the seashore . . . or in the synagogue." Jesus is the Teacher well qualified, the Source of wisdom and the Generator of light.

When the Lord speaks in today's Gospel about a student being subject to his teacher, He implies that there is much to learn and that one should value a teacher and respect human wisdom — realizing all knowledge doesn't come automatically from God solely by divine inspiration. Some modern fundamentalists, including some who appear on TV, minimize the need for scholarship in sacred matters and even regard it as suspect. I heard one say that he rejected the work of biblical scholars (and academic pursuits in general), for they get in the way of the Holy Spirit, Who reveals truths directly to the souls of real Christians. There is no doubt that such a view is tragically wrong and stupid.

Countless learned and holy teachers, both now and in the past, have dedicated their entire lives to the advancement of religious and biblical learning. They have excelled and become like Jesus the Teacher, bringing understanding, light and wisdom to others. We as students and learners owe them our sincere respect and should read their books and articles or attend some of their lectures. Learning can come directly from the Holy Spirit, but the normal way it comes to us is through others — teachers.

If an uninformed person tries to teach others who are seeking understanding, the results, the Lord says, are like one blind man guiding another. Both will fall deeper into confusion.

Knowledge, integrity and personal responsibility are necessary qualities for the good teacher. Jesus calls one a hypocrite who ignores serious matters and insists that others adhere minutely to minor things. In fact, if we would all concentrate on ridding ourselves of the big blotches in our personal lives we would have no time to gossip about or even see the small faults of others.

The true teacher enlightens rather than judges the students.

The ultimate test of a person who is both wise and virtuous is the effect they have on the lives of others. The true teacher will produce good results, for they will have shared a part of their life. The person who is uninformed, misinformed or self-centered cannot show any true or lasting results. They can only produce what Jesus calls "decayed fruit."

Out of its abundance the heart speaks; the quality of its fruit will reveal the nature of the tree.

NINTH SUNDAY OF THE YEAR (C)
1 K 8:41-43   Gal 1:1-2, 6-10   Lk 7:1-10

One of the vital factors which made the Roman army highly successful was the aggressive leadership offered by the centurions. They were the "captains" in charge of 100 men; named thus because "centurion" means "100." They served within a Roman legion, under the command of three tribunes (or generals). An entire legion at full strength numbered about 5000 troops, and so each would have 50 centurions.

In his pivotal position, the centurion had to be equally adept at both obeying and giving orders, which were issued not in writing but by the spoken word. When the tribune gave a command, it was the duty of the centurion to make sure that it was promptly executed. When he in turn gave a command to his troops, he could depend on prompt obedience. This military law, still followed today, was even more rigorously observed in ancient times. Once an order was given, it was as good as done; the accomplishing of the deed was just a matter of time.

The centurion in today's Gospel reading therefore dealt with Jesus from the viewpoint of his military training and completely trusted that the spoken word of a higher power would be fulfilled.

He desperately wanted his servant to be healed, and yet he didn't approach Jesus directly. He sent a messenger. The centurion's personal presence was not important, but only his word. Jesus consented to come personally into his house, but again it was not the person of Jesus he wanted but His spoken word or command, which he believed would be enough. It is easy to see why Jesus so lavishly praised this man's belief in the spoken word, and said that He had not found such faith in the people of Israel.

When the command for the servant's cure was uttered, the servant was cured; most likely, the centurion showed no surprise. It was like the inevitability of an enemy city falling, once the tribune gave the order to attack it.

The confident request (prayer) of the centurion can put us to shame for our weak trust in God and His word as spoken in the Bible. We often desire a spectacular and miraculous sign of His presence when we should simply be placing our faith in His words. God is as good as His word, for it is an extension of Himself. It's His way to reach out and touch us from a distance.

In the Old Testament (Is 55:10-11), the word of God is seen as a kind of missile which once spoken (or launched) goes its way to reach the target for which it was intended.

Whether or not we are worthy for the Lord to personally come to us is not the main point; rather, if we are burdened and filled with darkness, despair, fear and sickness, we can send a confident request and then know that God will "say but the word and our souls will be healed."

TENTH SUNDAY OF THE YEAR (C)
1 K 17:17-24   Gal 1:11-19   Lk 7:11-17

Jesus must have been a welcome sight in the neighboring towns of Nazareth. When invited to a wedding in Cana, just four miles north of His home, He supplied drinks for everyone. In today's Gospel reading He journeys to Naim, five miles south of Nazareth, where He stops a funeral procession and brings the dead man back to life. Is it any wonder that the people of that locality all shouted, "A great prophet has risen among us"?

The Lord doesn't say much at this funeral but He does tell the widowed mother and her friends, "Do not cry." This doesn't mean that crying is a sign of weakness; He also wept at the death of His friend, Lazarus. We might think that His instruction to refrain from crying was poor advice; modern psychology encourages us to cry and express our pent-up feelings in order to be free of them.

Jesus would no doubt agree with this, but in this case they need not cry because of what He's about to do. To the dead person He says, "Young man, I bid you get up." His divine command was stronger than death and "the dead man sat up and began to speak." This was one way that Jesus taught the existence of a future life and demonstrated His control over it.

Our bitter tears when death strikes our families or friends, express the numbing pain of loss; but we can also dry those tears, for Jesus still repeats the words to our beloved dead: "I bid you sit up." Eventually, we hope to hear them spoken to us.

We cannot give life to the dead, but we can to the living — by standing near and supporting those who grieve. The people of Naim generously supported the widow, for "a considerable crowd of townsfolk were with her." Our physical presence and consoling words give a needed uplift to those who are brought low by sufferings.

Because of the Risen Lord's power to grant new life to others, we see our earthly pilgrimage not as a death march heading toward the cemetery but as a joyful walk to glory, back into the heavenly city, to our Father's house.

We often refer to the miracle of birth, but death is an even greater miracle. It is our second birthday, when we are born into everlasting life. We should not cry over the fact that this earthly life will end, but simply live it to the fullest and patiently allow it to give birth to the next stage of our continuing journey. We are on a journey from one level to the next, from death to life; and Jesus is quietly with us repeating the message of Naim. A dead man was carried out and Jesus bade him to rise up, which he did. So can we, by our abiding faith in the great Prophet from Nazareth who has arisen among us and for us.

ELEVENTH SUNDAY OF THE YEAR (C)
2 S 12:7-10, 13   Gal 2:16, 19-21   Lk 7:36-8:3

In his Gospel, Luke tells of Jesus going to dinner at various people's homes at least seven times. There's Matthew's party with the tax collectors; His overnight stay in Jericho with Zacchaeus, His occasional dining with Mary and Martha of Bethany, etc. Today He's invited to dinner at the home of a Pharisee named Simon. Nothing is ever stated about the food at these gatherings, for the focus is on what takes place between Jesus and His hosts.

This particular meal takes place in Galilee. It appears that this Pharisee had some questions for Jesus and invited Him to his home, away from the ever-pressing crowds. Simon's apparent friendliness, however, was shallow. This was betrayed in his obvious lack of courtesy to his guest, Jesus. It is still today a capital rule in the Middle East that a guest in your home is to be given the very best treatment. Where friendship is honest, one does not have to worry about this — it comes naturally. Simon appears to be much more concerned about himself than about Jesus.

With no warning, an unnamed woman with a bad reputation enters the house and sits beside Jesus. Etiquette forbids Simon to dismiss her. Neither does Jesus, for she has brought Him a gift of ointment and is applying it to His feet. She becomes so emotional in Jesus' presence, that her tears fall on his feet. She delicately dries them with her hair and then kisses them. This display of genuine affection seemed strange, but she was expressing a grateful love for Jesus — which is more than could be said for Simon.

We don't know whether she was a local prostitute or merely a poor woman from a lowly family, or even why she was grateful to Jesus. Perhaps He had aided her with some timely advice or a forgiving blessing. In the secrecy of his own mind, Simon turned thumbs down on both the woman and Jesus. She was labeled a sinner and He a false prophet. However, Simon was automatically condemning himself — for the instant he was accusing Jesus of ignorance, the Lord was reading his calloused mind. Had his thoughts been more positive, Jesus would have given him a better rating. The little parable by Jesus put Simòn on the defensive. He had to admit that he was an unforgiven sinner. He gave Jesus only one tenth the love she did, and therefore received only one tenth the forgiveness.

Be careful when you condemn those "terrible sinners" in your neighborhood, whom you say the Lord will surely punish. We all suffer from "Simonitis" — recognized by solemn pronouncements of God's judgment; listing the evildoers of the world; and loudly stating our own righteousness. Since much has been forgiven us, we may be expected to be ten times more loving than we are. Would Jesus be welcome in your home? Can He peacefully relax in your heart?

TWELFTH SUNDAY OF THE YEAR (C)
Zc 12:10-11   Gal 3:26-29   Lk 9:18-24

One of the truly distinguished actors in the world-famous Oberammergau Passion Play was Anton Lang. He spoke the sacred words and carried the cross of Jesus with such depth of intensity that audiences would become entranced.

One day an American couple who had witnessed his sensational performance went backstage to congratulate him. After a brief chat he posed with them for a picture. As they were leaving, the gentleman saw the large stage cross leaning against the wall. "Snap a shot of me carrying the cross," he told his wife. Thinking what a nice memento it would be to show their friends back home, he briskly approached it as she prepared the camera. With both arms he tried to lift it to his shoulder, only to discover that he was unable to budge it. Embarrassed, he gave it another mighty heave but could not move the solid wooden cross even one inch. Now truly humiliated, he blushingly said to Anton: "I thought it would be hollow. Why do you carry such a heavy cross?" The muscular actor silently smiled for a moment and replied: "If the cross were not heavy, I could not play the part."

What kind of a cross do you suppose Jesus had in mind in today's Gospel, when He said: "Take up your cross and follow me"? A very heavy one, no doubt. In fact if the cross is not heavy, it's not really a cross.

In everyone's life there are many inconveniences, difficulties and trying situations — but a cross is something much heavier. It may be the previous death of a spouse or child that you cannot accept. Perhaps it's a malignant disease within your body, eating away your life — or a serious illness of someone close to you. It may be a bitter rejection you've experienced — something you've worked hard to obtain and now you know you never will. Maybe your cross is to be pregnant and have others urge you to have an abortion.

A fitting cross for one person may be totally unbearable for another, and for a third it may be only an inconvenience. Crosses, like people, come in all sizes — but regardless of the size, it's always a full load.

We hear Jesus tell His apostles today that He is the Messiah, the Son of Man: the One who must suffer, be rejected, die (on a cross) and rise to a new life. He's not John the Baptist, Elijah or one of the prophets as the crowd thought — for as great as they were, they would have been unable to lift and carry the cross of Jesus.

Can you identify the cross in your life? If it seems like you can't carry it one more day, don't give up. You can. It's your identification as a disciple of Jesus. He knows the deadening weight but He still wants you to shoulder it and follow, even if you can only take small steps.

THIRTEENTH SUNDAY OF THE YEAR (C)
1 K 19:16, 19-21   Gal 5:1, 13-18   Lk 9:51-62

Farmers have long observed the old traditional cycle of crop planting: corn one year, followed by oats, then by wheat and finally by hay. Although modern agriculture varies the sequence, the conventional cycle is still valid — for each crop replaces some of the nutrients into the soil which the previous one had taken out. The traditional rotation has other advantages, tested and proven through the centuries. A similar cycle was observed in the land of our Lord.

In today's Gospel, Jesus again alludes to farming, making a spiritual point about ploughing a field. The advice is to look ahead and not back, once you "put your hand to the plow" — for if you are constantly looking back, you will plough a crooked furrow.

This has an even deeper meaning for the disciple who follows Jesus. Look ahead, for that's where He is — and it's the direction one should be moving also. Looking back means that you have not yet let go of the past, and that you long to return — at least for a little while. The backward look, therefore, is an indication of faltering discipleship in the new life of Jesus, which you profess to have chosen.

Last year's harvest is over and done, and the plow heralds the first step for a new and better crop in the future. Don't lament yesterday and try to hang onto its joys which have passed away. The oat stubbles of last year are now ploughed under, and the cycle moves on to the new wheat crop of tomorrow. Your "wild oats" have been sown and reaped, for better or worse. If there were mistakes or sins, the plow will cover them forever, like the forgiving hand of Jesus. Now we think only of the new wheat and the many loaves of bread about to be produced, to both physically and spiritually feed a hungry world.

Jesus tells the young would-be disciple to not return to his former home even to attend his father's funeral. It's an overstatement — but one which makes the point that we are pilgrims, constantly moving forward. There's always another field to plough and a new crop to plant.

Jesus said that He had "no place to lay His head" in this world. His true home and ours is found on the other side of time — so when we think of the future, our thoughts should pierce the horizon and bridge the grave. The birds and animals call this world "home," and so build their permanent nests and dens. We seek another.

This land, for the Christian following Jesus, is but a place to pass through. We can find many places to lay our heads, but the question is: where do we want to lay them? Jesus laid His on the line for us, and promised all a room in His Father's house, His home. There's no place like home!

FOURTEENTH SUNDAY OF THE YEAR (C)
Is 66:10-14   Gal 6:14-18   Lk 10:1-12, 17-20

An article in the newspaper, some time ago, told of the various problems women face in their efforts to be successful models. There's the duty to play up to promoters for the good jobs; the need for strict diets and exercises to keep the right body measurements; the necessity of hours of delicate skin care to avoid all blotches and blemishes. One young lady expressed her continual fear of any little accident or injury that might leave a scar, which would cause her to lose her job.

In his letter to the Galatians today, Paul speaks of the appearance of a model Christian. None of the above qualities are necessary. In fact, the one thing the model dreads most is the very thing Paul says makes the follower of Jesus beautiful and valuable — scars.

Paul himself had plenty of them to display and he could remember and relate the story behind each one, like a wounded veteran of a military campaign. He was whipped, stoned and beaten for his faith, and he loves the scars, calling them the "marks of Jesus in my body." He doesn't want to hide them, for they bring him much peace and give witness to others.

Jesus warns in the Gospel that Christians will be liable to pains and injuries, as He was. The mind and emotions may also be scarred as well as the body, but it's all part of the unique discipleship required of each. Jesus doesn't alter the rules to make life easier, but continues to send us out like "lambs in the midst of wolves." Teddy Roosevelt's advice to speak softly and carry a big stick does not apply here, for Jesus tells us to speak out boldly and carry no stick. We are thereby in a good position for acquiring scars.

Once you take a definite stand, support an unpopular cause, help a suspect, etc. because you feel that Christ would do the same, then you'll begin your scar collection and most of them will be mental and emotional ones. They are the permanent records of past encounters.

Old-time railroad workers were considered mediocre unless they had some fingers missing. A coon hunter in the market for a new dog will pay out good money only if the hound's face, gums and ears display the marks of battle from sharp claws and gnashing teeth. The Liberty Bell in Philadelphia is much more valuable and inspirational because of its 1835 crack, for that "scar" tells a lot about the history of our country.

Of course Jesus, the greatest model of all times, was literally scarred from head to foot. The marks of the nails and spear became His best proof of identification when He appeared to His disciples. He loved His wounds so dearly that He transferred them to His glorified body and undoubtedly still displays them in Heaven today.

What scars do we have to show for our years of Christian living?

FIFTEENTH SUNDAY OF THE YEAR (C)
Dt 30:10-14   Col 1:15-20   Lk 10:25-37

The story of the Good Samaritan is a parable. That means, it never really happened. But since it is a parable, it has happened a million times. We can pull it out of its Middle East setting and place it in modern-day America and make it happen again.

A man was driving in the night and he stopped to stretch his legs at a rest area. Someone hit him over the head with a club and stole his car and money. Later, a well-known pastor of a church made a brief stop, saw the unconscious, bleeding man, but was afraid and drove off and left him. Then a businessman drove by in a fancy sports car, spotted the victim and sped on, not wanting to get involved. Finally a junky old pickup truck rattled into the area, driven by a scarfaced Cuban, recently deported from one of Castro's prisons. Seeing the victim, he ran to the pump and soaked his large red handkerchief, then wiped the man's face until he regained consciousness. He then lifted him into the truck and hurried to the emergency room at a hospital. Since the victim had no identification, the Cuban gave his own name and address, assuming responsibility for any bills not covered by the man's hospital insurance. Which of the three proved to be the victim's neighbor?

When Jesus asked that question, His audience so hated the Samaritans (half-breeds and heretics) that they would not even say "Samaritan," but only "the one who took pity on him." We may not like the story either, for it tells how people (like you and me) can ignore others, even those in dire need. It says that some "big people" are not so big — and that others, thought to be of little account, are tremendous individuals.

There are countless victims along the road. They suffer from ignorance, disease, violence, blindness, depression, old age, poverty, floods and fires. A teacher might choose to ignore the ignorant; a doctor could refuse the sick; a salesman can cheat the naive; the clergy can avoid the sinners; the rich can pretend not to see the poor.

Many need only a little help, like a dollar bill, some good advice, a genuine smile or just a minute or two of our time to hear "their story."

The road between Jerusalem and Jericho goes from above sea level to below; from the dusty desert to plush green fields; from long straight stretches to winding hills and valleys. In other words, it's a model of any road, any place, any time. Since we only pass by once, why not be a Good Samaritan along the way?

SIXTEENTH SUNDAY OF THE YEAR (C)
Gn 18:1-10   Col 1:24-28   Lk 10:38-42

The small valley-town of Bethany, where Martha, Mary and Lazarus lived, is located just over the mountain from Jerusalem. Today a large church occupies the site which tradition says was the original home of these three close friends of Jesus. Located about

500 feet up the eastern slope of the Mount of Olives is the tomb from which Lazarus was called forth, after he had died.

Our Gospel today tells of a casual visit Jesus made to this wrangling Bethany family. Exactly how or why He had developed such a personal relationship with these three people, we are not told; but John tells us that "Jesus loved Martha and her sister and Lazarus very much" (Jn 11:5).

This was not a typical family, since it consisted of two single women and a bachelor brother. Lazarus was possibly somewhat of a recluse, besides being sickly, and needed to be cared for by his sisters — for in the various passages we never have one word from him. Mary appears to have been shy and introspective, while Martha was aggressive, outspoken and undoubtedly the one in charge of the household. In spite of their varied temperaments and peculiar personalities, they shared a mutual love for Jesus — although their common love for each other left some room for improvement.

Martha shows her complete ease in the presence of Jesus by her chiding remark about His sitting and talking to Mary, while she has to do all the work. In essence she subtly said: "What I am doing is more important than what you are saying." Jesus, however, defended Mary's right to sit and talk — and indirectly invited the energetic Martha to join them and leave the housework until later. The Lord no doubt smiled and shook His head gently as He spoke her name twice with the suggestion that she sit down and relax. There is a time to work and a time to visit — and now was the time to visit, as Mary was doing. He would not ask her to clean the house or prepare a snack.

Don't we all get caught up to some degree in the Martha syndrome? We rush about, shouting at others, constantly on edge and filled with tension, doing all our "good works" with a lousy attitude. A change of pace is vitally important for all people. We are often asked, "What do you do?" Maybe the follow-up should be, "How well do you do it?"

Setting aside some time each day for personal meditation can help us to work more effectively and purposefully. The moments we sit at the feet of Jesus are not "down time," for being alone with the Lord in thought and prayer can melt away tensions. The more we look into His gentle face, the more we begin to smile — for then we realize that He's in charge and everything is not on our shoulders.

SEVENTEENTH SUNDAY OF THE YEAR (C)
Gn 18:20-32 Col 2:12-14 Lk 11:1-13

Many times Jesus told His apostles that they should pray, but had never explicitly told them how. Then one day, they silently observed Him at prayer and were greatly impressed. When He finished, one of them approached Him with the request: "Lord, teach us to pray . . ." Thereupon, Jesus taught them the Lord's Prayer, which is recorded by Luke in today's Gospel.

Jesus had previously told them how not to pray, for He had expressed His disappointment with the way hypocrites approached prayer. He said that when you pray, don't stand on the "street corners in order to be noticed . . . and do not rattle on . . ." (Mt 6:5-7). Prayer, we might think, is something simple: just talking to God. But that is really not simple after all. What qualities make up a good prayer? What are the internal feelings we should have? Is there a correct time or place to pray? Today's Gospel answers these questions.

1. In regard to the prayer itself; note that the Lord's Prayer begins with the proper address of "Father." It is followed with an expression of praise, "hallowed be Your name." It would seem thoughtless to begin immediately with a long series of "give me's," without first showing some reverence and praise to the Almighty One, Whom we are addressing. Following our initial praise, our

thoughts and words can move to petitions for spiritual or material blessings, or to expressions of thanksgiving or to requests for pardon for our sins.

2. Times to pray. It is the old Jewish tradition to pray at the 3rd, 6th and 9th hours of the day. This custom was incorporated into many monasteries and religious houses. Jesus, however, assures us that prayer at any hour is fine, for He is always "on call." In this Gospel, the Lord tells of someone shouting for help "in the middle of the night." We should pray when most awake and alert, in order to be at our best when talking to God.

3. Dispositions of the person praying. We're asked to view God as our Father (and Friend) with tremendous faith in His goodness and love for us. If we are offering petitions, the quality of perseverance is of utmost importance. We are told to continue to ask, seek and knock even when all the doors appear to be closed and bolted, with a dozen good reasons to leave them locked. Yet if we persevere, there is one better reason to open them. "Whoever asks, receives; whoever seeks, finds; whoever knocks is admitted."

These solid Bible teachings come from the One who hears the prayers of the world, and He says that these are the kinds He likes to hear.

Most gracious Father, all praise and glory be to You. Teach us to pray with confidence and perseverance, and lead us to Your Kingdom.

EIGHTEENTH SUNDAY OF THE YEAR (C)
Si 1:2, 2:21-23   Col 3:1-5, 9-11   Lk 12:13-21

At this productive time of the year, when fields, orchards and gardens are displaying the annual blessings of nature, the Church presents a timely parable of the rich man and his good harvest. Jesus told the story to teach people to "avoid greed in all its forms."

The rich man is censured not because he's rich but because he takes his abundant crop, which he received only because of God's generosity, and hordes it all for himself — having enough for many years. There is no thought of sharing it with the less fortunate or giving one tenth as a thanksgiving offering to God.

He is the image of the man who falsely thinks that he can control his own destiny, by wealth and possessions. Just when he thought everything was set for a prosperous future, he discovered that he would die before sunrise and there was nothing he could do about it. The parable implies that his abundant wealth made dying more painful, for he had to leave so much behind.

The philosopher Qoheleth, in the first reading, concurs with the parable. Much of what we think is so important, he says, is only "vanity" — i.e., worthless and transient; for the abundance of material wealth alone does not make for a meaningful life. It's not a question of being rich or poor, but to what degree we are possessed by our possessions. Some, who can well afford it, refuse to spend anything for others or even for themselves. They believe that money is to be saved, and it nearly kills them to spend a dollar. Others would unfortunately always be broke even if they were handed $500.00 a day. Somewhere between these extremes is a common-sense philosophy.

For a number of years, Sam Shulsky has written a newspaper column giving advice on investing money. Once he told a very affluent widow that she'd saved enough and should start spending. Later another elderly reader objected, saying that money should be saved and that one should practice self-denial. Shulsky replied that this was fine "when building for old age." But when you reach that age, "it's time to spend some money on luxuries and on little extras, which one denied oneself during the years of accumulation."

He further explained that many senior citizens are tightly grasping every penny, as they learned to do during the Great Depression, even though they are financially secure.

Jesus does not recommend that we work hard only for material possessions. He counsels us to labor day and night and go to extremes to grow rich in the sight of God. That is the guaranteed way to have blessings in reserve for years to come.

NINETEENTH SUNDAY OF THE YEAR (C)
Ws 18:6-9   Heb 11:1-2, 8-19   Lk 12:32-48

If you want an excellent definition of faith, then ponder and memorize the first sentence in today's reading from the Letter to the Hebrews. "Faith is *confident assurance* concerning what we hope for, and *conviction* about things we do not see." This one sentence can give you many hours of meditation. Think about the many things you hope for. Do you have confident assurance of obtaining them? Next you can try to imagine the many things that you think exist. See if you have real conviction of their existence. In such a fashion you can determine your depth of faith.

The author of Hebrews emphasizes that one can only have faith in another person if the other is trustworthy. Thus our first step in religious faith must be to determine for ourselves if God is 100% trustworthy. The author assures us He is. Faith means more than professing belief in creeds and rules. It means trusting God — as the coin says.

Examples of great people of faith are presented in this passage. There's Abraham, the all-time classic model, who took to the road without map or compass like a brave pioneer. He left everything behind and did not know where he was going, but he had faith in a better life because of his deep confidence in his directing God.

Sarah, his wife, was twice the age for bearing children and laughed at the thought. But when she was convinced that God was speaking to her, she fully believed God and gave birth to Isaac.

Perhaps we could have deeper convictions about religion if we simply had more faith in general, for we believe in many things we don't see. No one has seen electricity in itself, but only the results of its existence. The same is true of the wind, gravity and even of life itself. So we see that many an unseen mystery is a reality.

Someone told me some time ago that he was an agnostic. "Well, maybe not," he added, "perhaps I just question things and think too much." When you question truths and think about them, it doesn't mean that you're losing faith. Rather, your faith is healthy and growing. Faith is different from science and mathematics, for often it doesn't test out or add up.

The popular slogan, "Seeing is believing," is poor theology. Believing is precisely not seeing. Jesus told Thomas, "Blessed are they who have not seen and yet believed" (Jn 20:29).

When invited to something new and challenging, some people say, "I can't," or "I don't know how." Others reply, "OK, I'll try." We can murmur about uncertainties and innovations and then retreat to our familiar surroundings, or we can launch out in faith like the pilgrims of old.

Our trustworthy Lord came forth from the tomb and encourages every follower to hope against hope. Believe, trust Him.

TWENTIETH SUNDAY OF THE YEAR (C)
Jr 38:4-6, 8-10   Heb 12:1-4   Lk 12:49-53

We cannot dispute the fact that Jesus was a peacemaker. He proclaimed peace, prayed for it and counseled others to pursue it. He called peacemakers "blessed" and promised them the Kingdom of God. In contrast to this congenial image, we read in today's Gospel that Jesus said He came to "cast fire upon the earth." He adds: "Do not think I have come to give peace . . . but division." He declares that because of Him, people and families will be divided. How do we reconcile these two seemingly contradictory images?

The Second Person of the Blessed Trinity is amazingly complex. There exists within Him another kind of trinity — He is Priest, Prophet and King. As King, He calls for order and peace that the Kingdom may be strong. As Priest, He wants to unify people in faith and worship and establish harmony in the community. The role of Prophet, however, causes Him to speak a different language — for a prophet is on the cutting edge of society, expressing views which people don't want to hear. Therefore as Priest and King, Jesus is a peacemaker; as Prophet He is a "troublemaker."

Jesus the Prophet had a time-honored tradition to follow. There was Nathan, who had condemned King David to his face. Amos had angered the rich. Jeremiah continually berated the government. John the Baptist literally lost his head over an illicit marriage. To be a true prophet, Jesus could do no less than speak His mind and disturb the peace, for prophets were not concerned about being popular or agreeable. When He was yet a baby, the aged Simeon had predicted His prophetic role as "a sign of contradiction."

Ultimately, the aim of the true prophet is to achieve peace. The person who never objects or criticizes is less a peacemaker than the outspoken critic who is sincerely trying to improve the world. If we ignore a curable ill present in our city, church or family, we are not acting as Christians. It sounds strange to say and it take brave people to do it, but sometimes we have to be troublemakers, in order to heal and reform.

A good wife corrects her husband because she loves him. A loyal citizen condemns some national policies in order to help his country. Disunity is not to be avoided at all costs. It is often the price to be paid for progress and improvement. Jesus showed us that sometimes it is our duty to criticize and divide, that a greater unity and peace may follow.

TWENTY-FIRST SUNDAY OF THE YEAR (C)
Is 66:18-21   Heb 12:5-7, 11-13   Lk 13:22-30

When the players or coach of a victorious team are interviewed, we usually hear someone say, "We're a well-disciplined team." The speaker doesn't mean that they must be in bed by ten o'clock each evening or that they are physically punished for their errors. Discipline means that they are in control of their bodies, minds and emotions. They have repeated their plays a hundred times in practice and know what they can do as individuals and as a team.

The word "discipline" occurs five times in today's reading from the Letter to the Hebrews, where the author is encouraging the readers to live according to Christian standards. "Discipline" is more a positive than a negative term, since a disciple is simply one who is disciplined in the lessons of the Lord.

Jesus, like the good coach who always wants us to do better, may seem to be too demanding — but it's all for the purpose of ultimate victory. Success eventually goes to the team that can run faster, jump higher, throw further and coordinate it all into a common effort.

We are disciplined if we can offer our prayers in a spirit of calm confidence, knowing that God is faithful to His promises. If we can accept setbacks without falling apart, and not become smugly elated over success, we are disciplined. The follower of Jesus finds timely counsel in today's second reading: ". . . do not disdain the discipline of the Lord, nor lose heart when He reproves you . . . strengthen your drooping hands and weak knees."

Children are expected to recognize and appreciate the discipline given by their parents, teachers and others in authority. It is a necessary training for them in the ways of life, done from the motive of love. When correction is seen as a punishment or "putdown," then we miss its meaning and lose an opportunity to grow. We all need to recognize the value of good advice and guidance. When it is given, we should thank the person instead of condemning them as being bossy or domineering.

If we could pray sincerely the four words of the Lord's Prayer, "Thy will be done," we would be showing a great degree of spiritual maturity and strength of Christian character. These were the words Jesus prayed on the night before He died.

Out of discipline come disciples — those whom the Lord knows and recognizes, according to today's Gospel. The undisciplined He rejects, saying, "I don't know where you are coming from."

TWENTY-SECOND SUNDAY OF THE YEAR (C)
Si 3:17-18, 20, 28-29   Heb 12:18-19, 22-24   Lk 14:1, 7-14

We might think that the best way to encourage a person to like us is to give a gift, but today's reading from Sirach says that there is a better way — less expensive and more effective. *"Conduct your affairs with humility* and you will be loved more than a giver of gifts." A boisterous and aggressive individual is usually difficult for others to accept. He alienates people by his belligerent attitude. It is much harder to reject a person who is humble and quiet.

Sirach also writes that the greater you are, the more important it is to be humble. We often expect famous people to act in an aloof manner. When they don't, we say that he or she "is a regular person; down to earth; one of us." It's another way of saying that they are humble and we are glad about it.

Sirach shows that he is a straightforward realist when he advises us to admit that some tasks and positions are beyond the strengths and talents of some of us. To be told that we are unable to do a particular job can be discouraging — but if it's the truth, we should admit it. Such an honest admission is a vital part of humility. Although we are created equal as regards basic rights, we are unequal in intelligence and talents. Recognizing our abilities — whether superior, average or inferior — is another mark of genuine humility.

The Gospel complements this teaching by warning us not to push ourselves into positions of honor, especially where we are not invited. We might have the third row from center stage, but out of pride we push into the front seats. Just before the curtain opens, some dignitaries are ushered in to occupy these seats reserved for them and we must then go to the standing room section in the back. Aggressive pride and selfishness can be our own worst enemy.

Our lack of humility can also cause us to make statements and give answers about things we don't know about. We are too proud to admit our lack of knowledge. I like the quotation from the famous author Somerset Maugham: "It wasn't until quite late in life that I discovered how easy it is to say, I don't know."

So according to the Book of Sirach and the Gospel of Luke, if you want to be happy, successful and have a good reputation, "conduct your affairs with humility." He who humbled Himself unto death, said that it's the Christian thing to do.

TWENTY-THIRD SUNDAY OF THE YEAR (C)
Ws 9:13-18   Ph 9:10, 12-17   Lk 14:25-33

The vastness of space is beyond the comprehension of the greatest scientists. The Milky Way, for example, is 800 million billion miles across. It would take 120 thousand years to go from one end to the other, traveling at the speed of light. It contains millions of suns, much larger than ours, many with their own solar systems. It is so gigantic that we have no earthly words to describe it. Our precious space ship earth is but a tiny speck of dust compared to the rest of the universe. Space is a frontier that humanity can never conquer or even significantly explore.

Another exciting frontier enticing the modern mind is the world of the computer. Even in its infant stage of development, it can "think" so rapidly and store so much information, that we can only marvel in disbelief. Many of us cannot believe its multi-talented capabilities, even after numerous demonstrations.

Now I invite you to think of God in relation to the above. We believe that He in some way made the entire universe, set it all in motion and keeps it functioning smoothly. His mind, we also believe, is infinitely more capable of fantastic feats than the best computer that will ever be invented.

The author of the Book of Wisdom knew little of the boundlessness of the universe and nothing of computers. Yet, he knew of the omnipresence of God and His infinite wisdom, and so speaks of it in today's first reading. He counsels us not to be so arrogant that we think we can understand the mind of God and predict His plans for the future. "When things are in heaven," he asks, "who can search them out?" If we truly believe that God has all the stupendous qualities we attribute to Him, how can we so smugly think our little minds can comprehend Him? We — who are baffled by outer space, intimidated by the computer and unable even to understand ourselves — should bow in profound silence before the Almighty.

There are infinitely more things to know about God than are recorded in the Bible or taught by any Church. To think that a book or organization can comprehend Him, is to offer Him the greatest insult possible.

Those who claim to "have all the answers" would do well to ponder this reading from the Book of Wisdom. Deliver us, Lord, from human arrogance, and forget not Your helpless people on this far-flung island in space.

TWENTY-FOURTH SUNDAY OF THE YEAR (C)
Ex 32:7-11, 13-14   1 Tm 1:12-17   Lk 15:1-32

This parable, traditionally known as The Prodigal Son, is also called The Forgiving Father. It exemplifies compassion in action. Some of the following thoughts are credited to Dr. Kenneth Bailey of the School of Theology in Beirut, Lebanon. He notes that in Middle Eastern society, like our own, the father may or may not make a will, but in any case he would always retain the rights to and the interest of the money until he died. If the children were to request their share of the estate prematurely, it would be like telling their dad to "drop dead."

In this parable, the younger son insults his father in two ways. First, he asks for the money now, showing that he can't wait for him to die; secondly, in his demand for the share of the estate and his right to dispose of it, he has completely ignored his father's future needs. Yet the father complies with his son's request, and although deeply hurt, he is not angry.

Once the son had spent the money, we might wonder why he would not have come home earlier. One reason would have been that he was ashamed to return; another was that he would be subjected to the "shun" — no one would speak to or associate with him in any way. A man was subjected to the shun if he married an immoral woman or lost his money to the gentiles. In these cases the guilty one was to confess his sin, compensate for the loss and remain outside the community until proven worthy to reenter.

In this parable, the father initiates a new way of forgiveness. Rather than applying the shun, he runs (something old men normally did not do) to meet his son, who had openly and deliberately insulted him. The father does not wait for apologies but forgives him immediately and totally. The young man is delighted by this unexpected and overflowing love.

Jesus uses the story as an example of God's forgiveness to us and as a model of our forgiveness to each other. The father's love had healed the past; the son's present repentance and conversion would correct the future.

Note that the elder son did apply the shun; he refused to welcome home his brother. We can either imitate the compassionate father or the merciless elder brother when it comes to pardoning another person. We can hurry to meet them with open arms, or turn our back and refuse to speak to them. Which way do you choose — to run or shun?

Each time we remit and forget past hurts and offenses, we grow a little bigger and better. If we are living in the midst of bitterness and hatred, we are slowly starving ourselves. It is high time to "break away and return to the Father."

TWENTY-FIFTH SUNDAY OF THE YEAR (C)
Am 8:4-7   1 Tm 2:1-8   Lk 16:1-13

More than 700 years before the birth of Jesus, the prophet Amos was on the biblical scene, preaching the need for integrity. He was a farmer from southern Israel, who travelled to the rich north country, by divine inspiration. His mission was to condemn the selfishness of the rich who refused to help their struggling brothers and sisters. Amos had a three word formula for making money: *Make it honestly.*

He was infuriated with those people who cheated in their business dealings, and he predicted that God would take revenge on them. In today's reading we hear his anger blazing out against the cheats, the swindlers and all dishonest and selfish people.

Some are so greedy, Amos says, that they refuse to worship or rest on the Sabbath, lest they lose business. They are even impatient with nature, complaining that it takes too long for the wheat to ripen, before they can sell it.

Amos condemned the vendors who cheated their customers by using small measures (ephah) when selling grain by the bushel, and heavy scale weights (shekal) when buying by the pound. He also denounced those who offer bribes, pay-offs and kick-backs, and who entice the poor to do their "dirty work" by offering them a few silver pieces or a pair of shoes. Amos is an old-time preacher whose message needs to be heard in today's world. Hear him shouting to the contemporary charlatans, "God will not forget what you have done."

Generally speaking, is our society any better than the one Amos knew, 2700 years ago? Since we constitute our society, how would we answer the following questions? Am I an honest person? Have I ever *deliberately* cheated anyone? Am I 100% trustworthy with other people's money and possessions? Do I consider it sinful to take advantage of others, even though it's easy to do? If you don't rate well, you might be helped by reading the Book of Amos. It's only nine chapters.

Unfortunately, we live in an atmosphere of deception, which makes us suspicious of others' motives and fearful of being cheated. We face everything from deliberate frauds and vicious lies to psychological manipulations — like the price $19.99 to make us think it's much cheaper than $20.00, or the box of breakfast cereal twice the size of its contents.

Honesty is not only the best policy but the only one. The integrity we use in dealing with our neighbor determines whether or not we are honest with God. Don't we feel some obligation to be as good as our word and help people to continue to trust others? Jesus, like Amos, clearly taught that it is maliciously sinful to deceive or victimize the poor, the uninformed, the old, the young, or anyone.

TWENTY-SIXTH SUNDAY OF THE YEAR (C)
Am 6:1, 4-7   1 Tm 6:11-16   Lk 16:19-31

The style of today's Gospel is a lot like that of the old westerns. The bad guy (Dives) is all bad, and the good guy (Lazarus) is all good. Dives dresses in royal purple clothes, made of the finest linen. He does more than eat good food; he feasts splendidly — every day. Lazarus smells the food cooking and, although starving, he is offered nothing. Dives thinks only of himself and doesn't want to see Lazarus as he lies helplessly in the dirt outside the gate, covered with raw sores. He is so hungry that even dogfood would be a treat, but the dogs come first.

Finally Lazarus starves to death, and then everything is reversed. He is skyrocketed into glory, with the angels carrying him to the side of Abraham. Poor old Lazarus has paid the price of pain and now reaps a rich reward.

Dives later sinks into death and continues on down into the abode of the tormented. He suffers terribly for his selfishness, but his pain increases when he looks up to Heaven and sees Lazarus, the disgusting beggar, in the bosom of Abraham.

What does the story tell us? It does not teach that rich people are sinners and poor people are saints. The opposite could easily be true. Nor is it teaching the existence of Heaven and Hell. The story simply assumes their existence, envisioning them the way most of Jesus' contemporaries did. Originally this parable was addressed to the Pharisees, who — like Dives — considered themselves superior to others, especially the poor and ignorant. In this liturgy it is intended for those of us who think we are high-class people, when in reality we may only be selfish snobs.

Note that the first reading from Amos proclaims the same theme. The conflict between the rich and poor is no new problem. The Lazarus-Dives story may seem to be exaggerated, but sadly this is not the case. During the Great Depression, when the poor and unemployed formed long soup lines in New York City, the rich on Long Island held a surprise party for their dogs. The cost was $100.00 a plate, and the menu was "all you could eat" of the choicest steak — for the dogs.

We are not all equal financially, but we do share a natural and basic obligation to each other. We are our brother's keeper, and Jesus says that what we do for others we do for Him.

TWENTY-SEVENTH SUNDAY OF THE YEAR (C)
Hab 1:2-3, 2:2-4   2 Tm 1:6-8, 13-14   Lk 17:5-10

The canyon was exceedingly deep, with jagged protruding rocks anchored in its walls. A thin strong wire was tightly stretched across the 250 foot span which separated the two banks. Confidently, a 30 year old acrobat walked the slightly swaying wire, as the tense crowd watched and cheered.

Next, blindfolded, he performed the same feat, and the admiring crowd cheered louder. Finally pushing a wheelbarrow full of sand, he crossed the canyon again, with the wire sagging almost to the point of breaking. The moment his steady feet touched solid ground, the terrified people went wild with praise for his bravery.

"You can do anything on the high wire," one young man shouted, hugging the courageous acrobat. "You're the greatest I've ever seen." Picking up a shovel, the performer began to remove the sand. "So you really believe in my ability?" "Oh yes, I believe in you, man; I really do. You're the best there is." "Well then," replied the trapeze artist, "I'll cross the chasm once more and this time you get in the wheelbarrow." Suddenly the young enthusiast lost all his faith.

How easy it is to cheer at a distance for a particular person or project — but the closer we get to the real danger involved, the quieter we become. What we thought was strong faith, turned out to be no faith at all. We may have many faith-filled answers for others who are enduring a severe illness, a deep depression or a family death — but when problems touch us, we may be fearful, cursing and faithless. It is very hard to keep faith in both good times and in bad. Perhaps that's why Jesus says in today's Gospel that even a tiny bit of faith will enable us to do marvelous deeds. When the Lord explained the power of faith to His apostles, they on the spot prayed in unison, "increase our faith."

Our Christian faith must of necessity be firmly anchored in the person of the Lord Jesus Christ. If we try to build on another basis we will fail. How much confidence do you place in the Master? If Jesus were the trapeze artist on the high wire and He asked you to cross over the chasm with Him, would you be afraid to get into the wheelbarrow?

TWENTY-EIGHTH SUNDAY OF THE YEAR (C)
2 K 5:14-17   2 Tm 2:8-13   Lk 17:11-19

They earnestly prayed for the Master's pity. He could have said, "I sympathize with you fellows, for I know what you're suffering. Do your best and don't lose heart." Had it happened that way, the ten lepers might have felt a bit better because of His concern, but their problem would have remained. They needed more than verbal encouragement.

It was a most gracious cure which Jesus bestowed on these ten helpless men. Leprosy at that time was a very ugly and prevalent disease. Its victims became outcasts, shunned by all. Blindness often ensued, and life was shortened by 15 or 20 years.

At least today, the victims of such serious ills as cancer and heart attacks are cared for, touched and consoled by loved ones at their bedsides. The lepers, on the contrary, had already "died" to their families, and with lonesome hearts they painfully awaited death. To be cured of this dreaded disease, therefore, was more than a physical healing. It was a release from "death row," a rebirth into the excitement of normal life.

This Gospel records two cries for understanding. The lepers ask Jesus for His mercy, and Jesus asks for their appreciation. They needed each other — they could not heal themselves, and He could not thank Himself.

No doubt, all ten *felt* very grateful for their cures. Since the Lord could read their thoughts, we might think that would have been sufficient. However, just as they had needed a real cure, He needed real gratitude, expressed in actions and words. The lepers only managed to return 10% of appreciation for His 100% of healing.

Our unmaterialized good intentions and our unexpressed appreciations must hardly impress the Lord. We probably all cry for pity from God and humanity, at least 10 times more than we offer thanks.

Gratitude in action can take many forms — an appreciative visit to another, or at least a note or phone call. This is not only good etiquette, but good religion. Can't we all remember some uplifting words of thanks given to us, and how they made us feel happy and at peace?

Everyone has a need to be appreciated — even Jesus. "It is right to give Him thanks and praise," both in prayer and good works. We are reminded of this at every Mass.

TWENTY-NINTH SUNDAY OF THE YEAR (C)
Ex 17:8-13   2 Tm 3:14-4:2   Lk 18:1-8

Today's Gospel parable is Jesus' call to His disciples to pray and work with a positive attitude. Even if you're a poor "nobody," says the Lord, like the widow, don't stop fighting for your just rights. If it means opposing the powerful and wealthy establishment, go to it. The judge in this story is admittedly corrupt and the widow is innocent. She seems to be getting an unfair deal in her legal case because she is too poor to bribe the judge. Her opponent is no doubt an "important" citizen who can use his wealth and influence to manipulate the crooked judge.

The widow cannot compete with the insidious judge and her other adversaries on their own terms, so she decides to pick her own battlefield. She can outmaneuver them with her stubbornness. By hounding the judge continuously, she gets him to settle in her favor just to get rid of her.

Justice here is not achieved from any high motive — but nonetheless it is achieved. She really had him running scared, since he thought "she will end by doing me violence." How did she terrorize him? Maybe she carried a heavy cane and threatened to hit him.

If we know both what we want and how we can achieve it, and pray and work stubbornly for it, it will be hard to stop us. One thing is sure: if we don't know what we want and don't work to get it, we will never have it.

The widow operated on the principle of "make it happen." She did not hopelessly wring her hands over her misfortune and cry, "why, why?" She envisioned how things should be and relentlessly prayed, "why not?"

Jesus asssures us that determined prayer is powerful and can produce unexpected results. This parable is especially consoling to the little people in today's world who are so often unheard and ignored. Although political clout may seem necessary to get things done, here we are reminded of a clout even more powerful — persevering prayer. It can make the weak and poor triumph over the rich and powerful.

With Moses in today's reading from Exodus, we lift our hands to God and refuse to rest until the battle is over and the victory has been won.

THIRTIETH SUNDAY OF THE YEAR (C)
Si 35:12-14, 16-18   2 Tm 4:6-8, 16-18   Lk 18:9-14

I recently saw a poster of a powerful tawny-bearded lion, with a caption reading: "It's so difficult to be humble." That seems to be the case of the Pharisee in today's Gospel. He had many respectable qualities. He prayed in the Temple daily and gave one tenth of his money to charity. He fasted twice a week (Mondays and Thursdays), like the other Pharisees. He was faithful to his wife and honest in his business dealings. But all these good qualities were tainted by his inflated ego, as he proudly poured out his mind and heart to the one he loved most — himself.

Those who are truly holy think much more about God than about themselves, as is well noted in the lives of the saints. Their sanctity is attributed to God and not to their own efforts.

Since we profess God's mercy to all people, we assume that this Pharisee was forgiven. But had he not sung his own praises so loudly, he would truly have been the person he thought he was. We all must constantly fight against pride lest our good deeds become the cause of our downfall. It is so easy to condemn others and worship ourselves. When we begin to do this, we should remember the One who is infinitely better than any of us, and how He humbled Himself unto death.

The tax collector may have done evil, as the Pharisee thought. Perhaps he was adulterous or crooked, but he knew that he needed God in his life and he begged His forgiveness. His prospects for a happy future were better than the Pharisee's. If we want an ideal model for daily living, we should try to do the good works of the Pharisee with the attitude of the tax collector.

When we think of God, the Architect of the universe, we realize how futile it is to imagine that we can impress Him by our importance. We have not earned our salvation, for grace is Jesus' gift from the cross. He only asks in return our faith, love, humility and thanks.

Since no one pays his or her way into heaven, we should not brag about our great spiritual accomplishments. What little good we do, God will notice without our help. He should hear us praying, "God I need you," rather than hearing us make it sound as if He needed us. All of us have a full time job of "building up Christ within us," by admitting and eradicating our faults, especially pride.

"Oh God, be merciful to me, a sinner," and by your loving grace help me to return home justified.

THIRTY-FIRST SUNDAY OF THE YEAR (C)
Ws 11:22-12:1   2 Th 1:11-2:2   Lk 19:1-10

Jesus had a particular love for tax collectors. He chose one as an apostle (Matthew) and attended a banquet where many were present. He told a parable of a tax collector who was holier and prayed better than a devout Pharisee. Now, in today's Gospel, Jesus invites Himself to the home of Zacchaeus, the chief tax collector of Jericho. All of this infuriated the Jewish people, for they regarded these collectors as traitors and sinners.

They were especially hated because a significant amount of the taxes paid was sent out of the country — to Rome. Obviously it was not the fault of these Jewish tax collectors that Rome had conquered Israel, but because they collaborated with the Romans and did some cheating on the side, they received the vented hatred of their fellow citizens.

Zacchaeus was also hated and rejected for being greedy and dishonest. He was a small man in a land where biggest meant best, and this augmented his problems. We are not told why he was so anxious to see Jesus. Perhaps he had heard that Jesus favored "his kind of people," and the sight of Him would give him strength.

He had to be a competent, hard-working man to head up the

entire I.R.S. Department of Jericho, but the thought of seeing Jesus in person so captivated him that he became like a little boy and ran down the street and climbed a tree to see over the crowd.

A comparable situation might be if the President of the United States were driving through our town and the mayor, dressed in an expensive suit and tie, would excitedly shinny up a roadside tree with binoculars and camera. It's one of those situations where you want to achieve your objective so much that you forget about etiquette and propriety.

Zacchaeus must have nearly fainted when Jesus stopped right under his tree and asked to spend the night in his home. Typically, the people murmured, "He's gone to a sinner's house as a guest." This "sinner" confided to Jesus that he was not what the people said. He explained how he gave half his "belongings to the poor," and if he defrauded anyone out of ten dollars, he would repay forty. Jesus knew he was a kind man and praised him. He blessed his house and called him a "son of Abraham."

The Lord promises that those who go out on a limb for Him will not be left sitting alone. He too went out on a limb for us, becoming a most undignified spectacle in order to invite Himself into our lives. Love causes us to do unpredictable things. Sometimes it drives us right up a tree.

THIRTY-SECOND SUNDAY OF THE YEAR (C)
2 M 7:1-2, 9-14   2 Th 2:16-3:5   Lk 20:27-38

The ancient Greeks, such as Plato, had a clearer idea of personal immortality than the Israelites did. The Book of Wisdom, written about 50 B.C., contains the Old Testament's most vivid concepts of the future life; not surprisingly, this originated from a strong Greek influence.

The hazy Hebrew notion of the afterlife centered around the

word "Sheol," meaning "the grave." This was a vague and shadowy type of survival, a very unappealing one. It was much better to live on earth than in Sheol, which explains why the Hebrews interpreted a short life as a punishment and a long life as a reward from God.

Under Greek and Persian influence, Pharisees professed belief in the future life and in the resurrection of the body. The Sadducees, a more conservative group, believed in neither.

Jesus basically agreed with the Pharisees on this question. The Sadducees took exception to this and thus set the scene for the confrontation in today's Gospel. They tried to negate the possibility of resurrection and deflate the teaching of Jesus by posing the example of a woman who had been married to seven brothers. "At the resurrection of the dead," they gleefully inquired, "which one will be her husband...?"

Jesus simply restated His teaching on the resurrection, and then explained that life in eternity would be different and that such problems would not arise. Our Lord's answer was good, but His best answer would come later with His own personal resurrection from the grave.

In all ages and places, Christians have professed and proclaimed their belief in the immortality of the soul and the resurrection of the body. This central truth of our religion is dramatized liturgically at the annual Easter celebration and at every Mass which is offered. It's the message which gives meaning to our funeral liturgies, and is symbolized by the presence of the burning Easter candle. From early times, we as a Church have professed in the creed our belief "in the resurrection of the body and life everlasting."

As Jesus triumphed over the objections of the Sadducees, we too must triumph over doubt and opposition. We are citizens of both earth and heaven. Death is our second birthday — our birthday into eternity. Since we are not angels but humans, we are incomplete without our bodies. Jesus therefore assures us that there will be a resurrection of the body. Then we will finally have it all together — forever.

THIRTY-THIRD SUNDAY OF THE YEAR (C)
Ml 3:19-20   2 Th 3:7-12   Lk 21:5-19

If you're looking for a lively Bible discussion, this Gospel passage could serve as a good starting point, since it tells of future doom and destruction. Speculations about the end of the world occur in every age, but we are approaching a time in history where the predictions will increase. The end of the second millennium is near and the doomsday preachers are already at work. Unfortunately, the Bible — especially the Book of Revelation — is misinterpreted in such a way as to spread this kind of false fear.

Popular authors like Hal Lindsay, who wrote *The Late Great Planet Earth* and other works, continue to apply excessively literal interpretations to both the Old Testament prophets and the words of Jesus, concerning the destruction of the world. Others confuse innocent people and cause them to drastically alter their lives, give away all their possessions, and flee to the hills — all for no good reasons.

There are sensible reasons for wondering how long our present way of life can endure. Besides the fear of instant destruction by nuclear war, there is also the constant concern about overpopulation, food, housing and jobs.

It's a sad commentary on our intelligence and ingenuity if we are unable to solve these difficulties. It must be clearly pointed out, however, that no reputable scripture scholar accepts the theory that the Bible pinpoints the date of the end of the world. Jesus Himself says: "But of the day and hour no one knows, not even the angels in heaven, but the Father only." (Mt 24:36)

Actually, the important question to ask is somewhat different.

How are we using the time which we have, and what do we hope to accomplish in the years that lie ahead? So instead of gathering together to sing Auld Lang Syne to the passing world, we should expect that all of us will leave this world long before the world leaves us.

Jesus promised that He would remain with us forever. In Him we can securely anchor our future, as we patiently enjoy life and the world about us. Age-old fears can easily grab our attention, but Jesus' enduring love is what counts. "Perfect love casts out all fear" (1 Jn 4:18).

THIRTY-FOURTH SUNDAY OF THE YEAR (C)
SOLEMNITY OF CHRIST THE KING
2 S 5:1-3   Col 1:12-20   Lk 23:35-43

If the names Richard Rodgers and Oscar Hammerstein appear on a musical presentation, it's a sure guarantee that it will have class and quality. One of their most popular musicals is *The King And I*. Hammerstein, as usual, wrote the beautiful lyrics which Rodgers set to bouncy and exciting music. It was on Broadway for over three years and then made into a hit movie starring Deborah Kerr and Yul Brynner.

It's the story of a widowed English school teacher who goes to Bangkok to tutor the children of the King of Siam. She represents the western culture and he the east. They are in constant conflict because of their differences, yet there exists between them a tender love and deep understanding.

On the feast of Christ The King, we give attention to our relationship with Him. The Lord has reminded us of our differences when He said: "Your ways are not my ways; My thoughts are not your thoughts." Although there is a world of difference between God and His people, yet there is present a deep and mysterious understanding.

One of the well-known songs in *The King And I* is "Getting To Know You." Those same lyrics can have particular meaning for us in reference to our King.

We keep getting to know Him, all the time learning of His true, loving nature. Each day we try to probe a bit deeper into His ways. We are also getting to know all about Him in His works of creation — especially in people, where we see His image. If we truly like the King, then we will trust His words and try to live by them. We know that He likes us, too. Since He does, we can and should like ourselves. Everyone needs a good self-image and a sense of dignity.

Jesus came to make us feel free and easy by taking away our sins by His death. Sometimes we become our own worst enemies, and with our guilt feelings only see Him as our Punisher and Judge. It's a good sign of familiarity, when we can pray to God spontaneously, simply saying what comes to our minds and meaning each word. The result is that we become bright and breezy because of all the beautiful new things we learn about Him day by day. This bespeaks a happy relationship, full of life and excitement. There is nothing found here which is heavy, depressing or repelling.

Although each of us relates to God in our own particular way, these lyrics can provide some food for thought on what a truly beautiful experience life can be, in spite of all its pain and mystery. Each of us should think over this question: How strong is the bond of friendship which exists between the King and I?